Praise for [barcode: M000273689]

"A little like Bill Lederer (WWII-era author and also a former naval officer), former State Senator Fred Rohlfing exhibits a wry sense of what might have been when he depicts the trials and tribulations of being a minority party leader in post-WWII Hawai'i. *Island Son* offers insights on political infights won and lost, the failures and successes of a local boy, a Yale grad who earned his law degree at night school while serving in the Navy, a minority party underdog who held to personal principles rather than compromise to political ambition. Rohlfing reveals the personal history behind his empathetic views that led him in shaping key legislation on land reform and rights for leasehold homeowners…while losing two close elections for Congress from O'ahu.

It is all a matter of timing, Rohlfing further suggests in recounting his bid to better understand the issues in Vietnam by temporary assignment there as a Navy Intel reservist. He arrived in country Jan. 27, 1968 two days before Tet, the lunar new year observance that in 1968 marked a major offensive by the communist-led forces of North Vietnam."

—Edwin Tanji, Maui Bureau Chief for the *Honolulu Advertiser*
    and retired City Editor for the *Maui News*

"Fred Rohlfing helped define moderate Republicanism in the State Legislatures of the 1960s and early '70s. Fred understood that the progressive tradition came in Republican hues that were ideally suited to the multi-ethnic population of his Island home. *Island Son* reminds us of Fred's love of Hawai'i, his patriotic service to his country, and of the intelligence he brought to the public square."

—Dan Boylan, Professor of History, University of Hawai'i,
    TV political commentator

ISLAND SON

THE LIFE AND TIMES OF
HAWAI'I'S REPUBLICAN REFORMER

To Glen who became a lifetime friend but started with the politics of Hawaii in the late 60's; see p. 209. All the best to you. Aloha, Fred

ISLAND SON

THE LIFE AND TIMES OF HAWAI'I'S REPUBLICAN REFORMER

A MEMOIR AND COMMENTARY
BY SENATOR FRED ROHLFING

LAWYER, LEGISLATOR, NAVAL INTELLIGENCE OFFICER,
FEDERAL JUDGE, STATESMAN, COMMUNITY ADVOCATE,
AND LOCAL BOY

LEGACY ISLE
PUBLISHING

© 2010 Frederick W. Rolfing

All rights reserved. No part of this book may be reproduced in any form or by any electronic or mechanical means, including information retrieval systems, without prior written permission from the publisher, except for brief passages quoted in reviews.

ISBN 978-0-9844212-9-9

Library of Congress Control Number: 2010930532

Editor
Paul Wood

Design and production
Karen Bacon

Excerpts and editorial cartoons courtesy *The Honolulu Advertiser* and *The Maui News*

Hawaiian Lullaby copyright © 1974 by Siluco Music Co. All rights reserved. Used by permission.

Hawai'i Aloha song sheet courtesy Oahu League of Republican Women

Bright College Years (Yale University alma mater) courtesy Carolyn Claflin, Association of Yale Alumni

Superferry photo courtesy Terry White

Legacy Isle Publishing is a registered trademark of:

Watermark Publishing
1088 Bishop St., Suite 310
Honolulu, Hawaii 96813
Telephone 1-808-587-7766
Toll-free 1-866-900-BOOK
sales@bookshawaii.net
www.bookshawaii.net

Printed in the United States

CONTENTS

ISLAND SON

THE LIFE AND TIMES OF
HAWAI'I'S REPUBLICAN REFORMER

INTRODUCTION

Maui bookshelves carry little on the subject of Hawai'i's post-statehood politics. The best-known effort is *To Catch a Wave* by Tom Coffman, former *Honolulu Star-Bulletin* political reporter. Tom's book focuses on the long rivalry between Burns's forces and those under the leadership of Tom Gill. He also provides chapters about the Republican 1970 primary battle between Porteus and King in which he gives extensive coverage to D.G. "Andy" Anderson (supporting Porteus) and myself (supporting King).

Former Governor Ben Cayetano's recent book *Ben* emphasizes the years subsequent to the early eighties. Hence it relates to events occurring after my principal political activity took place. All Hawai'i citizens should read *Ben*, particularly to make themselves aware of the kind of power-plays and pressures that take place in our legislature. There is also former Governor Ariyoshi's short but well researched book *Hawai'i: The Past Fifty Years, the Next Fifty Years*, which emphasizes state planning.

Unlike Governor Ben, I did not grow up in rough-and-tumble Kalihi Valley but rather in staid middle-class pre-World War II Mānoa Valley. We Rohlfings weren't part of the haole social elite nor the "missionary boys." My dad often told stories at the dinner table of his battles on behalf of the Hawaiian Pineapple Company (Dole) versus Dillingham interests in the harbor area and versus Matson on shipping matters. Other stories about "understandings" between members of the "Big Five" occasionally got full review at the dinner table. (My mother was a good listener!) My father was his own man and called the shots as he saw them in the interest of his employer. If some top boss wanted to overrule him because of another firm's concerns as expressed by the boss's missionary cousins, so be it. But he always strove to do his job by putting forth the best solution to the problem. In his youth he had been a baseball player, and through life he used baseball terminology regarding the pursuit of results. Whenever I mounted the steps of an aircraft in order to return to college, his parting advice was always: "Keep your eye on the ball!" I tried to follow his advice in the political environment. *Remember who you're working for, Fred—namely, the people who elected you! It helps you sleep well at night.*

This book's organization differs markedly from that of most memoirs. We go first to my political life in chapters 1 through 3 and do not get to family and personal upbringing until Chapter 4. Why? Because I think you'll find it more interesting that way. Had I wanted to publish a resume, I'd have done it the traditional way.

Another note about the content of this book: you won't learn a lot about my personal life or that of my family today. They (and I) are entitled to privacy.

I believe that life reflects a certain symmetry. We, like the weather, pass through cycles—starting with stability, experiencing change, ultimately adjusting back to stability. Change can come in many different shades and hues. Heraclitus concluded five hundred years before Christ that "nothing endures but change." He also said that "it is in changing that things find purpose."

Over the past fifty years much change has come to Hawai'i's political landscape. During my time in office the "Big Five" played less and less of a defining role as the years passed. So too the ILWU, which had much power at the time of statehood through its ability to elect neighbor-isle legislators. The ILWU was overtaken by the increasing power of the government employee unions as the 1968 Constitutional Convention gave them the power to bargain collectively and to strike. Even more important in that equation was "the great equalizer"—the case of *Reynolds v. Sims*, which made both houses of our Legislature the mirror image of each other. This gave O'ahu control of both houses as "population" replaced "acreage" in determining representation. The reapportionment that followed *Reynolds* also ended multi-member districts, where Republicans could pick up more than a few spillover votes and thus gain a seat or two in normally Democratic-leaning districts. Republican Party activists actually pushed for this latter change, clear evidence of what could best be described as a "death wish."

Colorful leaders with political and financial muscle—Art Rutledge, Jack Hall, Ed Tangen, Hiram Fong, Lowell Dillingham, Spark Matsunaga, Neal Blaisdell, Ed Brennan, Frank Fasi, Hannibal Tavares, Sherry Ing, and many others—have passed on. Others, such as longtime HGEA head Russell Okata, have retired. Gary Rodrigues has been removed from leadership of the UPW. Gone too from active business management, much less political leadership, are the Cookes, Castles, C. Brewers, T.H. Davieses, Dillinghams, etc. Activities of most of these firms are directed now from the Mainland, and local managers even of sizable firms have little political muscle. Such influence is diffused even further by the contemporary attitude that progress requires consensus.

Further fragmentation has resulted from an increased number of "single issue" groups, and also from an aggressive environmental-interest lobby that I believe has overstepped its appropriate role. To this perplexing hand add a wild card, the Hawaiian sovereignty/Renaissance movement, and you have real problems in making substantial political progress. I know a little about these more recent organizations by having helped set up the Maui Open Space Trust during the late eighties and by acting as liaison with early founders of the Maui Tomorrow Foundation.

Today these citizen organizations have used their lobbying power to block positive activities such as the Hawai'i Superferry. The statutes through which these organizations derive such increased power need to be reviewed. The Superferry is a classic case of the frustration of public goals. Surveys at the time all indicated that a majority of the general Hawai'i public favored the ferry. The negative syndrome that these organizations have parlayed to power is illustrated by the bumper sticker I saw recently which simply said "STOP SOMETHING!"

Hawai'i's political parties—even the ever-dominant Democrats—have lost much relative power due to the above-described changes in the political mix. The Hawai'i Republican party, if judged by the number of its legislators that hold office, is within a couple of breaths of expiring altogether. I try to deal with that problem in "Looking Down the Road" later in this book.

The latest addition to the game of politics is the "Tea Party." It is too early to judge how effective this more fundamentalist and conservative organization will be in Democrat-dominated Hawai'i, but it is a sign of hope.

The Tea Party phenomenon might indicate that the good red blood in the veins of the people of these islands is stirring again, and with it a resolve to somehow "fix stuff." We *can* demonstrate spirit and resolve. After all, we collectively live and die for our Rainbow Wahine volleyball team whenever they face the mighty Amazons of the Texas plains and the Midwest. We also loudly rally our Samoan-dominated defensive line as it interfaces with the 375-pounders from Wisconsin and BYU. We have won our share of these unequal battles. *Yes, we can be Warriors!* If we can do that, we can change our political landscape as well. We are, in the end analysis, "Islanders"—just as I am an "Island son"—and on islands, no matter in which direction you travel you come to the ocean. Quite naturally, you realize that you must get along with your fellow Islanders and make do together!

Although elected as a Republican in 1959, and always serving in the minority party, I was an activist when it came to the employment of government power to solve problems that free enterprise or ordinary citizens could or would not solve. I had no compunctions, for example, about writing to the mayor or to the City traffic agency concerning the need for a second turn lane at the intersection of Kilauea and Wai'alae Avenues. Many legislators would have said that this was a City problem and thus ducked the issue. Nor did I decline to act on a bipartisan basis—all of my constituents received equal treatment regardless of their party affiliation.

I was an unabashed supporter of "liberal" positions on leasehold land reform, State land management, affordable housing, mass transit and procedural reforms such as a unicameral Legislature. I "crossed the aisle" (as they say in Washington) to work with Democrats such as Dave McClung, Walter Heen, George "Scotty" Koga, Nelson Doi, Sakae Takahashi, Tom Gill, Kenny Brown and Vince Yano to accomplish results on many a legislative measure.

I pressed for transparency in our school system and for accountability through system decentralization. I was on the field early with comprehensive environmental legislation. I pushed hard for affordable housing, and I co-sponsored (together with Senator Vince Yano) an omnibus bill to effectuate it.

When it came to labor-management relations, I relied on a guiding philosophy inherited from my dad: *Each side is entitled to half the road.* Go over the centerline, though, and you are in for trouble! My nine years' experience representing the Hawai'i Nurses Association further contributed to a perception that I was a "different kind" of Republican. Through this association with the nurses' union I became more aware of working people's problems in our society. One of my most prized awards was being named an "Honorary Registered Nurse" at the HNA's annual convention! Moreover, I was particularly proud to receive the endorsement of every major Hawai'i union except one (the Construction Laborer's Union) in my 1976 congressional race against Cecil Heftel.

On the other side of this activism was my fiscal conservatism. I consistently argued and voted against large budgets, once calling the budget "a grand *shibai*" (great hoax). I also voted consistently for local (i.e., County) control of government functions—"Home Rule"—rather than the absorption of local authority into the jurisdiction of State agencies.

I believed that political parties should have an agenda and should stick to it. I never approved of cozying up to the other side to gain perks for individual officeholders. I also accepted Otto von Bismarck's wisdom when he said that "Politics is not an exact science but rather the art of the possible."

What, then, lies ahead for you as my reader?

We begin this book with my early interest in politics, then we jump right into the legislative years and two exciting congressional campaigns—first versus Sparky, then versus Cec Heftel.

After that we reverse engines to the year before the Great Depression. We catch up on my early years at Punahou, Yale and George Washington University Law School. Along the line, you will be exposed to the highlights of my thirty-six-year commitment to the United States Naval Intelligence Reserve beginning with 1951. Military service was my third career, after law and politics.

Further on I recap my full- and part-time work for the Territory of American Samoa, my presidential appointment as alternate representative on the South Pacific Commission, and finally, after a stint as Maui Corporation Counsel, official retirement. In Chapter 7 I talk about some part-time jobs such as service on the Maui Reapportionment Advisory Committee and my work as U.S. magistrate judge.

The finishing chapters and appendices provide commentary on current issues facing the state and those who have served it with me.

So let us now climb into our time capsule. Let us set the control time clock for the mid-1930s....

PART ONE

SERVICE TO
THE STATE OF HAWAI'I

Ua mau ke ea o ka 'āina i ka pono
The life of the land is perpetuated in righteousness
(Hawai'i state motto)

A POLITICAL CAREER TAKES SHAPE

Early Interest in Public Affairs

My interest in politics began early. World events were a topic of discussion at our family dinner table for as long as I can remember. As the only child in the family, I was expected at the dinner table at six-thirty p.m. every evening, with no excuses permitted. I had to be sure to wash my hands (and feet) ahead of dinner time and put on a clean shirt. (Kids never wore shoes in Hawai'i except for events and—after we reached seventh grade—for school.) Growing up in Hawai'i during the 1930s meant being aware of the threat of war with Japan while, at the same time, watching from afar the Nazi buildup to war in Europe.

The potential for war with Japan became more personal when my father traveled to the Philippines in the late summer of 1940. He had been directed to appraise the possibility of an investment by his employer —Hawaiian Pineapple Company, Ltd. (Dole)—in the southern Philippine Islands, which at the time were affiliated with the United States. My mother and I were sworn to secrecy about the trip. (Dole didn't want any of its competitors alerted to its idea.) When my father returned, he recommended that the company not invest in the Philippines for many reasons, but most prominently because of the potential threat posed by Japan. His prediction of war with Japan by early 1941 was not far off the mark.

There were other involvements and studies related to public affairs. After having been "evacuated" from Hawai'i to the U.S. Mainland in July of 1942 (after the Battle of Midway), I kept the order of battle chart for the Russian front in my public school in Palo Alto and paid close attention to our military progress in the Battle of the Pacific.

While at Yale I focused on courses in history and political science. One instructor, Professor Henry Turner, taught a popular course in history that opened my eyes to the connection between worldwide religions, native cultures, and the politics of our time. I then majored in political science/government. During territorial days, Hawaiʻi's delegate to Congress, Joe Farrington, came to visit New Haven and gave an interesting talk focused on the status of the long campaign for statehood for Hawaiʻi. Joe, a dedicated Republican, invited us to visit him whenever we were in Washington, D.C., which I did in 1948 after the surprising Truman re-election.

There were some Hawaiʻi boys at George Washington Law School when I resumed my law studies in 1952. Among them was future U.S. Senator Daniel Inouye and a Chinese-Hawaiian lawyer-to-be by the name of Alvin Shim. After classes Alvin and I frequented a bar/restaurant called Bassin's on Pennsylvania Avenue. There we explored the ramifications of the Eisenhower years and the political changes that were about to come in Hawaiʻi. He was already a Democrat, and he was destined to become a member of the group of Asian war veterans who swept into power in the elections of 1954 before I returned to Hawaiʻi. I was still uncommitted party-wise, but I had great faith in President Eisenhower and thought he had changed the image of Republicanism from the "just say no" crowd to a modern progressive governing force. As a businessman my father had leaned to the Republican banner. My grandfather (the first Frederick William Rohlfing) had been appointed postmaster in Placerville, California, through association with California Republican Senator Hiram Johnson, a railway-baron fighter.

Upon returning to Hawaiʻi in 1955 and passing the bar, I joined the firm of Blaisdell and Moore, primarily a labor-law firm that represented employers, and Alvin became a member of a firm that represented AFL-CIO-affiliated unions. We never faced each other head on, however, mostly because by 1963 I had become a "union lawyer" myself, representing the Hawaiʻi Nurses Association for collective bargaining at four Oʻahu hospitals.

While still in Washington, my wife Joan and I were invited to the

Eisenhower inauguration ball by Randolph Crossley, who at the time was aspiring to become the governor of Hawai'i—a position that was then a presidential appointment. Joan had been a classmate of Meredith Crossley, Randolph's daughter. I was the wide-eyed tag-along.

Entrée into Politics

After returning to Hawai'i in 1955, I was recruited in 1956 by a business executive named Howard Hubbard to help a young thirty-eight-year-old lawyer named William F. Quinn with his campaign for the Hawai'i Territorial Senate. This was my first experience with door-to-door and other grassroots campaigning. Quinn ran a good race, but he lost. However, in a strong sense he actually won, as he was subsequently considered potential gubernatorial material by President Eisenhower, who was looking for a "new image" that contrasted with that of then-Republican Governor Samuel "Sam" Wilder King.

In 1957 my old high school friend Dr. Robert Gibson had another vision for me: election as Chairman of the O'ahu Young Republicans (YR). My opponent was deputy attorney general Wallace Fujiyama, who had garnered the support of those who served in the King administration. I was the candidate for the largely "haole" faction that Dr. Gibson and his group of friends recruited to show up on election night. While I won, it was some time before I bridged the division created by this election. In due course, Fujiyama became a Democrat as well as a highly effective plaintiff's trial attorney.

It was not long after my selection that political lightning struck. In 1958 President Eisenhower announced that he was appointing Bill Quinn as governor, replacing Sam W. King. The O'ahu Young Republicans, under my leadership, held a dinner at Queens Surf honoring Quinn. One of the speakers at the dinner was former Territorial Secretary Farrant Turner, a World War II leader of Japanese-American troops who praised Sam King for his leadership. I was impressed with his direct honesty and, as a result, had some second thoughts about where my loyalties lay. These feelings stirred again when I led an effort to recruit Sam P. King, the former governor's son, in the 1970 primary contest against my Senate colleague,

Minority Leader Hebden Porteus, with the winner to take on Governor John Burns. But that's a later story.

Around this time a group of young attorneys and friends met at my house in lower 'Āina Haina on Saturday afternoons in an effort to develop some guiding principles and programs for revival of the Hawai'i Republican Party. Those that I recall participating included Percy Mirikitani, Bill Yim, "Kinka" Harlocker, Clint Ashford, Dwight Rush, "Red" Schaefer, and Barney Smith. We took our "manifesto for change" to the State Republican Party's annual platform convention and got it considered as a resolution with the passive consent of party chairman Arthur Woolaway. The resolution included some strong phrases that I had fought for, including statements in support of land reform in Hawai'i. The strongest opponent of the resolution was a colorful senior lawyer named O.P. Soares, who took the floor in the Farrington High School auditorium and blasted our proposal as being "communistic." Soares was particularly concerned with the threat that might be posed to the Roman Catholic Church and its substantial holdings. As best I remember, the resolution was amended substantially.

During this pre-statehood time we also had the 1958 territorial legislative election. In my home Seventeenth Representation District three Republicans were elected (we had multiple representation districts that carried over to statehood)—Webley Edwards of *Hawai'i Calls* fame, Frank Judd from a longtime kama'āina missionary family, and young part-Hawaiian lawyer Ambrose "Amby" Rosehill. These men were in session when the Hawai'i Statehood Bill passed Congress in March. The bill called for primary elections in early June and a general election in July as well as a vote on approval of statehood.

Also pending at the time was a lawsuit brought by Honolulu lawyer Jack Dyer seeking reapportionment of the Legislature. The outcome of the reapportionment case was of great interest to me. If the plaintiffs won this case, my district would gain a seat. I could then run without damaging my friendships with the incumbents and their friends, especially Amby Rosehill. In the end I decided to run, believing that the reapportionment case would be resolved favorably and if it wasn't, I was still willing to take the risk. My decision caused some concern among our friends, but it became a non-issue when the court gave our district an additional seat.

The Statehood Election of 1959

My campaign was off and running by early April. I emphasized grass roots—first in my home precincts in ʻĀina Haina—vowing to visit every home personally to talk to the owner/occupant, even if I had to go back after working hours to catch people who were not home in the late weekday afternoon. I asked precinct leaders to organize walking groups throughout the district on their own schedules, but I found that system too hard to implement effectively. Instead I organized Saturday morning walking teams, which I accompanied.

My print media guy was Jack Young, a kamaʻāina businessman, and my dedicated campaign manager was longtime best friend and fellow naval-intelligence colleague Barney Smith, who lived in Waiʻalae Kāhala. I obtained some innovative signs from an oil dealer that turned in the wind if properly rigged; however, they were hard to keep in service since kids had a penchant for taking them home. We kept expenses to a minimum and finished a strong third place in the July general election behind Edwards and Judd but ahead of Rosehill. Total expenses for the campaign would make today's candidate extremely jealous—just over $1,300! This was quite a contrast to the $250,000 or so that I subsequently raised and spent in my congressional race of 1976 against television mogul Cecil Heftel, who spent over $600,000!

Early Sessions of the First State Legislature

Being a member of the first State Legislature was exciting. We were poised to lay the legislative groundwork for a new State government: establishing the nature and scope of all the departments of the State as well as the State's relationship with the various County governments. We were to set the overall direction of the state, which continues—both good and bad—to this day.

There were eighteen Republicans and thirty-three Democrats in the House. Republicans controlled the Senate by only a slim margin. They were a curious lot and failed to practice party discipline well, unlike the

Democratic senators. Senator Julian Yates from Kona was in his mid-seventies. Neighbor island representatives included "Doc" Hill from Hilo, Senator Marques Calmes from Maui, Yates and Bernard Kinney from the Big Island, and Senator Noboru Miyake from Kaua'i. The younger Democrats included such luminaries as Hilo's Nelson Doi, an ILWU attorney named Nadao Yoshinaga, and my friend-to-be Sakae Takahashi. Back in the House, Representative Elmer Cravalho was elected speaker, hav-

I ADMIRED SENATOR NELSON DOI FOR HIS FORTHRIGHTNESS AND SUPPORT FOR AN UNICAMERAL LEGISLATURE.

ing previously won that job in 1958 in a vicious intra-party fight with a group backing Vince Esposito for the position. Representative Tom Gill, who aspired to higher office and was a leading liberal crusader, was prominent in the Esposito faction. Our caucus elected veteran legislator and sugar man Joe Garcia from the Hilo area to be minority leader, Representative Web Edwards as floor leader, and Representative Al Evensen as whip.

Bill Quinn was our state's first Republican governor—and the last until Linda Lingle was elected in 2002. I had worked on Quinn's unsuccessful campaign for the territorial Senate in 1958 and had hoped for a close cooperative effort upon our mutual election in 1959. I was to be very disappointed when it turned out that he listened more closely to Senate Republicans than to our younger group from the House, and failed to bring us into his inside planning circle. His closest advisor was Howard Hubbard, a Castle & Cooke ("Big Five") executive who along with others of Quinn's close advisors lacked local political perception.

My interest in urban land planning and residential leasehold reform

Praise for *Island Son*

led me to choose the House Lands Committee at the outset. I was also an active member of the Transportation and Labor Committees. The Lands Committee was chaired by Representative David McClung, a colorful labor attorney who had grown up in Michigan, and the Transportation Committee was chaired by Representative Billy Fernandes from Kauaʻi, whose father had been a colorful territorial legislator.

It is to state the obvious to say that island land is limited in quantity. It is axiomatic that economic, social, and political goals of human beings must be met within the space available. Over the years in Hawaiʻi, more than most American places, this shortage of space and governmental supervisory structure has led to clashes between various urban and agricultural interests. To understand the significance of the bills we worked on in the first several years of the new State Legislature, a brief history lesson is helpful.

Originally taro farming, animal husbandry, and other Native Hawaiian land uses were adapted to the *ahupuaʻa* boundary system. An *ahupuaʻa* was a roughly triangular land division running from a point on a mountain ridge to two points along the shoreline. Other land divisions were developed over time and were given a big push by the declaration of the Great Mahele in 1848 (the approximate time Great Grandfather Rohlfing left Germany for America!). In essence the Great Mahele imposed the Anglo-Saxon concept of fee simple ownership in the place of the traditional, very practical native land-holding pattern wherein the aliʻi (chiefs) held sway. Non-native Hawaiian interests soon took advantage of the new law to acquire large tracts of land for sugar and ranching. Many large tracts found their way into haole and in due course Asian citizens' hands through marriage, purchase, foreclosure, and adverse possession. With the collapse of the whaling industry in the mid-1800s, sugar and ranching became the bread-and-butter economic activities for Hawaiʻi. The Great Mahele helped those so engaged acquire the necessary large tracts of land.

Hawaiian history also tells of the establishment of a large land trust known as the Bernice Pauahi Bishop Estate, provided in her will by the Hawaiian princess of that name. The princess was a Kamehameha. Other members of the family, including her haole husband, joined in assigning lands to the trust. It is estimated that lands in this estate total approximately ten percent of the state. The proceeds from the trust were set aside in perpetuity to the Kamehameha Schools.

The Great Mahele led to the acquisition of many large tracts by the ensuing governments of the Hawaiian Islands. The overthrow of the Hawaiian monarchy in 1893 added more acreage to the government's total, estimated at forty percent of the state.

The initial challenge before the House Lands Committee was the State Land Management Bill, which would define how that forty percent would be sold, leased, or otherwise managed. "Old-line" rules and practices under territorial and prior land regimes were a target for the McClung (and Gill) Democrats, and I must admit I agreed with them most of the time. The leading senators on the conference committee for the main 1961 bill (Senate Bill 3) were neighbor islanders headed by Kaua'i's Francis Ching. The House conferees, of which I was one, pushed hard to keep State-owned lands within State control through leases, rather than sales, and other practices that favored private use. After numerous extensions of the legislative session, on the final night the pork barrel (capital improvement projects) bill passed, but Senate Bill 3 died when the conference committee draft was not voted on in the Senate. (For more information on this action see the book by Horwitz and Meller, *Land and Politics in Hawaii*, published by Michigan State University in 1963). In the budget session of 1962 a bill similar to the conference draft did finally pass, under pressure from Governor Quinn.

The State Land Use Act (Act 187 SLH 1961) was another big piece of legislation that we dealt with in the early statehood days. Called the "Greenbelt Law," it was a comprehensive statewide code for the zoning of all lands. The law divided the state into three major categories— Agricultural, Urban, and Conservation. Later a fourth category, Rural, was added. This law was meant to be responsive to a state plan, but no such plan was adopted. Over time the "Greenbelt Law" agency—the Land Use Commission (LUC)—has filled the planning role for the state, but the quality of that effort is debatable. From my observation Maui County at least, and probably the other counties, have improved the quality of their own planning agencies markedly since the LUC came into existence.

LUC emphasis was placed on protection of agricultural lands, and this spirit extends to this day. Our four-acre Maui property is zoned agricultural, which means it can be subdivided only into parcels no smaller than two acres. Also, under this law only one ʻohana unit (cottage) is permitted on an agricultural lot.

The Maryland Land Law

Also receiving Land Committee consideration in those early statehood days was the Maryland Land Law. This was a highly publicized Democratic Party platform plank. As indicated by its title, the bill had been adapted from a Maryland statute that gave long-term renters (lessees) an option to buy the fee-simple title to their real property interest. In Hawaiʻi this idea had broad implications for residential lessees, many of whom in my district had Bishop Estate leases, or leases from other large landowners. Subdivisions in the Waiʻalae Kāhala and Hawaiʻi Kai areas had all been built on lands leased from the Bishop Estate. ʻĀina Haina was leasehold under the Hind Estate, and Niu was leased by the Pflueger-Cassiday interests. The original residential leases were usually set for thirty years with reopenings after a set period (usually fifteen years) to adjust rents in line with increasing values. In time, fifty-five-year leases became customary. When my wife Joan and I bought a home in ʻĀina Haina in 1956, for example, the property came with a fifty-five-year lease with reopening for rent adjustments at fifteen and thirty years. At the outset we paid only 250 dollars a year for rent. Our lessor (the Hind Estate), however, sold its fee residual interest in these East Oʻahu lands to a Mainland-based company that seized the opportunity it had been given. Now as re-openings came up, the new company demanded drastically increased rents—increases of over one thousand percent! People felt trapped and insulted by this, as they had purchased property in contemplation of leasehold rents and mortgages that they could afford over the long term. The new landowner offered to keep the rent increases down somewhat by allowing reopenings earlier than that which had been scheduled under the lease agreement.

The ʻĀina Haina developments provided stimulus for legislative action on the Maryland Bill (House Bill 16). When the bill was brought to the floor of the House, I rose to speak for it. Strangely, no one on the Democratic side got up to herald their longstanding support for action. The bill passed easily in the House. Patsy Mink, who was in the gallery when the Maryland Bill was voted on, was visibly excited by my speech. It was, however, a different story in the Senate. Native Hawaiian groups (supporters of the existing system that favored the Bishop Estate and Kamehameha Schools) marched in torchlight protest parades around 'Iolani Palace as the Senate considered the bill. In the end, Senator George Ariyoshi cast the deciding vote against the bill.

With the failure of the Maryland Bill, the residential leasehold issue became more pressing. I decided to prepare a bill that would regulate the residential leasehold process rather than try to resolve it by purchase option, as provided by the Maryland proposal. I called it the "Lessees' Bill of Rights." It contained provisions for arbitration of rent increases and for payment to lessees of the value of their homes if leases were not renewed, as well as other controls on the process to make it fair and balanced. Unlike many of my bills, which were often relegated to the legislative refuse bin simply because they were Republican-sponsored, this bill turned out to have a future after I was elected to the Senate.

Looking (Way) Ahead: Mass Transit

As early as 1961 I introduced bills calling for a pilot study of express rail transit for the Kalaniana'ole Highway corridor in East O'ahu. I had attended the Seattle World's Fair in 1960 and ridden the monorail built in connection with that event. I thought that before traffic congestion overwhelmed the people of Hawai'i, their government should condemn sufficient land when creating highway rights-of-way to enable the inclusion of rail or bus transit lines, and I introduced legislation to this effect. When these bills came up for hearing in Billy Fernandes's Transportation Committee, the officials of the Department of Transportation pooh-poohed their necessity, saying that the people of Hawai'i will never get out of their cars, and that all funds and planning should go to highways and road improvements. As these officials were appointees of Republican Governor Quinn, the Democrats who controlled the committee had an excuse not to act on my bills and resolutions and later proved, by inaction, that they were no different from the Republican-appointed state officials. To this day Honolulu has failed to deal with the

REPUBLICAN DINNER IN EARLY 1960S WITH U.S. SENATOR ED BROOKE OF MASSACHUSETTS AND GOVERNOR QUINN OF HAWAI'I.

need for a mass transit alternative and is facing billion-dollar numbers and hefty tax increases with the current idea to do so. I am now opposed to this overly expensive and poorly designed plan, which I call "The Giant Rail Rat Hole." While no one wants to hear it—"I told you so" some forty-five years ago!

If we'd done it then, it would have required a fraction of today's cost, and it would have benefited a larger number of people.

The Maui Special Investigative Committee

Any account of my three terms in the House would be incomplete without briefly noting my service on the House Maui Investigative Special Committee. This committee was created by Speaker Elmer Cravalho to deal with a political battle on Maui between two major labor unions—AFL-affiliated construction workers and the very powerful ILWU. The conflict involved the awarding of a construction contract for the War Memorial Gym in Wailuku by the County of Maui with funding by the State. The committee's official mission was to see if undue influence had been exercised by County officials in favoring a contractor whose workers were connected to the AFL and, presumably, to opine on whether legislation should be passed to right any injustices in the bidding/contract-award process. Rep. Walter Heen was named chairman of the four-Democrat, three-Republican select committee. My Republican colleagues were Representatives Joseph Dwight, Jr., and Dorothy Devereaux.

Headlines in the *Honolulu Advertiser* discussing the situation went so far as to proclaim "Fear Stalks the Streets of Maui," so we knew we had a hot issue to investigate. At the outset we took sworn testimony in Honolulu under subpoena from those involved, including Maui County supervisors. Several "sang like birdies" such that when we eventually held standing-room-only public hearings in the Planning Department's hearing room, there was not much "wiggle room" for them.

Upon receiving the report of the committee, whose conclusions as best I can recall were relatively innocuous but favored going ahead with the proposed contract, Speaker Cravalho first dismissed the three Republicans, and then let the committee languish. He had accomplished his intended purpose on Maui, which was to make certain that everyone understood who was really the boss—he, not those "peons" on the Maui Board of Supervisors. More importantly, he had further ingratiated himself with the powerful ILWU for representing their complaints over the award. Cravalho went on to become mayor of Maui County for two terms, and he still calls shots within the Democratic Party.

"Young Turks"

"Young Turks" is the nickname given by the political writers of the day to our group of young representatives who had been elected to the first State Legislature. Our group, as I recall, included Amby Rosehill, Bob Teruya, Joseph Dwight, Jr., Percy Mirikitani, Wadsworth Yee, Bill Bains-Jordan, Dick Kennedy, Katsugo "Kats" Miho, and several others. The more traditional "old-timers" group included Minority Leader Joe Garcia, Webley Edwards, Frank Judd, Eureka Forbes, Al Evensen, Dorothy Devereaux, and several more. Within this group I was particularly close to Percy Mirikitani and Dick Kennedy. Percy later served in the Senate with me. Ken Nakamura (an ex-University of Hawaiʻi football player who later became my law partner with Don Low, later a per diem District Court judge) joined us in 1962.

In 1963 at the beginning of my second term (the first term was three and one-half years in length instead of two years because of the timing of statehood in 1959) we reorganized the leadership of the then-eleven-member minority with Rosehill as minority leader, me as floor leader, and, I believe, Kats Miho as whip. D.G. "Andy" Anderson had been elected to the House in 1962 and was the "swing man" in the contest for leadership with the older group. Miho and I frequently conflicted on program and general manner of doing things. In 1964, after Rosehill ran and lost for the Senate, Miho was named minority leader. When the session concluded, our caucus decided that it wanted change, and I was elected minority leader. Anderson was named floor leader and Jimmy Clark, an old Punahou football buddy of mine, was named minority whip. The turnover got lots of press coverage, including a *Honolulu Star-Bulletin* early edition headline: "Miho Fired." Miho went on to become a well-respected Family Court judge.

Campaign Research

I was always interested in progressive policy. Hence as minority leader I hired staff people on the basis of merit and ability rather than sheer loyalty. One of the people we hired in 1963 was a talented young lady by the name of Margita White, a native of Sweden who had worked in the Dillingham campaign of 1962 and who was a first-class researcher/writer as well as natural political operative. She put together documents and wrote speeches that helped us immeasurably in our public appearances. She also prepared a post-session review organized by issues that provided ammunition against the majority Democrats. This was very useful in preparing for public appearances between sessions. Unfortunately, she returned to the Mainland in 1964 with her Navy husband, Stewart. She immediately went to work for the Goldwater presidential campaign. When Richard Nixon came into office, she went on to work in the White House in the communications office. In that capacity she assisted me tremendously in making contacts with key Nixon administration figures on

Hawai'i issues when I was getting ready to run, or was already running, for Congress in 1972 and 1976.

Australia and Laundromats, 1964–1965

My first trip to the South Pacific occurred when I joined the Honolulu Chamber of Commerce's 1964 Australia–New Zealand trade mission. The mission departed Honolulu on April 5, 1964, with the charge of exploring trade and investment opportunities with "Aussie" and "Kiwi" business leaders and government officials in Sydney, Melbourne, Canberra, Brisbane, and New Zealand. (I only stayed with the group through the Australia portion. New Zealand would come later, twice in tourist-style trips and then in 1997 on a great hiking trip called the "Routeburn/Greenstone Trek" with my sons Fritz and Karl.)

Our group leader was chamber president Slator Miller, and our group included "heavy hitters" such as Chinn Ho, "Molly" Mollenhoff (Honolulu Roofing), Max Pilliard (Bank of Hawai'i), Herbert Taylor (First Hawaiian Bank), Richard M. Towill (R.M. Towill Corp.), Shelley Mark (director of State Planning and Economic Development), Fred Lowrey (Lewers and Cooke), Kim Jacobsen (*Hawai'i Business Magazine*), William Foster (Malia, Inc.), and several others.

The meetings went well, and I became interested in making an investment in Australia. I noted that there were very few Laundromats in the big cities, and I began asking questions about those in the business. I was introduced to a gentleman named Spencer Grace, who had the Westinghouse franchise in Sydney. We talked about my possible participation in building more Laundromats via creation of a Hawai'i investment hui (cooperative). Spencer was an ex-Australian Rules athlete, and we got along well. But we didn't have enough time to get into details due to the tight tour schedule. So I made a return trip to Australia the following year by myself.

This time I drove all over Sydney looking at existing Laundromats and scouting locations for new "stores." Spencer brought a new potential partner into the mix, an Englishman (whose name I have forgotten), and we worked to develop a plan.

However, as negotiations stalled between the three of us, I decided to see more of Australia. I took a three-day tour of the Snowy Mountain scheme out of Canberra. This scheme was a series of dams and conduits used to transfer water from the Snowy Mountains in the state of New South Wales to make fertile the broad valleys of the state of Victoria to the south. It was a long bus tour, and by the time it was over I never wanted to inspect another dam, walk through another pipe, or see another wattle tree as long as I lived. (Ironically, I now live in Kula, where wattles grow like what they are—weeds!) I also did a side trip to Brisbane and the "Gold Coast," where I purchased a small lot on an internal canal. I held onto this property for several years then sold it for a good profit. The negotiations with the Englishman having broken down again, I headed for home the long way—via the Philippines and Japan.

Did I learn anything from this experience? Yes. I got to know a number of my fellow tour people well. Bill Foster, for example, became a member of my campaign finance committee and raised a bundle of money in subsequent campaigns. I learned about the Australian economy and met important people, some of whom visited me in Honolulu in later years. Even more important, I learned that I never wanted to leave Hawai'i and that a life of operating Laundromats in a foreign land wasn't my thing after all. It was time to settle down in my Hawai'i-based law practice or politics or both.

State Senate Campaign

Pat Saiki, who later became Hawai'i's only Republican U.S. Congressperson, was one of our legislative staffers. She was also a good friend of *Honolulu Star-Bulletin* political correspondent Doug Boswell. In 1965 Pat told me that Boswell thought I would lose a State Senate bid. She said if I ran she would help me, and she was true to her word.

With my longtime worker and legislative clerk Henry Ho we began our house-to-house efforts in Kaimukī in July. The race was multi-candidate and multi-seat (four persons were to be elected). Web Edwards and I were the Republicans who won, and Vince Yano and Walter Heen won for the Democrats. I believe I finished number two to Yano. I

SENATE AND HOUSE REPUBLICAN LEADERS MEET AT THE TAHITIAN LANAI.

subsequently hired Pat Saiki for a secretarial position in my Senate office. In 1968 I walked house-to-house with her early in her campaign for the constitutional convention.

The Senate and the Land Reform Act of 1967

In the Senate I continued the work I had begun in the House on land and transportation issues. My best friends across the aisle again were David McClung and Walter Heen. I worked with David on land-reform issues and with Walter on district concerns, one of which was the silting of Paiko Lagoon. After several years of efforts we obtained budget consideration for the dredging of this lagoon before it filled up and destroyed property values in the area. Another local district success was the return of the Coast Guard property in Wailupe to the State (then later to the City of Honolulu for use as a park and to provide ocean access for fishermen). Credit for the final success of this effort went to Senator Hiram L. Fong, with whom I had partnered.

The land-reform effort was a horse of a different color. As the 1967 session began, I redrafted and strengthened my "Lessees' Bill of Rights," a regulatory alternative to the Democrats' earlier proposals. Also, newly elected Senator David McClung totally redrafted the Maryland Bill by inserting State powers of eminent domain to effectuate conversions from leasehold to fee-simple.

McClung's scheme in the new bill provided that a majority of residential lessees in a "development tract" could petition the State to initiate the fee acquisition. Thereafter, the State would proceed in court for the condemnation. Large landowners (Bishop Estate, Campbell Estate, Pflueger-Cassiday, Kāneʻohe Ranch, and others) were, of course, opposed to the forced sale of the fee underlying their leasehold properties, but they realized that something had to give. The Democrats had made land-reform a major issue in their climb to power, and some ten years after gaining that power they had failed to produce a solution. The landowners were primarily concerned about any action that would cause them to be deemed dealers in property. On the other hand, if the sale in fee of the leased residential property were forced, the estates would pay capital gains taxes and not taxes on ordinary income. Furthermore, if deemed to be property dealers, they could lose their charitable exempt status with the IRS.

The Bishop Estate, with its support from the Hawaiian community, was particularly anxious about loss of charitable status. As a consequence, the Bishop Estate hired a highly respected law professor, Dean William Warren from Columbia Law School, to set up discussions with the IRS in Washington for our Land Committee. Warren was an expert in tax and trust law. The IRS was forthcoming in saying that what we were proposing was positive, but they couldn't guarantee that our approach would produce the desired result.

McClung wanted to get more than down-the-line Democrat support for his bill. So he must have figured that if he gave me something, he could enlist some Republican support. I think he also recognized that my bill filled a gap in his party's proposals—i.e., protection for those lessees who did not want, or who could not afford, to buy in fee simple. So he incorporated my "Lessees' Bill of Rights" provisions in the final bill. His assumption was correct, as a substantial number of Republican senators voted in favor of the bill.

"Government by Hui" and the "New Elite," 1966–1968

As Republican policy leader in the State Senate, and being naturally outspoken, I received numerous invitations to talk to groups about the Legislature and the current political scene. In one of these speeches in 1967 I characterized the State administration under Governor John A. Burns as a "hui government." ("Hui" is an oft-used Hawaiian word meaning club or association.) I have not been able to locate the text of that speech, but I have found a contemporary talk to the State Chamber of Commerce in which I pointed out that a "new elite" had taken over our state.

My "new elite" phrase was picked up by *Honolulu Star-Bulletin* political writer Doug Boswell in an article dated June 21, 1966, entitled "Gill approaches showdown with political 'new elite.'"

Boswell referred to Gill's bid for lieutenant governor after having lost in the Senate race to Senator Fong in 1964. The writer noted that another defeat for Gill "could spell retirement from elective politics." The story went on, "But a victory could point Gill toward the governor's office in 1970 and the ultimate collapse of a power structure which Republican Frederick W. Rohlfing has described as the 'New Elite.' Built by Governor John A. Burns over the past three years, the 'New Elite' is the precarious three-cornered political balance shaped in an alliance between the Democratic Party, the ILWU, and Island business.... Business and industry shudder at the thought of Gill in the governor's office, as does the ILWU.... [Republican strategists] believe a Gill victory could destroy the New Elite and funnel new energy into the drive to rebuild the GOP." (In due course Gill won the lieutenant governor's office over Burns's man Kenny Brown, but he lost to Burns for the governorship in 1970.)

In both of the speeches my thrust was that Burns's political operators had teamed up with labor unions, land developers, and business interests to control development in the Islands. The hui's goal was to reap rewards not available to the general population. Suddenly, business was no longer in the Republican camp. Indeed it was in bed with Burns and his Democrat majority in the Legislature. I avowed that hui-controlled government was resulting in traffic congestion, pollution, lack of affordable housing, and a general downgrading of the local lifestyle that is our birthright. My use of the word "hui" was calculated to stir images of backroom maneuvering by various interest groups whose primary objective was personal gain. For local people "hui" denoted a grouping of self-interested people in a money-making cause.

I pointed out that businessmen were told frequently they should participate in politics. But when they did, their decision often resulted in "abject surrender to the ruling political power group, a surrender usually rationalized as being realistic."

A letter to the editor at the time (*Star-Bulletin*, Feb 23, 1966) went even further. The writer described my remarks as "reassuring in that they signaled awareness that [State government] is now controlled lock , stock, and barrel by vested interests—the magnates of big business, big labor, and the Democratic Party. It makes no difference to this clique of convenience what the true needs of the people may be."

In early January 1968, shortly after our New Year and as I was getting ready to go to Vietnam on temporary active duty—see Chapter 5 for my firsthand account of the infamous Tet Offensive—the *Honolulu Advertiser* published a series of interviews with political figures. Entitled "Hawai'i Politics," the series included fifteen articles in all, their interview with me being last in line.

The series began with Governor Burns and continued with Lieutenant Governor Tom Gill. It included Honolulu Councilman Matsuo Takabuki, Senator David McClung, Speaker (later Maui Mayor) Elmer Cravalho, Speaker Tadao Beppu, ILWU head Jack Hall, U.S. Senator Dan Inouye, State Representative Stuart Ho, Former GOP head Art Woolaway, Governor Bill Quinn, GOP Chair Ed Johnston, Mayor Neal Blaisdell, and U.S. Senator Hiram Fong. Most of these subjects were asked about my characterization of "government by hui" and of state control by the "new elites."

The questions posed by Jones, also the responses from interviewees, follow:

Jones: "What about Rohlfing's charge of 'hui government'?"
Burns: "I get hit for government by consensus. But I know you

are not going to get anywhere unless the majority of the people are with you. I guess Rohlfing is just hitting out at what he fears is entrenchment by Democrats. It may look like management and labor and the administration are all together. I don't think that's true."

* * * *

Jones: "Then you agree with Fred Rohlfing that we have government by hui?
Gill: "Rohlfing put his finger on it when he talked about government by hui…. That is about the shape of the problem we have."

No question was posed to Takabuki on the subject, but he brought it up himself:

Takabuki: "The Republicans have been the minority party for a long time now, and with the growing weakness of the Old Guard, you find the Fred Rohlfings taking the lead. Their image and their program is different. Rohlfing talks about government by hui, where we used to hit at the Big Five."
Jones: "Is Rohlfing symptomatic of something new in the Republican Party?"
Takabuki: "Well, I don't know that he is symptomatic yet, but he is part of a new breed of Republican—people like Lindsay, Rockefeller, and Percy—the Republican liberals. Some things he proposes may just reflect his special constituency. But his proposals on leaseholds are quite, quote, radical, unquote—more so than the Democrats are willing to go."

* * * *

Jones: "Is there no philosophical difference [between the parties]?
McClung: "There are two basic factors. One is the increasing role of outside pressure groups to influence elected officials. The other is the rise in the Republican party of more liberal-minded people who are not part of the old establishment. Rohlfing, Toshi Ansai—even if he is an old-timer—and James Clark come to mind."

Jones: "What do you think of Rohlfing and his charge of government by hui by the Democrats?"

Cravalho: "His speech was the usual thing about the outs complaining about the ins. Throw the rascals out and let us rascals in. He doesn't have the intellectual capacity, the ability to move and to reach rational decisions. He is more interested in headlines than results."

Jones: "How do you think the Republicans stand now?"

Cravalho: "I think they are trying. I think Rohlfing is trying…. Rohlfing sounds like a pioneering Democrat of 1954…. The question is, are the young Republicans going to have the patience and the perseverance?"

* * * *

Jones: "Do you think Rohlfing symbolizes a new mood of Republicans?"

Beppu: "I don't think one man can do it. Rohlfing has been trying to take leadership for the past seven years. But I do not see any results in the foreseeable future."

* * * *

No question.

Hall: "Fred Rohlfing attacks on hui—consensus—government, but that won't win him many supporters."

* * * *

Jones: "What do you think of Fred Rohlfing's charges of government by hui, naming Takabuki and your father and others?"

Stuart Ho: "That's a sensitive question. I think he's fishing for issues as a base for a future campaign. This one—although it's not true—is an issue which he probably thinks will appeal to some people in the community."

* * * *

Jones: "What do you think of the charge that we have government by hui?"

Blaisdell: "I don't know what Fred Rohlfing means by hui. I think it's absolutely necessary that we have a good deal of rapport with all levels of government…."

* * * *

Jones: "What do you think about Rohlfing and his charge of government by hui?"

Woolaway: "There are huis in every political party. That's the way it works. What he is talking about is that business supports the Democrats. Business isn't Republican anymore. When you have five thousand stockholders, they sure aren't all Republicans."

Interview number fifteen, January 22, 1968: "Rohlfing Charges Secrecy and Waste."

I am not going to repeat my long interplay with Jones. The use of the word "hui" had made the picture clear. But I will restate my response to Jones about public education:

"Our school system is a bomb that may go off at any time. We have raised pay and spent a mint on buildings, and we have a competent administrator. Yet we have, despite quantity, a lousy quality over all. The schools, in some cases the districts, are running autonomously.... There are too many cooks—the Legislature, the board [of education], and cross-references between teachers' organizations and PTAs. It is the biggest business in the state, and I think it's going to blow up. People are not getting their money's worth out of the education dollar."

That paragraph could easily fit in with the discussion of education's current policy and performance in Chapter 8.

Ah, yes, things do change slowly in Hawai'i!

My theme continued into the 1970s as revealed by a speech on October 22, 1970, to the members of a group called "Zero Population Growth." I said that the Burns administration had a "land developer philosophy" that promoted "more people, more houses, more hotels, more money," and that "the criteria for everything is the almighty dollar." I added that the administration also had an "open arms immigration policy" that was "creating a burden on Hawai'i's ecological and social balance." By that point I was beginning to take leadership on a number of environmental issues.

'68 Events

The year 1968 was full of surprises. In addition to Tet, there was the seizure of the *SS Pueblo*, an intelligence ship, by North Korea, who imprisoned the crew for a substantial time period. Then on February 27, after my return from Saigon [see Chapter 5], Walter Cronkite announced on the CBS News that the U.S. should negotiate a settlement of the Vietnam War. In March Senator Eugene McCarthy defeated President Lyndon Johnson in the New Hampshire primary. Two weeks later, LBJ announced that he would not run for reelection. A week after that Martin Luther King, Jr., was assassinated.

And it was only April 4!

Race riots were occurring all over. In June Sirhan Sirhan assassinated Robert F. Kennedy, Jr., the former president's brother and a former attorney general. In August the Soviet Union invaded Czechoslovakia. Seven days later anti-war demonstrators fought Chicago police in the streets and areas associated with the Democratic Party's national convention. The national culture was in the throes of violent change. The two political parties each moved toward their extreme elements, with Nixon eking out a win over Humphrey in the general election. It was an amazing year!

I was a player in the game, too. I was selected—along with Democrat legislator Dickie Wong (later Senate president and, ultimately, Bishop Estate trustee of dubious credentials)—for the Eagleton Institute of Politics program at Rutgers University. From July 28 through August 3 at a conference facility in Key Biscayne south of Miami, Florida, I attended the Institute's seminar for "outstanding state legislators."

While at this seminar I met prominent Democrats such as Jesse Unruh (long-time speaker of the House in California), Willie Brown (mayor of San Francisco), and some top Republicans (such as then-governor of Rhode Island John Chafee) some of whom were to be my contacts at the national convention a week later in Miami.

The GOP National Convention
Miami, Florida, 1968

Andy Anderson and I were both elected delegates to the Republican National Convention of 1968. Andy was head of the Nelson Rockefeller for President Committee for Hawai'i. I, too, supported Rockefeller over Nixon.

The contacts I had made at Rutgers the week before proved most useful. I could talk easily with politicians of prominence in New Jersey, Missouri, Washington, Rhode Island, Alaska, and other places. Andy would sit in his hotel room, where he maintained communication with top Rockefeller people, and then contact me on the floor of the convention by phone. I would then communicate with my friends on the floor. But we couldn't match the Nixon machine, and Rockefeller was knocked out.

Our delegation stuck with our Senator Hiram Fong, but eventually he threw Hawai'i's votes into Nixon's column.

Three sidebars from this convention: one, a lei presentation I made to Julie Nixon at a campaign breakfast with our delegation; two, a confrontation outside the convention hall with Vietnam veteran protestors; and three, my son Fritz's appointment as a page.

The second event involved my being physically surrounded by a group of shaggy guys, some of whom were smoking pot and all of whom felt animosity towards Nixon specifically and Republicans generally. When I told them that I had served, albeit briefly, in Vietnam, the atmosphere cleared up dramatically and we parted as "friends."

1968 Mayoral Race

When longtime Honolulu Mayor Neal Blaisdell died in 1968, his position came up for grabs. Democrat Frank Fasi, out early on the campaign trail, appeared to be the man to beat when Senators Wadsworth Yee, Andy Anderson, and I met at Trader Vic's to decide which one of us would take him on. The nod went to Andy. I did not covet being in City government. I believed it would be a diversion from my lifetime goal of representing my state in Washington. This same rationale led me to decline Fasi's later offer of an appointment to the job of City prosecutor.

Having encouraged Andy to run for mayor, I put my shoulder to the wheel by making numerous speeches and appearances on his behalf over a period of at least three months. In addition, I prepared position papers and speeches for him and attended countless meetings. My law practice suffered a lot. Even so, in the end Andy was defeated.

Affordable Housing 1969: Bipartisanship Carries the Day

I spent much of my legislative effort in 1969 on affordable housing matters. I worked hard in drafting and setting policy for what we dubbed an "Omnibus Housing Bill." I had done my homework, which had included a one-on-one with George Romney in his role as secretary of Housing and Urban Development (HUD), arranged by my friend Margita White in White House communications.

One of my staffers, courtesy of the Chamber of Commerce legislative intern program, was a young go-getter named Gayer Dominick. He was related to U.S. Senator Peter Dominick (R) of Colorado, and he was very liberal. (He is now a Democrat and lives in Olympia.) I got to know him when we both worked for Rockefeller in the 1968 presidential campaign. He worked diligently on the bill and helped me make contact with Senator Vince Yano's people. Yano was an AJA lawyer whom I got to know as we campaigned competitively in the same multi-member district. Yano led the ticket in our first encounter (1966), but I think I beat him in 1970 or '74.

Our bill was like those big tax bills in Congress—a heavyweight, as it was modeled on the legislation that established the U.S. Department of Housing and Urban Development. The Legislature didn't pass Yano's and my bill, but much of it showed up in a Democrat party bill introduced by Senate President John Hulten. When Hulten's bill came to the Senate floor, most of my fellow Republicans, and even some Democrats, said the bill went too far and gave too much power to the housing commissioner. I was quoted in floor debate as saying that since "the bill had been

amended to tighten control over the program [and] would allow for a 'little Capehart' construction program," I would vote for the bill. I added that "I have been critical of this administration for not acting on this problem…. In this bill the ball is tossed to the governor once again, and I am willing to have him have another go at it since I prefer constructive action to criticism."

It was clearly a time to put up or shut up.

Representing Labor

A subchapter in my legal career had political implications that were later to bear fruit in my congressional campaigns of the seventies. In 1963 I received a call from my friend and Senate colleague, Wadsworth Yee (Hiram Fong's nephew). He asked if I'd be interested in representing nurses in contract negotiations. He explained that he had contacts within the leadership of the Hawai'i Nurses Association (HNA). These contacts had asked him to take on such work, but he wanted to keep them as insurance clients and instead oversee another lawyer who would actively do the negotiations work. I replied, "Okay, when do I start?"

Almost immediately I was deeply involved with negotiations at Kuakini Hospital in lower Nu'uanu Valley. A more unusual place for collective bargaining would have been hard to find. Kuakini was run by, and principally for, the Japanese community in Hawai'i. While open to other ethnicities, it was very traditional in all that it did. As I remember, the Hawai'i Employer's Council provided a "hired gun" to represent the hospital. Nevertheless, it was Mr. Kenji Goto, the chief executive officer of the hospital, who clearly called the shots from the other side of the table.

In those days nurses made only about $3.50 per hour, and the argument was always about how many cents-per-hour more they wanted. I recall a spirited negotiation that resulted in a long impasse. The HNA had a policy against strikes at the time, so we had very little leverage. We ended up with a very unsatisfactory bargain, and I became emotionally committed to doing better at my next negotiations.

As an aside, much later Kenji Goto supported my campaign for the House Thirteenth District (1982) by stating: "For a number of years, as administrator of Kuakini Hospital, I sat across the bargaining table from Fred Rohlfing, chief negotiator for our nurses. I found him to be a tough and resilient negotiator and spokesman for his side. But I also came to respect highly Fred's capacity for bringing divergent views into a constructive consensus."

The opportunity to improve my negotiating skills came soon enough at St. Francis Hospital, which had a totally different, and even more encompassing, philosophy of existence than did Kuakini—St. Francis was still very Catholic. The director of nursing, also a registered nurse, was a nun by the name of Sister Maureen.

I will never forget our first meeting in the St. Francis conference room. At the head of the table Monsignor Daniel Dever opened the meeting with a prayer. He then stayed on to oversee the presentation of each side's initial proposals. As time went by, he excused himself from our sessions, as Sister Maureen was obviously a strong and intelligent leader who could handle our strike-less band of penitents with dispatch. At one session I got into a doctrinal debate with Sister Maureen about how one should treat those in poorly compensated positions. The discussion became particularly heated when I began quoting at length from Pope John's encyclical on labor.

Some years later, when we had reached a particularly deep impasse at St. Francis, I called Father Dever. We met at Ciro's restaurant on Hotel Street to discuss options available to both sides and possibly seek some common ground. I told him that his strategy at that first negotiations meeting—trying to "psych" us out by acting as the controller of the meeting—had backfired. Instead of being cowed, the nurses had dug their heels in deeper to prove that they merited equal footing. He got the message, and we talked frankly about ways to break our impasse and resolve the issues. St. Francis was well connected with Democratic leaders in Hawai'i, so it was somewhat ironic that they had to contend with what amounted to a high-class labor union whose chief negotiator was, of all things, a Republican legislator!

The executive directors I worked with over the years in collective bargaining included Rose Ann Poyzer, Margaret Cookson, and Chris Taylor.

It was my experience that the nurses generally were concerned more with the practice of their profession than with their economic rewards. This was particularly true at Kaiser-Permanente Hospital, then in Waikīkī, and at Kapiʻolani Hospital in the Punahou district. This professionalism was amazing to me given the woeful level of pay they were then receiving. I argued and pressed for common dates of contract expiration so that we could have joint negotiations or—if still separate—at least during the same time period. We were able to do this. And we finally exercised our legal right to strike, thus overcoming former HNA policy. I walked the picket line with our women at night at both Kapiʻolani and Kaiser, and in due course we obtained a decent settlement. Some time after this a resolution was passed at an HNA convention naming me as an honorary registered nurse!

Towards the end of my duties with HNA, nurses began organizing at Queen's Hospital and at government-owned and -operated hospitals. We initially lost a representation election at Queen's, but we filed an unfair labor practice action with the Hawaiʻi State Employment Relations Board (HERB) for coercion at mandated staff meetings. The opposing lawyer, Bob Katz, was with the successor firm (Torkildson, Katz, et. al.) to my old law firm (Moore, Torkildson, and Rice), so it was particularly satisfying to win the case.

When HNA won the vote for State nurse representation, however, I was faced with a potential conflict of interest. I served on the Senate Ways and Means Committee, which would have to recommend to the Senate any funding agreement with HNA. I submitted the issue to the State Ethics Commission. They opined that there was an appearance of conflict (in that we ultimately voted on the State budget, which would include State nurses' salaries). They brushed aside my point that I was a minority-party senator and had little influence on the outcome. I withdrew from representing HNA shortly thereafter.

I thoroughly enjoyed the negotiations work, and I treasure the memory of those professional associations. I continue to have great admiration for our state's hardworking (and still underpaid) nurses.

Senator Clark Switches Parties

Probably the most emotional speech that I ever gave followed upon the announcement by my fellow senator James K. Clark that he was switching parties. (See Appendix Four for speech text.)

I had known Clark before politics, as we were both Punahou graduates. We had played together on the 1945 Punahou varsity football team. Clark was a sophomore who played first-string tackle, and I was a senior guard who started only three games but got better as the season progressed. Jim was married to Velma "Jiggy" Blaisdell (Mayor Neal S. Blaisdell's daughter), also from Punahou. Jim had invited me to his home in Papokolea (Hawaiian Homes housing on Punchbowl) where we had sung Hawaiian songs along with Jim's father, Herman Sr. (also a legendary semi-pro football player). After Punahou Jim had attended Oregon State along with his younger brother, Herman Jr. (a.k.a. "Buddy"), who ultimately played for the Chicago Bears. Jim was named an All-American and was subsequently drafted by the Washington Redskins. When I was in the Navy in Washington, I watched him play for the Redskins at Griffiths Stadium. My wife Joan and I had dinner one night at the Clarks' apartment. As a politician Jim had served in the House as our minority whip. In a nutshell, he was my friend.

My speech was the keynote at the convention of the Oʻahu Young Republicans. A Tom Coffman byline story in the *Honolulu Star-Bulletin* in early March 1969 read in part as follows:

"State Sen. Fred Rohlfing today positioned himself against what he called an 'intolerant, loud and abusive' faction of Hawaii's Republican Party.... While welcoming 'responsible' conservatism, he called for driving toward a broad-based, cosmopolitan party—despite the recent GOP setback: the defection of his friend State Sen. James K. Clark to the Democrats.

"Rohlfing's keynote address to the convention appeared to be a rare personal outpouring precipitated by Clark's bolt Tuesday away from the GOP. [Rohlfing] said that 'those who talk loudest about their 100 percent Republicanism make me sick.' Rohlfing said, too, that he was 'through taking a conservative stance "for the sake of the party." I will never accept that

Sen. Rohlfing raps 'intolerant' faction of Isle Republicans

By Tom Coffman
Star-Bulletin Writer

Fred Rohlfing

State Sen. Fred W. Rohlfing today positioned himself against what he called an "intolerant, loud and abusive" faction of Hawaii's Republican Party.

And, while welcoming "responsible" conservatism, he called for driving toward a broad-based, cosmopolitan party — despite the recent GOP setback: The defection of his friend, State Sen. James K. Clark, to the Democrats.

Rohlfing's keynote address to the Young Republicans' convention appeared to be a rare personal outpouring — precipitated by Clark's bolt Tuesday away from the GOP.

Rohlfing said Republicans must struggle with the problems of both the affluent and the poor.

In this context, he said that those "who talk loudest about their 100 per cent Republicanism make me sick."

ROHLFING said, too, that he was through taking a con-

See editorial on page A-10

servative position "for the sake of the party."

"I will never accept that negative role again."

He recalled that he and Clark "were schoolmates and played on the same football team in 1945.

"We have played and sung Hawaiian songs together at his parents home in Papakolea.

"I am deeply saddened, both emotionally and intellectually, by Jim's decision."

And, he said, "Those who would be quick to throw verbal brickbats, and those who would gloat, have missed the underlying message of this event.

"THE LOCAL talk-talk station element is now delir-

ously happy with the implications of victory of so-called Republican 'conservatives' over the so-called GOP moderates and liberals." (The reference was to Radio KTRG.)

"Is the party, Rohlfing asked, "now to undergo a purge so it can be made up of all the same type of people?

"David McClung (Democratic Party chairman) says we still suffer from the plantation image, but that is an old wives' tale.

"Our problem today is instead, an intolerant, loud, and abusive dissident element."

This group, Rohlfing said, "is either unwilling or unable to really understand the people of these Islands or their needs."

HE POSED to the young party members a dire alternative to dealing realistically with urban problems:

"Does the Republican Party respond by saying that its theoretical principles do not admit that these problems

Rohlfing dipped into his own family background as he confronted the conventi describing himself as a of "immigrants from Cali nia.

"My grandfather wa one time postmaster of cerville, Calif., in the H Johnson era. Hiram Jol was a great Republican senator who fought the opolistic railroads, an was a believer in tru mocracy.

"In fact, he was esse a Populist.

"MY DAD worked iron works, Cast Cooke, and retired president of Dole. Bo parents instilled in r losophy of honest qu of the sacred cow era.

"Also they tran

The Honolulu Advertiser

Established July 2, 1856

THURSTON TWIGG-SMITH — *President & Publisher*
GEORGE CHAPLIN — *Editor*
BUCK BUCHWACH — *Managing Editor*
JOHN GRIFFIN — *Editorial Page Editor*

THURSDAY, APRIL 16, 1970

U.S. land for campus?

State Senator Fred W. Rohlfing's effort to get Federal land in central Oahu returned for use as a second University of Hawaii campus deserves strong support from both political parties and the board of regents.

His proposal envisions space for both the educational institution and the supporting community around it — which could possibly grow to a population of 100,000—without encroaching upon prime agricultural lands.

PRESENTLY, THE regents have approved "in principle" a site offered by the Bishop Estate at Waiawa. The Campbell Estate has also submitted a proposal for putting the campus on some of its land.

Rohlfing is proposing an alternative which would be excellent if it can be achieved. He has three sites in mind, all of them lands ceded by Hawaii to the Federal government without compensation at the time of annexation.

● "The underde....
Schofi....

tures." Acreage is large but specific figures were not listed.

● "Wheeler Air Force Base—now virtually deserted; 1,404 acres which adjoin State-owned land.

● "Schofield East Range — a developable and under-used area adjoining the urban area of Wahiawa town. Approximately 1,500 acres."

The Manoa campus is about 300 acres. The second campus area is being discussed in terms of 1,000.

ROHLFING BELIEVES that under Federal law, the administrator of the Department of General Services, "acting in concurrence with an agency or department head", can return any of the three sites to Hawaii without the need for Congressional action.

The Federal government, he notes, owns, leases or otherwise controls 25 per cent of Oahu. For most of this land, there are important and necessary uses. But at least some of the sites listed....
fa....

Rohlfing Charges Secrecy and Waste

By GARDINER B. JONES
Associate Editor, The Advertiser

Last of 16 articles

Republican State Sen. Fred Rohlfing, who accuses the Democrats of "government by hui," says their leaders are guilty of:

Secrecy, actions against the public interest, waste in highway construction, questionable legal ethics, conflict of interest, favoritism in government contracts and fostering "do-nothingism" in the government service.

As for Democratic claims of having improved the school system, Rohlfing says that "it is a bomb that may go off any time"; that the schools are poorly run and education in "of lousy quality over-all."

Rohlfing, who sounds like a young Democrat of 1954 attacking the Big Five, charges that the men running the government today have little of the feeling of being Democrats. Those who seek well as the common bond of being Democrats. Those who seek to do business with the government, he says, must go through the right persons "to maintain their eligibility."

The "government by hui" accusation is mentioned as a "comer" in the Republican party. It is widely believed in political circles that he is grooming himself to run for Congress in 1970.

The "government by hui" accusation was made in a speech a few months ago. In a current interview, Rohlfing amplified the accusation and also made these other points:

● The Republicans are being revitalized by an influx of new, young faces, and the Democrats correspondingly are

being weakened because they offer little opportunity for the young politician.

● The Democratic party split between Gov. John A. Burns and Lt. Gov. Thomas P. Gill is essentially a case of the old machine operation vs. the brash young reformer.

● Island politics today is more tolerant in the area of race; a Caucasian today can win Oriental support he could not have expected 10 years ago.

● Because public needs have outrun revenues, govern-

HAWAII POLITICS
A Candid, Inside Report

ment will have to enter joint ventures with private capital to meet some future requirements.

Here is the interview:

Question—Your recent speech about "government by hui" caused a lot of comment. Specifically, who were you aiming at?

Rohlfing—I was talking about Governor Burns, Chinn Ho and City Councilman (Matsuo) Takabuki. I am critical to a degree of the newspapers for not opening these things up.

I think those who have been in critical positions of State executive power and the power of the City Council — well, first there is an inter-relationship, not just because they are Democrats; there are all sorts of business and economic relationships.

Where I really admire them is that they have shown a tremendous ability not to get rattled by what little criticism that has come out openly.

Generally speaking, the most knowledgeable businessmen in town who either work with the State Government directly under contracts or who sell to the State fully understand that they have to deal through certain lawyers or other representatives to maintain their eligibility.

During the last campaign various contractors were asked for contributions to Burns on a percentage basis of the work they had done for the State. This has been reported to me.

You will find that the attorneys who represent these interests are Democrats who have either past or present associations with people in high political office. In some cases there is a question of what I would call conflict of interest.

In some cases, there is questionable legal ethics. I think the ethics committee of the bar has been weak in enforcing and interpreting ethical violations.

I am not suggesting there has been illegal conduct. But is it improper for an official to represent his constituents first, rather than special interests?

Question—Are you saying people have acted against the public interest?

Rohlfing—Yes. I think the very climate, the power structure, the process one must follow to relate to the government is the backdoor approach.

Things are underground, done in secrecy. I don't think the State Administration enjoys debating things. You don't

See ROHLFING on A-4, Col. 8

---

negative role again…. I am deeply saddened, both emotionally and intellectually by Jim's decision…. Those who would be quick to throw verbal brickbats, and those who would gloat, have missed the underlying message of this event. The local talk-station element is now deliriously happy with the implications of victory of so-called Republican "conservatives" over the so-called liberals…. David McClung (Democrat Party chairman) says we suffer from the plantation image, but that is an old wives' tale. Our problem today is, instead, **an intolerant, loud, and abusive dissident element.**'

"Rohlfing said that 'a Republican legislator represents all the people of his district, not just the Republicans. He represents people whose backgrounds and environmental conditions are as disparate as Pālolo Public Housing and Walupe Circle.... The less fortunate must count on the understanding of their legislator.'"

The *Advertiser* commented editorially on March 4, 1969: "Affluence reaching right into the ranks of blue collar workers has made a whole new group where the Republican Party might flourish. But it may well be that members of this new middle class are scared off by rightwing talk that bears so little relation to life as the majority here sees it."

A week or so after this speech there was newspaper speculation that I might run for governor. One article concluded:

"At a recent press conference announcing minority legislative plans, Porteus took his seat as minority leader at the head of the table.... He said his lines and then Rohlfing said his.... To oversimplify a bit, Porteus seemed to view the minority program as a 'series of helpful suggestions,' a phrase he uses often. Rohlfing portrayed it as the beginnings of an alternative to the present administration."

When will they ever learn? You don't win political ball games by playing "footsie" with those in power.

1970: King vs. Porteus vs. Burns

We Republicans looked forward optimistically to the gubernatorial race of 1970. John Burns had been in office since decisively beating Bill Quinn in 1962, and he had accumulated some scars. In the prior election (1966), Burns had put his very considerable power and prestige on the line by selecting Kenneth F. Brown as his running mate for lieutenant governor. Brown was an architect/businessman who until then had never run for public office. Worse for Burns, Brown had been beaten soundly by the outspoken upstart in the Democratic Party, Tom Gill. This was a tremendous "loss of face" for the ruling Burns faction. "Face" is important in politics anywhere but particularly so in multi-racial Hawai'i. On Election Day, Gill received 90,900 votes for lieutenant governor. Burns himself received only 86,000 votes in the governor's race!

As 1970 approached, those from business, labor, and community interests were increasingly testing the waters on whether Tom Gill would take on and could have the wherewithal to defeat Jack Burns for governor. Gill, an issues man (even more than I), believed in his remedies for the uncontrolled growth of tourism and rapid land development, both of which were inundating "Old Hawai'i" in the dynamic 1960s. Gill was the architect of the Land Use Law (the only statewide land zoning law in the nation), and he sought to provide affordable housing via condemnation of large tracts owned by the powerful estates, kama'āinas, and businesses. He was strongly for rail mass-transit, anti-trust controls, and other government activism. He railed against the oil companies for both high prices and pollution. The intensity of the Burns-Gill face-off had its impact on our side of the aisle. Some thought the internal battle of the Democrats would destroy their winning formula. We needed, therefore, to choose our candidate wisely and get on with it.

At this juncture in mid-1969 Andy Anderson, our Senate minority floor leader, made his move to push minority leader Hebden Porteus into the race. Porteus came from the old school of politics and had served for years in the territorial Legislature. By "old school" I mean he was ready to compromise early on, avoid strong stands on issues, and to "go along to get along." Anderson put the heat on Porteus by contacting and ultimately hiring the political management firm of Spencer Roberts as early as May of 1969. He also prevailed upon some business contacts to come forward with pledges of $100,000 for Porteus's startup funds. Representatives of Spencer Roberts began arriving in Honolulu in September of the year before the election.

I had strong reservations about Porteus' chances of winning. Tom Coffman's book *Catch a Wave* was on the mark when it said on page 125: "Rohlfing in a 1968 speech made a splash by condemning the Burns style consensus as 'Government by Hui,' meaning a new closed system ruled by an elite clique. And Rohlfing also became increasingly skeptical of the Senate as a bipartisan club—for good or ill, it was that in many ways. Fred Rohlfing, in effect, thought the comforts of the Senate's clubbish lifestyle paled in comparison to the chance for the Republican Party to become a vigorous opposition party—perhaps to one day become the majority party. To play that role of vigorous opposition was no easy thing."

Coffman went on to say that "One part of the [Republican] party had its heart buried in the past, a second had its head buried under a wing of the Democrat—often the Burns wing—although there were those such as Rohlfing who grudgingly admired Tom Gill, feeling that Gill was fulfilling the responsibility of the loyal opposition which the Republicans had largely abdicated."

As the year progressed, I endeavored to put pressure on Sam P. King to run for governor by working with Ed Brennan and Phil Spalding, the Republican National Committeeman. Sam was still a State Family Court judge, so this decision would have been a big move for him. In time, being a political animal and disgusted with Democrat leadership, Sam took the bait and set up a lunch with Porteus. According to Coffman's book, Sam deferred to Porteus, but later, at another lunch, took back his deferral. The end result was a stimulating primary which Sam won, but not by the margin that we had hoped for. On the other side, Burns and Gill went at it, and the famous video *Catch a Wave* helped to save Jack Burns from the Gill assault in the primary. Senator Larry Kuriyama was brutally killed in his own garage a week or two prior to the general election, and Sam tried (unsuccessfully) to paint a picture of crime due to poor leadership by the Burns machine. The final election results were Burns 137,000 and King 101,000.

I still admire Sam King, who snatched victory out of defeat by being appointed a U.S. District Court judge, where he has served with distinction.

CHAPTER TWO

TWO CONGRESSIONAL CAMPAIGNS

Lead-Up to the 1972 Congressional Campaign: The Cost of Living Council (COLC)

In the period before my first congressional campaign, Margita White set up several meetings with prominent persons who were in a position to make decisions affecting Hawai'i. One of these meetings was with George Romney, Secretary of Housing and Urban Development. Affordable housing was one of my main interests even this early, and during this time frame I introduced a comprehensive State Housing Act. Romney was an "old shoe" kind of guy and was wearing a fuzzy sweater when I met him in his office. He called in a deputy to work with me on my bill.

I also met with key figures in my return-of-federal-lands initiative that focused on land for the second University of Hawai'i campus in West O'ahu. These key figures were Darrell Trent, an assistant to President Richard Nixon, and a representative of Housing and Urban Development by the name (I believe) of Nicosin. We located several parcels of federal lands that were vacant or underutilized in the vicinity of Wheeler Air Force Base on O'ahu's central plain (Wahiawā). These lands had been ceded by the Hawaiian republic to the federal government at the time of annexation. A broader return of federal lands was developed, along with the smaller Hickam package, and was pushed through the Conference of Elected Republicans (COER), of which I was chairman. This gave us some numbers to back up our efforts. Both major Honolulu newspapers endorsed my efforts and published feature articles praising them (*Honolulu Star-Bulletin* April 30, 1970, and *Honolulu Advertiser* April 16, 1970).

My strategy was twofold. First, I wanted to get our Legislature to adopt a resolution that pressed for the reclaiming of those lands. (This I accomplished.) Then I wanted to push the U.S. General Services Administration and a department head to release the key parcels without an act of Congress.

Meanwhile, Congressman Spark Matsunaga co-opted our efforts by writing to the Department of Defense and reiterating our proposal. This brought about the usual routine rejection and thus defeated our efforts.

Additional contacts that Margita set up for me would have major influences on my political career. These key contacts grew out of the Nixon administration's war on inflation and consequent creation of price and wage controls in approximately 1971. The Cost of Living Council (COLC) was created at this time under leadership of Donald Rumsfeld (Secretary of Defense under George W. Bush) and Bob Tiernan from the Bay Area, who would later become my Navy Reserve Intelligence commanding officer.

Due to a series of West Coast dock-work stoppages, businesses in Hawai'i were really hurting from interruptions of shipping services. Prices in the Islands started to rise because goods had to be brought in by air. We were experiencing shortages of essentials such as toilet paper and rice (a universal staple in Hawai'i). This shipping trouble was a big deal as far as Island business and the public was concerned. I realized that a single change in federal policy would really help Hawai'i—exemptions from the strict rules of the COLC (which, ironically, had been designed to control inflation).

Through my Washington contacts I was able to get the federal administration to send two outstanding officials to hold public hearings to find out whether Hawai'i should be granted a special exemption from the wage/price rules. This team of Frank Zarb and Dr. Harold Passer traveled from Washington, and we arranged for hearing space in the State capitol. As a result of my efforts, Hawai'i won a temporary exemption from the strict rules of the COLC.

On one of my trips to Washington to argue for this special treatment I met with Secretary of Labor James Hodgson. (This meeting was arranged by then-Assistant Secretary of Labor Lawrence Silberman, who is now a senior federal appeals judge and who, much earlier, had also worked for Moore, Torkildson & Rice in Honolulu.) Hodgson later sent me a letter which stated that "your bold initiative...resulted in a study team being dispatched to Hawai'i to review your special problem arising from the West Coast dock dispute.... As a result of your efforts the Cost of Living Council has become more sensitive to the extra dimensions of the Hawai'i economy."

We used a photo of Hodgson and me with this letter excerpt in our big print ads during the 1972 Matsunaga campaign. Frank Zarb later went on to head the NASDAQ stock exchange and NASD.

MAYOR FRANK FASI SHARES HIS MANA'O (VIEWS) ON HAWAI'I'S ECONOMY WITH ZARB/ PASSER TEAM.

The COLC activity occurred at the same time that I was moving forward with my intention to challenge Spark Matsunaga for the U.S. House first district seat. The positive results I achieved with the COLC underscored, for those paying attention, the contrast between what I, a mere State senator, had been able to accomplish through the Republican-led U.S. administration, as compared to the failed attempts by the Democratic incumbent. Unfortunately, as it ultimately turned out, not enough people were paying attention.

The aforementioned series of dock strikes presented further political opportunity for me the longer our U.S. Congressional delegation failed to act. At the outset I knew that challenging the popular Spark Matsunaga would be tough, but I felt I had to go beyond my State Senate district if I eventually wanted to serve in U.S. Congress, which had been a long-time goal of mine. Fortunately, I could run without giving up my Senate seat. So I would not be politically "dead" if I lost.

With the help of the group of women that Barbara Marumoto (later to be a State representative) had assembled, I created a staff. The leaders included Leinani Bortles (public relations/advertising), Diana Snyder (scheduling), Patty Bond (campaign headquarters manager), banker Frank Manaut (finance chair), Castle & Cooke executive George Miyasaka (campaign chair), and Dan Ichinose (campaign manager). Barbara Marumoto handled research. Others who joined or were already a part of my team were Willson and Sally Moore, Barney Smith, Murray and Marge Grune, Bob and Nancy Harlocker, Robert and Patsy Gibson, Keith and Polly Steiner, Ken Luke, Bobby Choy, Frank Barros, Elmer Punohu, and Tom Nekota. My mother and her friend Mrs. Watson Ballentyne would get into their town-going clothes and work on addressing envelopes or whatever Barbara had on for the day.

Dan Ichinose was the brother of universally known boxing promoter "Sad" Sam Ichinose, and he was one of a kind. He became totally dedicated to my campaigns, often sacrificing his personal income. (He worked as an insurance agent with Occidental Life.) Pat Saiki had recruited him originally when I ran for reelection to the State Senate in 1970. An example of Dan's dedication occurred when he committed himself to convincing a staunchly Democratic voting precinct in Kaimukī-lower Pālolo to vote for me. Ethnically the precinct was heavily Japanese, with some Chinese, Koreans, and an absolute lack of Republican-inclined haoles. The Japanese were voting about eighty percent Democratic. Dan would walk this area house-to-house on his own time, and he walked with me in other areas as well. We came close to winning the precinct, as I recall. And yet, despite his efforts, I believe Vince Yano beat me out in the final balloting. However, over the entire district we led the multi-office race.

The 1972 Campaign

Highlights of my first campaign for U.S. Congress flash through my mind: having a high-school student drive me to appearances in a puke-green Subaru wagon donated by Dutchy Schumann from Schumann Carriage; walking house-to-house in Democratic areas like ʻAiea in January, when people had absolutely no interest in politics; also, struggling to raise money in a race that all the experts said I couldn't win, early polls indicating it would take a miracle to do so. (I had around twenty percent of the vote in the early summer.) We had a media/policy advisor in San Francisco with whom we consulted long-distance by telephone (before the days of email). Mostly I remember a huge effort to raise the necessary funds. Despite these many challenges we plunged ahead.

President Nixon became a part of our plan when he came to Hawaiʻi to meet with Prime Minister Tanaka of Japan at Kuilima on the North Shore. We tried to get an audience with the president to discuss legislation to alleviate the dock strike and some federal land issues, as well as to present a petition from a Hawaiian group given to me by "Uncle" Charley Maxwell of Pūkalani, Maui. I was able to get the petition to the president through aides, but I couldn't get in myself. I was promised a meeting as he departed from Hickam Field for Washington, D.C., but this meeting never actually materialized. Later we did have our picture taken together at the Republican National Convention in Miami.

Our own polls, as well as those appearing in the press, indicated that Nixon was going to win in Hawaiʻi against McGovern. So Sandy Weiner, our San Francisco-based advisor, said we should grab onto his coattails. (Weiner's firm normally worked for Democrats.) Thus, in the final weeks of the campaign, we ran a series of large newspaper ads proclaiming benefits from my various contacts with the Nixon administration. We tried to tie Matsunaga to wild McGovern proposals to slash $32 billion from the defense budget and the negative impact that would have on Hawaiʻi. We also mounted a major attack on Matsunaga's inability to protect us against dock strikes and on his general softness on labor issues. Since he was always proclaiming how powerful he was due to his vaunted Rules Committee membership, we asked, "Why isn't he doing more for us?"

I came up with a plan to create a single federal agency focused on overseeing shipping between the U.S. Pacific islands and the Mainland, an agency that would oversee rates and terms of service. It would replace existing federal agencies, and it would have the power to mediate—and in extreme cases arbitrate—wages and working conditions. I also suggested amendments to the Taft-Hartley Act that would apply "cooling off" provisions to shipping emergencies in a single state instead of requiring a national emergency.

Money was another problem, but Frank Manaut and I negotiated for a badly needed $50,000 from the Republican Party at the critical point of the campaign. This funding would later (in the 1976 campaign) become contentious when the Party claimed it was a loan, not a grant.

We publicly challenged Matsunaga to debate on commercial television stations, but we were only able to get him to agree to debate on our National Public Broadcasting System (PBS) affiliate, Channel 11, for one hour. The electorate was not conditioned to watching PBS, so we knew we had to try to get the word out. We did the best we could with radio and full-page newspaper ads. I don't know how many people watched the debate, but clearly not enough actually did. (Either that, or I didn't do as well as my supporters and I had thought!)

Sen. Fred Ro...

HONOLULU ADVERTISER Thursday, Oct. 26, 1972 A-15

★ ★ ★

Matsunaga, Rohlfing debate issues

shipping strikes and seniority

U.S. Rep. Spark M. Matsunaga and State Sen. Fred W. Rohlfing last night drew their campaign battlelines in the 1st Congressional District race across the issues of dock strikes and congressional seniority.

Democrat incumbent Matsunaga and his Republican challenger also clashed on the issues of national economic and welfare policies and Hawaii's population crisis during their first television debate, sponsored by KHET-TV.

DURING THE hour-long debate, with a panel of four newsmen asking questions, Matsunaga for the first time lashed out against Rohlfing's proposed solution to dock strikes—the creation of a new Federal regulatory agency—saying "it is full of loopholes."

Rohlfing, in turn, charged Matsunaga with inaction in the Congress on the dock strike issue and inability to

recognize that the solution and prevention of shipping strikes requires new legislation, not reliance upon the Taft-Hartley law.

Rohlfing contended that President Nixon was unable to impose the cooling-off period in last fall's 100-day West Coast dock strike because the shipping strike did not "imperil the health and security" of the nation until the East Coast shippers became involved.

Matsunaga clung to his position that the strike could and should have been averted if Nixon used the Federal law as was done by four presidents in the past.

ON ROHLFING'S proposal that a new Federal agency be created which would have powers to call for mediation at the threat of a strike, Matsunaga said the plan would not avert strikes and would only add another Federal regulatory body.

The congressman said the answers to dock strikes remain in "the laws we now

have," although he favors an amendment to the Taft-Hartley law to mandate the President take action immediately upon threat of a strike.

ANOTHER HOT issue in the hour-long debate, which

ROHLFING

often times appeared as a mini version of the presidential campaign, was Matsunaga's claim that best representation for the district rests with an incumbent with seniority.

Rohlfing took issue with Matsunaga's claim that his five-term seniority in the

MATSUNAGA

House and his seat on the Rules Committee insures better representation for the district.

Rohlfing, a 13-year veteran of the State Legislature, said Matsunaga's position in the House may be shaky, with the national reform movement, led by Ralph Nader, attacking the seniority rules of Congress as a tool which has left Congress with "no leadership."

He said the voters have no guarantee that Matsunaga will not seek a U.S. Senate seat or that his seniority may be disposed of through reform, urging the voters to choose ability over seniority.

ON OTHER ISSUES debated between the opponents for Honolulu's House seat, Rohlfing steadfastly supported President Nixon's policies for economic growth and welfare reform, while Matsunaga voiced many of the proposals urged by the Democratic presidential contender, Sen. George McGovern.

Rohlfing contended the answer to growing welfare rolls is Nixon's family system plan which he said would encourage getting the working poor off welfare.

Matsunaga countered that Nixon's welfare reforms are useless with growing unemployment in the nation. He cited the unemployment rise from 6.2 million Americans in 1969 to 10.3 million people this year.

"The fact is people get on to welfare because there are no jobs to get into," Matsunaga said.

MATSUNAGA also claimed that new jobs, plus the creation of new industry in Hawaii, is the answer to keeping Hawaii's young people in the Islands.

Rohlfing said the growth influx into Hawaii is in part caused by the State's high number of immigrants which he said the Federal government is responsible for aiding with innovative programs.

My memory fails me with respect to the context of the debate. I do remember scoring points on Matsunaga's weakness on defense issues and his talk about a peace department in Washington. This fit into the overlay of Nixon vs. Mc Govern as well. On other points related to the COLC and his failure to protect Hawai'i from dock strikes, I believe we had him on the defensive. (We had done a mock debate in preparation for the real thing, with Barbara Marumoto starring as Spark—Harvard accent and all! So much of what he actually said I'd already heard.)

In the end, as expected, we lost by 12,700 votes. However, earning 43 percent of the vote after trailing 60 to 22 percent at the early stages was a respectable showing. Matsunaga was quoted a number of times in later years as saying this was the greatest electoral challenge in his Washington years.

In *Sparky: Warrior, Peacemaker, Poet, and Patriot*, author Richard Halloran makes these comments about our challenge in 1972: "The next time out, however, Sparky ran into the fight of his life when he was challenged by an aggressive Republican state senator, Fred W. Rohlfing. From the start Sparky acknowledged the strength of his opponent, saying, 'I plan to run as though I was the underdog.' Both campaigns were well financed—Sparky reporting a war chest of nearly $100,000, and Rohlfing $85,000. Race undoubtedly played a part in the campaign—the western portion of Sparky's district being heavily Asian-American, which favored him; while the eastern part was heavily haole, which favored Rohlfing.

"Rohlfing was no racist by any means, denouncing right-wingers as 'an intolerant, loud, and abusive element' as he sought to revive Republican hopes by building a multi-racial party. In some ways Rohlfing was a 'Republican Matsunaga'—independent, outspoken on certain issues, and a reformer. During a debate they clashed over Sparky's ability to win favors for Hawai'i in Washington, and Rohlfing accused Sparky of losing touch with Hawai'i. Sparky defended his place on the Rules Committee. The outcome of the election was the closest in Sparky's career: 73,800 to 61,100."

This summary is not inaccurate, but it omits a couple of details that would help the readers understand a little more. First, it discusses the district in terms of differences of race—an obvious fact—but doesn't mention that the party orientation in the western and central area was heavily Democratic. The quotation critical of GOP right-wingers came from my speech bemoaning the loss of Senator Jim Clark to the Democrats in 1969. (See Appendix Four.) Halloran misses the main point of my criticism of Spark: an inability to fix the dock strike situation—an issue that we attacked with full-page ads towards the end of the campaign.

Poho (Out of Luck/Money)

Our good showing in 1972 against an entrenched local AJA veteran and successful politician led to the determination that another try was in the cards. But we had other important matters to attend to: 1974 was going to be a big governorship election year, and there was a residual debt from the completed campaign as the Republican Party had reneged on its promise to grant us the $50,000. My recollection is that we were facing a $46,000 promissory note at the conclusion of the 1972 campaign. We whittled this down with various fundraisers. Even so, at the start of the 1976 campaign we were about $30,000 in the hole.

That Republican Party "grant" was later earthily described by Gummie Johnson, my Mainland advisor in the 1976 congressional campaign, as the "turd in Fred's pocket."

In retrospect, this willingness to go out on a limb was the price of admission to the upper ranks of candidates for office in Hawai'i. Dan Tuttle, University of Hawai'i professor and ultimate Hawai'i political guru, rated me at the forefront of gubernatorial prospects in a speech that was reported by the *Honolulu Star-Bulletin* on November 10, 1972.

1974: Hiram Says "No"

My Senate seat was up for grabs in 1974, but that was the least of our concerns. The Republican Party was in dire need of a strong gubernatorial candidate. A low-key drama developed as I, along with many others, encouraged U.S. Senator Hiram Fong to enter the race. George Ariyoshi had succeeded Jack Burns as governor and was generally thought to be fairly vulnerable to a strong challenge. Hiram Fong would have made a great choice, but he really wanted to leave Washington, D.C., and return to farming in Kāne'ohe. I had a personal interest in seeing him run, as I would then have run for lieutenant governor. In addition to being able to assist Fong in preparing and selling a legislative program, I would get statewide exposure and be positioned to become the "heir apparent" when Fong retired. Also, it appeared that he might serve only one term.

I met with Fong on several occasions and communicated my intentions should he decide to pursue the election. He was always gracious, but it was not to be. The nomination of Fong would have unified the Republican Party and could have brought victory. But on June 1, 1973, Fong held a press conference and officially announced he would not run for governor in 1974, and that he would retire when his U.S. Senate term expired in 1976. The announcement caused all sorts of new speculation. Gerry Keir, *Honolulu Advertiser* political writer (later to become editor-in-chief), focused immediately on Andy Anderson and me: "With Fong out, Anderson probably is in the best position to become the GOP candidate. With the help of anti-Frank Fasi Democrats he ran a strong race for mayor in 1972.... The other key prospect, Rohlfing, is probably stronger within the Republican Party than is Anderson. But political observers feel that Rohlfing might not do as well as Anderson in the general election.... Other than the two state senators, it would appear that no other island Republican has more than a remote chance of making the race for governor" (*Honolulu Advertiser* June 1, 1973).

Because I had criticized U.S. Representative Matsunaga in a speech around this time, there was an assumption by some in the press that I would run against him again and not for governor. I sought to clear that up with a letter to the editor published in the June 13, 1973, *Star-Bulletin* in which I said: "The most vital problem today is to put our state back on an even financial keel, and to lessen the burden on our people for over taxation and inflation." (That thought would be as valid today as it was in 1973!)

Probably the most complete analysis of the situation facing our party at that time with respect to potential candidates was performed by Tuck Newport in two articles published by the *Hawaii Observer* (now defunct) on June 12 and 26, 1973. The analysis of both Anderson's and my strengths and weaknesses in these articles was excellent. However, I believe there was an over-emphasis on the political significance of the issue of population control, which no one was able to implement anyway.

During the late summer and fall Andy and I talked about whether one of us should run for governor; but neither of us was decisive when he should have been. At one point Andy said it was my first option. But his supporters (including mutual friend, Bank of Hawai'i's John Anderson) were urging that he run for governor and that I run for lieutenant governor. That might have been a solution had we not previously disagreed dramatically over Porteus and King in 1970. There was no question that the loyalty bond between us had been shattered then, although we could still work together on specific items. I felt that Andy was just too close to the "machine." We had long endured this kind of rule under Burns, and it had prevented the change that our urban population needed.

As for our differences on the way government should operate, Larry Mehau was Andy's very good friend. Larry Mehau was a controversial Big Island ex-police officer who ran a private security agency that sought and obtained highly visible government contracts (e.g., airport, harbor security). Charles Marsland, Honolulu's first elected prosecutor, charged Mehau with being "The Godfather" of Hawai'i crime. The charge was never proved. Mehau was a close associate of Governor Burns and exercised considerable power and influence from a seat on the Board of Land and Natural Resources (DLNR).

The bottom line: why should I be a "water boy" (as lieutenant governor) for a repackaged, relabeled new developer/special interest-supporting regime, even if it was nominally headed by a Republican? The very essence of our policy differences was thus exposed.

We continued to jockey for position until the 1974 session when, out of the blue, Andy and I were both upstaged by an announcement from Randolph Crossley—former State senator, businessperson, and 1966 GOP gubernatorial candidate—that he would, again, run for governor at age seventy. I remember being speechless as Crossley walked into our Senate minority caucus room bedecked with leis. Crossley seemed like Methuselah to me. But I had a close friendship with his daughter, Meredith Young, and her husband Jack, and I didn't want to rock that boat.

As expected, Crossley and Ben Dillingham (GOP candidate for lieutenant governor) conducted an expensive but futile campaign, and the Democrats easily maintained their stranglehold on our government with George Ariyoshi in the catbird seat. We Republicans had blown it again.

In that election year our four-man team (Tom Kay, Sarge Kahanamoku, Tennyson Lum, and I) went up against the Democrats in the Senate

Seventh District race. With a house-to-house campaign run well by attorney "Willie" Moore, I again led the ticket, followed by Democrats Kenny Brown and Dennis O'Connor and by Republican Lum.

So it was back to preparing for a second congressional run, unless I just wanted to vegetate in the State Senate. Vegetables were not my favorite food, so the choice was clear.

Leasehold Land Reform Revisited

If we thought we'd solved the problems of residential leaseholds with the passage of Act 307 S.L. 1967, we were wrong. Disinterest in pursuing acquisition of development tracts by the Burns administration was not helpful. By 1975 I was back at it again with a comprehensive series of bills and resolutions. These included:

1. A resolution directing the Hawai'i Housing Authority (HHA) to make a report on the implementation of Act 307.

2. A bill creating a Residential Leasehold Commission to review lease rental rates on renegotiations, oversee compensation to be awarded upon termination of leases, and hear complaints for violations of Act 307.

3. A bill creating a revolving fund to assist in conversions to fee simple.

4. A bill authorizing investment of retirement system funds in development tracts acquired by HHA under Act 307, with an appropriation of $2 million in funding.

5. A bill providing for priority condemnation of smaller tracts.

6. A resolution requesting Congress to amend the Internal Revenue Code to promote the sale of residential leaseholds by encouraging voluntary sales.

7. Several bills to assure lessees of their rights under real property and income tax provisions.

The 1975 Legislature toiled away on these proposals and others. Ben Cayetano (future governor) was active on the House side and, as I recall, contributed to the final package. By March 13, 1975, we were acting on four third-reading bills in the Senate dealing with leasehold issues. My comments included the following: "Unfortunately, we thought we'd gotten a handle on things with the 1967 Land Reform Act.... At that time there were about 16,999 single-family residential leaseholds, up from 500 or less in 1940. Today this figure approaches 27,000, or an estimated 35 percent of all owner-occupied housing on Oʻahu. The rapid increase has resulted because developable suburban areas of Honolulu are all owned by large landowners who, for one reason or another, have not been willing—or if willing have been unable—to sell lands in fee. The resulting situation is unique in the annals of American real estate, and unique problems require imaginative solutions."

I went on to criticize the bills being considered as "incomplete and inadequate" in that "nowhere does [the package of bills] provide a means of assisting the homeowner in his ultimate problem: how to pay the bill. Nowhere is there any money for the condemnation test case that got headlines last week; nowhere is there...encouragement for the state retirement system...to buy the bonds of the state authorized by Act 307...[nor] is there any relief from the burden of real property taxes currently imposed on lessees...nor is there any assistance in forming a legal entity to simplify direct negotiations for purchase of the fee interest with a landowner who has an affirmative IRS ruling...for a partial liquidation and is willing to sell, etc. Mr. President, if it were late in December, I'd say that this Christmas will be in honor of Scrooge. The package under the tree is small, threadbare, and worn."

Just a week or so before the debate on the bills, I traveled to Washington for a meeting of the Inter-governmental Committee of the National Conference of Legislatures. While there, I met with numerous high officials from the Joint Committee on Internal Revenue Taxation, the U.S. Treasury, and the IRS, also with White House staff (Dick Cheney, first deputy to then-presidential chief of staff Don Rumsfeld). I was armed with our Senate's SCR 47, which called upon Congress to enact legislation that would assure that any landowner selling lands to a lessee pursuant to the provisions of Chapter 516 HRS (Act 307 S.L. 1967) should be taxed on profits at a capital gains rate—unless qualified as a charitable institution, in which case such landowner would not be taxed on profits. I was fortunate to be accompanied at some of these meetings by Dean William Warren from Columbia Law School (consultant to the Bishop Estate). Senator Fong and Representative Patsy Mink helped greatly in setting up these meetings.

Upon my return to Hawai'i on March 10, 1975, I filed a six-page report of my activities. The conclusion of the report read in part: "It is highly unlikely that the residential leasehold system would have developed in the first place but for the Internal Revenue Code and its potential application to proceeds from the sale of lands acquired before there was an income tax. The values of these lands have risen from almost zero to hundreds of millions of dollars. The consequent failure of landowners to make any more than a few isolated sales in fee has created a unique feudalism in home ownership in this state. Ironically this, in turn, has led to a 'loss' of revenue to the federal government, since no income is realized upon the execution of a residential lease by any landowner. It is suggested that capital gains taxes on such sales (by non-exempt trusts) will be at least some help to the deficit plagued U.S. government."

In due course, many of the technical aspects of "breaking up the estates" through land sales enabled by enactment of Act 307 S.L. 1967 and its follow-up legislation were resolved, and the biggest trust of all—the Bishop Estate—made multiple millions of dollars through sales of leasehold properties.

This created another problem when trustees (appointed in recognition of their political connections and influence by the State Supreme Court justices) wallowed in money, which they misdirected or took advantage of in personal ways. For that story see *Broken Trust* by Sam King and Richard Roth and *Ben* by Ben Cayetano. The first of these documents the worst aspects of what I had much earlier labeled "hui government."

On the other hand, the increased income to the previously land-rich but cash-poor Bishop Estate brought big changes to the education system that now benefits the Hawaiian people—Kamehameha Schools on the neighbor islands never would have been built without the income from land sales.

Not all landed estates have been so generous.

The work of many years and of many individuals had finally paid off. Through my "Lessees' Bill of Rights," lessees were accorded justice in that they could not be ripped off every time there was a rent reopening. They had rights to organize and defend their interests. They could join together and force the big landowner to sell them the property, or else they could require the government to condemn the land and sell it to them for residential purposes. I am proud of my role in this important change to democratic land practices.

I did not care that seeking such change was a big item in the Hawai'i Democratic Party platform and not mentioned in the Republican platform. David McClung was chief architect of this change. I helped him when it counted. What was right was right, and my constituents deserved to be protected.

Early Start on a Second Congressional Race

It wasn't long after the ballots were counted in the 1974 races that I started planning another run for the U.S. House. Senator Fong had announced his retirement, and Spark Matsunaga had jumped into the breach for his seat in the U.S. Senate. This meant there was an open House seat in the first district, the same seat that I had unsuccessfully pursued in 1972.

I served in the Hawai'i Senate through the spring session of 1975. In this session, besides the normal host of issues, we had to deal with continuing problems in the leasehold field. Would I continue to serve in the Senate while seeking the U.S. Congressional seat? Much controversy had surrounded this type of issue due to runs by Frank Fasi for governor while serving as mayor. I gave it a lot of thought and decided I would feel better if my constituents were represented in the 1976 session by a full-time legislator, rather than one running for Congress at the same time.

This was definitely not the way most politicians viewed this type of issue. My dilemma became clearer as I discussed the possibility of a resignation before the 1976 session with my advisors and troops. Meanwhile, my friend Bill Walker from the White House contacted me and, on behalf of then-President Ford, offered me a non-paid position as Alternate Representative on the South Pacific Commission. I knew little about the work of this commission but would soon find out more about it at an October conference in Nauru (a small island in the central Pacific known for its production of phosphate from bird guano).

I decided that I would attend the conference in Nauru and then, upon returning to Hawai'i, announce my resignation from the State Senate as well as my intent to run for the U.S. Congressional seat, all in one fell swoop. The advantage of this strategy was that it would allow sufficient time to appoint a new senator before the next session in January—hopefully someone I could endorse (my candidate was Buddy Soares, House Republican Leader). Also, of course, I could then concentrate on raising the necessary funds and "get out there" at the front of the line.

I discussed this approach, along with other plans, with my then-top advisor Ed Brennan and others. Brennan was pressing me to employ a qualified and experienced Mainland political advisor—Gummie Johnson from the Seattle area. My 1972 advisor, Sandy Weiner, would have been an obvious (and a lot better!) choice, but for some reason now beyond my recollection he was not available. Brennan wanted Johnson because he was a known professional. Brennan referred to my staff leaders in the

PRESIDENT FORD, SENATOR FONG, AND I DISCUSS NATIONAL ISSUES AT ADM. MCCAIN'S PEARL HARBOR QUARTERS IN 1976.

1972 campaign as "cookie cutters" (most were female), but I said they had done the job and that most of them would return in 1976.

After attending the week-long South Pacific Commission conference (my first) in far-away Nauru, and after spending a day and night at Majuro in the Marshall Islands, I returned to Hawai'i with a bad head cold. The next day we held our press conference and I announced my resignation from the Senate as well as my intent to run again for U.S. Congress. We held this conference at 'A'ala Park in downtown Honolulu. That proved to be a bad decision, as there was at least one drunk nearby sleeping off his long night of boozing.

Another irrelevant "surprise" was the presence of Richard "Ike" Sutton, a perennial Republican candidate who had a habit of horning in to get publicity. He asked Dan Ichinose for the lei Dan had brought for me, and then he put it on himself. He edged his way into position so he could be seen in any photos. Our blockade totally failed. Ike was good at that sort of thing.

Even worse was the hacking cough and drippy nose that I had exacerbated on the long trip home from the very center of the Pacific. My performance was definitely sub-par. Not a good start.

We fared much better with Governor Ariyoshi. He appointed Buddy Soares to my vacant seat.

And so the big campaign began in late November. I started walking house-to-house in 'Aiea while trying to pay off what was left of the 1972 campaign debt and build a fund for the campaign.

Was the early resignation the right decision? In retrospect, I would say no. It would have been far better to have had the media exposure of the Senate session of 1976, and I could have more effectively remained on the political forefront for whatever later opportunity might have arisen. The brownie points I had earned with the "drive-by" (liberal) media were fleeting and shallow, and scarcely a soul remembered my decision a year later. My advice for future candidates: don't resign from public office until you are ready to give up politics entirely.

The Campaign Commences

At the time of my decision to resign from the Senate, the leading elected Democrat considering the U.S. Congressional race was Dennis O'Connor, my fellow State senator from East O'ahu. Dennis was an old friend—we had both attended Punahou and had played sports together. In fact, people would get us mixed up since we were both fair-skinned haoles from Punahou. In addition to these similarities, we were both naval officers and Honolulu attorneys (and graduates of George Washington Law School). Having graduated from the Naval Academy, Dennis had spent more time in the regular Navy and at sea. By contrast, I had received my commission as a graduate of Officer Candidate School and added many reserve years to my three years of active service as a young officer in the Office of the Chief of Naval Operations in Washington, D.C.

The second Democrat looking at the race was Cecil Heftel, the multimillionaire owner of KGMB, one of our major television stations, and a political protégé of Senator Dan Inouye. "Cec" (pronounced like "cease") was a unique mix—he was raised in a Jewish family but had converted to Mormonism (LDS). The good news for me was that however long he'd been in Hawai'i, he still gave off the "vibes" of a Mainlander. But the bad news was that he had lots and lots of money. Also, he had previously run for office—the U.S. Senate race against Hiram Fong. Worse yet, he had, with lots of help from Dan Inouye, given Fong a scare in the U.S. Senate race.

As the owner of a big television station, Heftel could get statewide media exposure any time he wanted. His news staff under Bob Sevey proved to be loyal to the boss. His writers slanted stories so they were pro-Cec or anti-Fred. During the lead up to Heftel's candidacy, editorials featuring Mr. Heftel were conveniently inserted at the end of news programs.

Early in 1976 he did one of those public issue-type programs in which he was asked what he would do with his television station if he ran for office. His answer did not promise a specific course of action, but he firmly committed "not to run while still owning and operating KGMB." I, of course, took note, as did my advisor, and we repeatedly wove that into our early campaign speeches. In retrospect, we did that far more than we should have—Heftel made a big show of taking himself out of active management of Channel 9 (but not necessarily giving up his

ownership) after announcing his candidacy in early June. Someone came up with the idea of putting a broadcast tower on our headquarters in an area near the Ala Moana Center, and we featured it when I gave a formal headquarters opening speech (our own broadcasting tower in answer to Heftel's). But then we were really putting the emphasis on him, rather than on me.

FIRST IN THE BLOCKS

Heftel pretty much stayed with a media offensive. We pursued an ongoing "ground game," canvassing house to house every day after work and on Saturdays. By the time we were finished, we had covered almost the entire area from 'Aiea to Hawai'i Kai. We also made visitations to innumerable business offices and governmental offices. We had to. Heftel spent over $600,000, mostly on media, while we spent about $230,000 for all purposes, including the consultant's salary. Heftel's expenses broke the record for any previous or contemporary U.S. House of Representatives race in the entire country!

Heftel's advertisements cleverly had him in an aloha shirt walking on a pretty beach (in "ritzy" Kāhala, I think), but otherwise giving the

impression he was a good old "local boy." Meanwhile, in my television ads I was dressed in a suit walking corridors in the Capitol Building to stress my work as a senator—showing that I had the experience and knowledge about the needs of the people and how they wanted to be represented. Clearly we screwed up. At least some, if not all, of our videos should have played up our stronger local connections than his. After all, I was the "keiki o ka 'āina"—not he!

Early polls (spring and early summer) showed we were substantially ahead of Dennis O'Connor and a little less ahead of Heftel. But this began to change by September, and we knew it was going to be close. Then O'Connor didn't run after all, but Heftel did.

Very late in the game we were surprised to learn that a third candidate, Kathy Hoshijo, was also planning to run for the seat. She was from Maui and was a member of an independent movement (Independents for Godly Government) that involved Wayne Nishiki (one-time gubernatorial candidate and, later, longtime Maui County Councilperson). The movement had "hippie" connections and advocated legalization of marijuana. (I guess pot was considered God's remedy to civic distress.) Hoshijo, too, had enough money for a last-minute TV blitz—in which she presented a young attractive figure in a "Kathy Cares" mode.

Most of my advisors and other so-called experts wrote off the importance of Hoshijo, and I certainly didn't have an opinion one way or the other. It turned out to be a huge mistake on our part to take her lightly. Hoshijo staged a last-minute attack on me (as did Heftel) when we had little time or money with which to respond. This attack put us on the defensive at a critical stage. The basis of her attack was that I had represented Hawaiian Electric Company (HECO) in a power-plant eviction case that affected between ten and twenty families in Windward O'ahu. This claim was true but terribly overblown—those people had remained on HECO property long after they were entitled to, and they had been given ample advance notice. But Hoshijo had emotion on her side. We did not respond.

The second last-minute attack—by Heftel this time—was based on a more significant issue: the collective bargaining act for State and County workers and its impact on the civil service system. During the debates on this bill in the Senate, I had offered an amendment that would have

removed the restrictions on subjects that could be discussed and negotiated in the context of collective bargaining. Knowing that my amendment had little chance of passage, I had tried to show commitment to
the bargaining process as contrasted with civil service rules by broadening
the topics that could be decided at the negotiating table. At a later meeting of public administrators I proposed: "Why not allow the collective
bargaining contracts to provide for the terms and conditions of employment, and then give the public administrators the tools to carry out their
responsibilities; [including] the right to hire and discipline as in private
employment, subject to contractual rights of employees?" Heftel conveniently (and unethically) left out the underlined phrase in his attacks,
thus conveying the message that I wanted to give administrators a free
hand, which subsequently alarmed civil service workers. Spokespersons
for the government employees unions (including Maui's David Trask, Jr.)
spoke out in my defense. Their explanations, however, were too detailed.
As with any such last-minute attack, our defense was not well prepared,
packaged, or otherwise pursued.

A significant negative for us was Bill Quinn's campaign against Spark
Matsunaga. This was a loser from the outset (as the polls told those who
read them). But Republicans and independents poured a lot of money
into this hopeless contest against an entrenched Nisei veteran rather than
ours for an open seat. Quinn was a great guy and a good candidate, but
not for the U.S. Senate against the popular Sparky.

I know. I tried in 1972.

These events had been preceded by a large bump in the road—by
the end of September we clearly were not ahead in the polls and had in
fact lost ground. Heftel's media barrage was having its effect, and I was
concerned that our ongoing campaign would be perceived as negative.
Heftel, the big media mogul, was getting all the attention—not the hard-
working, longtime "local boy" public servant.

In later years, Don Clegg, who did many polls for Frank Fasi, labeled
Democrats who returned to the fold after flirting with support for a
Republican as "bungee cord Democrats." It became unfortunately an apt
term in relation to our hardnosed criticisms of Cec's use of his TV station
to foster his campaign.

So I decided to perform a major campaign overhaul with only a little over a month to go until the election. I terminated Gummie Johnson and formed a new committee to oversee the campaign. I was able to convince Walter Dods of First Hawaiian Bank, a strong Dan Inouye supporter/advisor, to assume the chairmanship of the campaign. Joining him were other well-known Democrats—Stuart Ho (a prominent legislator and son of legendary developer and financier Chinn Ho) Stanley Hong, and media person Jack Kellner. This prominent Democratic support was buttressed by endorsements of my candidacy by all the major unions (except for the Construction Laborers Union). This support was highly unusual for any Republican, but I think the unions remembered my involvement as a bargaining agent for the Hawai'i Nurses Association for over nine years, my role in supporting collective bargaining legislation for government employees, and the fact that I was seen by many labor people as a Republican rebel. In contrast, particularly for an alleged Democrat, Heftel had a reputation for disliking organized labor. He fought with the unions at his enterprises, and they didn't like him.

We immediately changed our media emphasis to the positive Fred Rohlfing record, as a State legislator with achievements and programs for the future, with no mention of our opponent and his manipulation of news via his TV station. Nice guy "local boy" ads ran in the newspapers. Try as we might, though, we were unable to prevent the bungee cord from springing. We had waited too long to change our presentation. The delay, the bungee effect, and/or Heftel's concluding massive TV blitz did us in.

The Outcome

The results came in early on election night. We were close in the first printout, about 300 votes behind. After 78 percent of the votes were counted, we trailed by about 3,000. By then I knew it was over. The final numbers were Heftel 59,690, Rohlfing 53,406, Hoshijo 23,699.

I gave the predictable, brave concession speech a little after the second printout. I quoted from "my kind of Republican" (Teddy Roosevelt): "The credit belongs to the man...who at the worst, if he fails, at least fails while daring greatly; so that his place shall never be with those cold and timid souls who know neither victory or defeat."

After my speech, when most all of my supporters had gone home, my legal secretary/longtime campaign supporter/house-to-house buddy/ future (1983) spouse Patty Bond and I sat in the campaign trailer together with a few die-hards and watched late TV coverage of the results. On Heftel's channel 9, he was claiming that he hadn't won because he'd out-spent Rohlfing by three times (more than any U.S. House candidate in history) but because of the "support of ordinary people and the proud traditions of the Democratic Party." Finally, having had enough of this, Patty threw a full glass of red wine at the television set. It "burped" loudly, gave a fizzling sound, and turned stone black. None of us said a word for a full minute. Then we laughed for at least five minutes. Nothing could have expressed the way I felt any better. That little toss endeared Patty to me for the rest of my life.

Aftermath of the 1976 Election

It's too bad we didn't have a political pro with the time and insight to fully analyze why we lost. (Our own man Alf Pratte, a newspaperman by trade, made a good try. See Appendix 1 at the end of this book.)

But if there is a first clue to my defeat, it has to do with money. Yes, it is true that money is the mother's milk of politics. In this race I was limited by what I could *raise*, while Heftel was limited only by what he chose to *spend* of his money that he "loaned" to himself—in this case over $600,000. My money raisers did a great job in the face of this blitzkrieg. Key fundraisers included Frank Manaut (Bank of Hawai'i), Ed Brennan (Gold Bond Stamps), Jack Fuller (Hawaiian Trust Co.), Phil Spalding (Western Steel), Sheridan Ing (Aloha Airlines), Henry Rice (Bank of Hawai'i), Sigfried Kagawa (Occidental Life), Dave Heenan (T.H. Davies), Clarence Tom (City Mill), Dan Case (attorney), George Miyasaka (Castle & Cooke), and many others—many lawyers and doctors whose names I will recall, unfortunately, AFTER this book is published. Friends in various organizations to which I had belonged over the years came through with sales of fundraiser tickets that provided most of our funds. There is one donor who always comes to mind—Mrs. "Doc" Lyons of Makawao, Maui. All I needed to do was send out a couple of tickets to a fundraiser—one that she was not going to come to Oʻahu for—and she'd generously send $500. What a morale builder! Her son Mike Lyons (Bank of Hawaiʻi), now deceased, became a good friend after I moved to Maui.

Raising money in general was not my particular talent, but I would accompany my best guys on some high-level calls where I talked issues and status of the campaign, not money.

What are we to do about the power of money in politics? I'm afraid most regulatory laws on this subject can be circumvented. Even McCain-Feingold is a "paper tiger." I now have come to the conclusion that "full disclosure" is the only medicine that will work. Trying to restrict amounts raised, and from whom, and to limit amounts spent is an exercise in futility.

Back to 1976, how much effect did Heftel's final ten-day media blitz have? Were we doomed from the outset by the Supreme Court ruling in January (after I had resigned my seat and declared for Congress) that eliminated the ceiling on expenditures for the race (previously set at $180,000) and that removed any restraints on rich candidates using unlimited amounts of their own money?

At the time of my second defeat I was quoted at some length in the press regarding the effect of a Supreme Court ruling. This ruling had nullified a federal statute that had previously set limits on campaign spending. In particular, the court had opened to door to unlimited use of any candidate's personal funds.

In the interview, published in the *Honolulu Star-Bulletin* and written by Grace Feliciano, I am quoted as follows:

"I knew there was a case pending, but you don't really rationalize these things ahead of time. We were counting on a maximum ceiling of about $180,000 and felt we would have no real problems raising that. I could conceive of the Supreme Court ruling against limits on personal money, but I could not conceive of overall spending limits being removed—that was a shocking thing to me, and we certainly felt the impact."

The article went on to note: "[Rohlfing] added that the ratio of television commercials and newspaper advertisements between him and Heftel was ten to one in Heftel's favor. 'In handshakes, I had him thirty to one.'"

Rohlfing Declares He'd Counted on Spending Ceiling

By Grace Feliciano
Star-Bulletin Writer

It was an encouraging start. Republican congressional candidate Fred W. Rohlfing trailed his opponent, Cecil Heftel, by only about 300 votes in the first computer printout.

Hopes were high when Rohlfing arrived at his Piikoi Street headquarters at about 7 p.m. yesterday, amid cheers and 48th birthday greetings.

He had time for a short interview with the Star-Bulletin and discussed his 13-month campaign which began with his resignation from the State Senate in October 1975.

"In the final analysis, I don't think many voters really remembered that (the resignation)," Rohlfing said.

"MAYBE WE underplayed it. I'd like to live with the results, whatever we do and just hope people understand. I don't like self-promoting types of advertisements any more than necessary," he said.

Rohlfing resigned three months before the U.S. Supreme Court nullified a federal law setting limits on campaign spending.

"I knew there was a case pending, but you don't really rationalize these things ahead of time. We were counting on a maximum ceiling of about $180,000 and felt we would have no real problems in raising that.

"I could conceive of the Supreme Court ruling against limits on spending personal money, but I could not conceive of over-all spending limits being removed—that was a shocking thing to me and we certainly felt the impact," Rohlfing said.

REFERRING TO Heftel, a broadcast executive and recent owner of KGMB-TV, Rohlfing said that it was "of some real concern to me that an extremely wealthy person can exert the kind of influence that has been exhibited in this campaign."

He said the media faced a "very difficult problem in this campaign."

"And I have to say that the fact that one of the candidates was a major broadcasting executive had a bearing on how they treated the candidates—I was not happy with the coverage of channel 9 (KGMB), the most powerful in the state," Rohlfing said.

He added that the ratio of television commercials and newspaper advertisements between him and Heftel was 10 to one in Heftel's favor.

"In handshakes, I had him 30 to 1," he added.

ROHLFING JUST recently finished paying off a $30,000 loan for his 1972 congressional campaign against Spark Matsunaga, which he thought the local Republican party organization was going to repay.

Asked if he had better help from the party this election, Rohlfing said "from individual Republicans and from the national party—yes; from the local party organization—no."

He said that other than a telephone survey, he got no Republican help, "no money, no grass-roots support."

Asked if public recognition of his 16-year legislative record was hindered by his membership in a minority party, Rohlfing said there were a number of new voters in the State, "younger people. Mainland transplants who have no feel for my legislative record.

"EVERY TIME we have tried to emphasize my record, it was not news to members of the press. So unless we did it through paid advertising, it never got aired," said the Honolulu-born Rohlfing.

"We were in a dilemma as to how much to emphasize what I had done as opposed to what I would do in Congress," he added.

Asked if the heavy labor endorsement of himself and Republican senatorial candidate William F. Quinn marked the end of labor as a Democratic party stronghold or whether it was strictly a personality choice, Rohlfing said it was "personality and their identification with the candidate's basic record and what the candidate can do in Washington for their stew-and-rice problems."

He said he could not tell at the present time how Kathy Hoshijo, Independents for Godly Government congressional candidate, had affected his election chances.

ROHLFING DREW contributions totaling about $176,000.

"Our contributions are from upwards of 4,000 people and even the group contributions we got were made up of small contributors.

"To me that's better than any one person buying an election," Rohlfing said.

At about 8 p.m. the second computer printout showed Rohlfing behind Heftel by some 2,000 votes.

The air around the pre-fab building was heavier and even when Rohlfing was asked if there would be another campaign if this one was lost, he said, "I didn't say 'never,' but I didn't say there would be."

At 8:35 p.m. he began his concession speech with words from "my kind of Republican—Theodore Roosevelt":

"The credit belongs to the man . . . who at the worst, if he fails, at least fails while daring greatly; so that his place shall never be with those cold and timid souls who know neither victory nor defeat."

ELECTION STORY—Weariness and disappointment show on Fred Rohlfing's face. —Star-Bulletin Photo by Craig Kojima.

What if Bill Quinn had not run in a hopeless race against Senator Matsunaga, thus enabling a concentration on the more winnable House seat? What if Sandy Weiner, architect of our media message in the 1972 campaign, had been aboard instead of Gummie? What if Hoshijo had not run—did she really take votes from Heftel, as I was being told, or was she really taking my votes? These and many other questions will never be answered with authority. My answers (with thirty years of hindsight) are that the loss of the spending limit alone made Heftel the odds-on favorite, that Quinn's candidacy drained significant financial support from our campaign, and that Hoshijo took more votes from me than she did from Heftel.

Needless to say, I had severe wounds that needed to be licked in some way. The television set that received Patty's douse of red wine recovered much better than I did. (It had belonged to Diana Snyder, who was my campaign scheduler. She good-naturedly accepted her loss—maybe she had already been in the market for a new one!) So it was time to regroup and reflect.

CHAPTER THREE

THE LAST HURRAH

Four More Years in the Legislature

As 1980 approached, I realized that my political viability in Hawai'i was steadily eroding due to lack of activity. When you spend the amount of time, energy, and wherewithal that I had in political life, your effort becomes a wasting asset if you just sit on the bench. So I ran in 1980 as a "team" with long-time associate Barbara Marumoto for the Kāhala/Wai'alae/Kaimukī two-seat eighth House district. We readily "ate up" the opposition Democrats. But when it came to organizing the Republican minority, we were not as successful. At that time Kinau Boyd Kamali'i was the prior session's (1979) Republican leader. She had been the chair of the Ronald Reagan campaign organization in Hawai'i, and Reagan's victory had given her considerable status. She had even offered to support me for an appointment to the U.S. District Court, but at the time I was not yet ready to call it quits in the elective field of play. I still had in mind a possible run for the governorship (obviously, as things turned out, a dumb decision!).

So in 1980 Kinau was re-elected minority leader and I, as the returning warrior, was named minority floor leader. Kinau was a Punahou graduate whose earlier appointment as a Senate staffer I had helped make possible. By 1980 she had become immersed in the Hawaiian Renaissance movement. As GOP leader she, together with Donna Ikeda, attempted to call all the shots on personnel for the research office. When a vacancy occurred in a prominent position, she attempted to put her choice, Warren Nakamura, into the slot. My supporters in the caucus agreed with me in a tense vote that the job should go to Craig Travis. Kinau was furious with this challenge to her leadership, and sour grapes poisoned the effectiveness of our minority efforts for the balance of the 1981 session. One of the up-and-coming young legislators in our group was Mike Liu, with whom I became close political friends. Unfortunately, Mike lost his attempts at higher office. He then took a H.U.D. assistant secretary position in the Bush administration and now is a lobbyist for a private firm out of D.C.

House minority organization continued to be a problem after the 1982 election. In that election we had single-member districts for the first time. I moved from Waiʻalae Kāhala to an apartment on Puʻulei Circle on the west side of Diamond Head and was elected to the House from the thirteenth district—Kaimukī/Kapahulu—while Barbara Marumoto returned via the Waiʻalae Kāhala/Waiʻalae Iki area. Only eight Republicans were elected (multi-member districts had always yielded more Republicans). When we went to choose leadership positions, we split into two groups of four. I had the votes of Barbara Marumoto, Marvin Dang, and Hal Jones plus my own. Donna Ikeda was supported by Whitney Anderson and John Medeiros from Windward Oʻahu and Virginia Isbell from Kona. I recommended that we hire Jill Frierson as our research director, and she performed admirably.

After several days of haggling we reached agreement on a scheme which gave the Ikeda supporters some key committee spots and our group the leadership positions—me as minority leader, Barbara as floor leader and Marvin Dang as whip.

Being minority leader put me in frequent contact with Henry Peters, the first Native Hawaiian speaker of the House since statehood. Peters was not yet a Bishop Estate trustee, but he was clearly angling for more power. Wherever he could, he took advantage of our lingering four-to-four minority caucus division and made things difficult for us. Peters even demanded to review my speech in advance of the opening session. I gave it to him, but told him not to expect any changes should he request any. He authorized more "goodies" (trips, best offices, etc.) for the dissident GOP group members. It seemed as though he would "mess" with me whenever he had the opportunity to do so. I was not the only legislator who found Peters to be a pain in the butt. Ben Cayetano's book

Ben provides a (literal) blow-by-blow account of how Peters bullied his Democrat colleagues. At least in my case he did not engage in physical threats but rather relied on more subtle intimations. His rise to moneyed status and power as a trustee of the Bishop Estate, and his subsequent fall from grace (see *Broken Trust* by Sam King and Randy Roth), could have been predicted from his manipulative practices in running the House.

The Bi-Partisan Coalition 1981-82

In the run-up to the 1981 session the Democrats were unable to organize the Senate despite their majority of seventeen to eight over the Republicans. Bitter infighting ensued. This led to the formation of a bi-partisan coalition headed by Senate President (and Democrat) Dickie Wong (my buddy from the Eagleton Foundation Seminar of 1968). Wong's group included comers Ben Cayetano and Neil Abercrombie. Republican coalition members were Anderson, Saiki, Soares (who had been appointed to my seat in 1976), Henderson, George, Ajifu, and Yee.

The left-out-of-leadership Democrat faction was led by old-timer John Ushijima from Hilo. It included outspoken Milton Holt (who had

SPEAKER HENRY PETERS   OPENING OF THE HOUSE

GREETING PRESIDENT REAGAN 1983.

starred on the football field for Harvard against my school, Yale) and my old Punahou/Navy/Outrigger chum Dennis O'Connor, who was the group's negotiator.

In the House, unfortunately, our outnumbered and out-fire-powered Republicans—a piddly eight to the Democrats' forty-three—were not exactly equipped to help push the Senate coalition's successes through the House, as we ourselves had split into two factions. On occasion we asked our Republican Senate colleagues to kill bad bills being sent to the Senate from the House. Inevitably, though, the Peters-led House allied itself strongly in the camp of Governor Ariyoshi.

The coalition played itself out in the 1982 session. On the sixtieth day of the session, Anderson and Saiki declared for governor and lieutenant governor, respectively. Coalition initiatives—such as a state lottery and a hotel room tax—died with these declarations.

Republican Death Wish Granted

More important than the coalition itself in long-term political impact was the decision, mentioned earlier, by U.S. District Court Judge Martin Pence in a Republican-pushed lawsuit. Pence upheld the assertion that all districts must be represented by a single member. A reapportionment committee then produced a map for all districts.

This single-member plan was the worst thing in the world for the state's minority Republican Party. As this is written, the GOP is now down to an all-time low of six seats in the House and a piddly two seats in the Senate—so few, out of a total of seventy-six seats!

Back in the sixties and seventies—when I was running for the Senate in a multi-member district of four senators—I would pull votes solidly from Republican areas in the valleys of East Oʻahu and then campaign in places like Pālolo Valley and Kapahulu for Democrat support. The Democrat ticket rarely had more than two strong vote-getters, so I would end up getting Democrat votes that would carry me into first place in the vote count.

I predicted at the time that we would rue the day our overly eager reformers would succeed in the single-member disaster.

While I have no regrets about having returned to the House for my final four-year stint, I found the atmosphere there less refreshing than during the heady early-statehood period and the aggressive policy-directed period of the run-up to my congressional campaigns. The reality is that most of today's legislators are politicians first, last, and always. Their second jobs, if any, are less significant. Compared with the Democrat leadership of the early statehood days—the Dois, Gills, Takahashis, Cravalhos, McClungs, Heens, et al.—today's lawmakers do not seem to be strong in their professions or in their private enterprises. Staying in office is their first and last motivation, which means they are subject to pressure from donors of campaign funds. And these donors (the candidates being Democrats) are usually the employee unions.

Moving On

In the meantime my personal life suffered a mid-life crisis. After almost three years of voluntary separation, I was divorced from Joan effective September 27, 1982. Joan Halford Rohlfing was a devoted mother to our three boys and a loyal wife. I have fond memories of our early Navy days in D.C. as well as in Hawaiʻi. She supported my political endeavors despite the sacrifices they brought in income and family time. She was a leader in democratizing the Honolulu Junior League and has given much to the Honolulu community. I will always be grateful for her support. How then to explain my restlessness during my early fifties? Simply put, I cannot.

I was able to find redemption and true marital happiness with my second wife, Patricia Ann (Santos) Bond, whom I married on August 23, 1983, in Los Altos, California. The service was conducted by a Naval Reserve captain who was also a minister, someone I found after a frantic hunt through the phone book. It was quite a rush to get rings and clothes suitable for the wedding, which took place only three days after I had proposed during dinner at the Bath House Restaurant in Monterey!

Patty's first husband, Rick Bond, had died young in November 1978.

My divorce settlement had provided that I would receive an undeveloped four-acre parcel of land in Kula, Maui. In due course that parcel of land became the foundation of our move to Maui in 1984.

While I don't recall when Patty and I actually began planning our move to Maui, by session time in 1984 we were already building a cedar home on this hillside parcel. It has a "million-dollar view" of Maui, Lanaʻi, and the tip of Molokaʻi. We were most fortunate to engage Mike Gerry and his brother Don as our builders. They were very straightforward and highly skilled guys whose work is still holding up well twenty-five years later. The house is a two-story, all-cedar, three-bedroom home purchased from Linwood Homes from Canada. Norm Woods was their representative in Honolulu, and he turned out to be great to deal with. We would talk to Mike by phone before going to the law office or the Capitol, and then we would come to Maui (usually staying with Bill and Pam Monahan in Makawao) to work on the place as it moved towards completion. We put all the "Deft" finish on the inside ceilings and all wood surfaces ourselves. We paid the subs directly as their work was approved by Mike.

When the legislative session was coming to an end, I received an offer to work for the administration of the County of Maui. This came from Rodger Betts, the corporation counsel for Mayor Hannibal Tavares, who offered a deputy position. So I resigned my legislative seat again. (To remain in step with the retirement system, I had to be on the job by the end of June!)

Governor Ariyoshi appointed kamaʻāina businessman Lowell Dillingham to fill out my term. This was a safe (for Democrats) appointment since Dillingham would not run the following year. (But I was able to talk Dillingham into letting me use Aloha Stadium seats given us for Rainbow football games that fall!)

My resignation led to the inevitable farewells on the final night of the 1984 session. My retirement party was well attended, but it was small and quieter than that of Democrat stalwart Yoshito Takamine. Yoshito was a hard-working labor leader from the Big Island and a reliable trooper for the majority Democrat machine.

HOUSE REPUBLICAN DINNER ON MY RETIREMENT IN 1984.

The press gave me a good final sendoff. The *Honolulu Advertiser* editorial on April 26, 1984, read as follows:

> "TWO GOOD LEGISLATORS—Fred Rohlfing is a Republican who was first elected to the House in the statehood election of 1959. He later moved to the Senate, ran for Congress, and subsequently returned to the House where he was minority leader in the last session. As a Republican, Rohlfing had little power. But he was, at times, an effective moderating force on both the Democrats and, in relation to more conservative elements, the GOP. It is likely that if the Republicans had had more candidates like Rohlfing, the party would have done better over the years. Rohlfing's service also includes terms as attorney general of American Samoa and as a U.S. delegate to the South Pacific Commission, and it is possible he could receive a diplomatic appointment from the Reagan administration. He is moving to Kula on Maui, so there is a chance he may serve government in some capacity there."

The *Honolulu Star-Bulletin* (more conservative than the *Advertiser*) offered this editorial on April 19, 1984:

> "The Republican Party may have gained strength with the addition of Frank Fasi, who in all probability will be its nominee for Mayor of Honolulu. But the retirement of Fred Rohlfing from the legislature is certainly a loss. Rohlfing has been a stalwart of the GOP in the Legislature for many years. He was first elected to the House in 1959 and served there until 1966, when he was elected to the Senate. He lost a bid for a seat in U.S. Congress in 1976. After serving as director of the Honolulu liaison office of American Samoa and as its attorney general, he returned to the House in 1980. Rohlfing plans to move to Maui and practice law there.

His retirement from politics may not be permanent. We hope not."

Another publication entitled the "Yellow Pages Guide to Hawai'i's 76 Legislators," published by lobbyist Rev. Frank Chong, had this intriguing comment:

"Republican Minority Leader Fred Rohlfing is a 'misplaced Republican' who, except for an accident of history, would probably be a Democrat. Because of his party, Rohlfing cannot get many bills passed, but he is a good representative of the 'loyal opposition.'" (What was that "accident of history"?)

As it happened, I moved to Maui before the electricity in our new house was on. I slept on futons for the first several weeks and used a propane stove! I "batched it" until Patty came over to stay around Labor Day 1984.

A Terrible Loss

In the late spring of 1985, at the age of fifty-seven, I took one last look at running for the governorship. I held a fundraiser at a restaurant in north Kīhei on Maui, and I convened a meeting of key people in Honolulu. However, it was not to be—not because of the state of politics but because of a call I received the evening after that Honolulu meeting, a call from my former wife Joan. She told me the terrible news that our third son, Brad, had died from a self-administered overdose of nitrous oxide.

How does one write about such a thing?

Like all parents who lose a child, I felt his death was totally unnatural. For quite a while I was besieged with guilt feelings. Couldn't I have done better for him? Was it because I had been the one to push for the divorce? I think about Brad often with deep sadness. Things had been going well with him at a new job with American Hawai'i Cruises.

Relatives and friends gathered for a meaningful service for Brad at Central Union Church in Honolulu. I could not speak. I passed the eulogy to my son Fritz.

Several weeks later Patty and I attended Easter services at Hui Aloha Church on the desolate coast of south Maui, where special prayers were offered to Brad and to us as survivors. Eddie Kamae was there and dedicated a Hawaiian hymn to Brad. I'd be honored if he were to sing at my funeral.

I had no energy left for politics, or much else, for a considerable period after this terrible event.

PART TWO

LOCAL BOY

HAWAI‘I ALOHA

E Hawai‘i, e ku‘u one hānau e,
Ku‘u home kulaīwi nei,
‘Oli nō au i nā pono
    lani e.
E Hawai‘i, aloha e.

Hui
E hau‘oli nā ‘opio o Hawai‘i nei
‘Oli e! ‘Oli e!
Mai nā aheahe makani e pā mai
    nei
Mau ke aloha, nō Hawai‘i.

E ha‘i mai kou mau kini lani e,
Kou mau kupa aloha, e Hawai‘i.
Nā mea ‘ōlino kamaha‘o nō luna
    mai.
E Hawai‘i, aloha e.

Nā ke Akua e mālama mai iā‘oe,
Kou mau kualono aloha nei,
Kou mau kahawai ‘ōlinolino mau,
Kou mau māla pua nani e.

BELOVED HAWAI‘I

O Hawai‘i, O sands of my birth,
My native home,
I rejoice in the blessings of
    heaven.
O Hawai‘i, aloha.

Chorus
Happy youth of Hawai‘i
Rejoice! Rejoice!
Gentle breezes
    blow
Love always for Hawai‘i.

May your divine throngs speak,
Your loving people, O Hawai‘i.
The holy light from
    above.
O Hawai‘i, aloha.

God protects you,
Your beloved ridges,
Your ever glistening streams,
Your beautiful flower gardens.

This is one of the many songs composed by the Reverend Lorenzo
Lyons, known as Makua Laiana, who had a church for many years
at Waimea, Hawai‘i. He died in 1886. A variant title for the song is
“Ku‘u One Hānau.” The song is so popular with Hawaiians that the
melody is used in other songs.

CHAPTER FOUR

THE EARLY YEARS

Hauʻoli la hānau (Happy Birthday)

Paul Harvey, the famous radio storyteller, would say, "And now it's time for the rest of the story." Accordingly, we set our time machine back to the year 1928.

I was born on November 2, 1928, at Children's Hospital in Honolulu, Territory of Hawaiʻi. My mother was Kathryn Coe Rohlfing, and my father was Romayne Raymond "Ted" Rohlfing. They were thirty and thirty-three years old, respectively, at the time of my birth. My mother had a pretty hard time bringing me into the world, and I have a reminder in the form of a forceps mark on the left side of my head that attests to her ordeal.

I was given the name Frederick William after my grandfather, who lived in Placerville, California, with my grandmother, Clara. I could have added "II" to my name officially—my son and grandchild of the same name have "III" and "IV" attached to theirs.

At the time of my birth my father worked for a company called Honolulu Iron Works, an industrial supply house. He knew a lot about plumbing, tools, paint, etc., and he was always tinkering around the house on Sundays fixing this or that. (I inherited none of this capability.) He had come to Hawaiʻi from California in 1915 or 1916 after graduating from the University of California at Berkeley. To be more precise, right out of college he took a job with a food brokerage firm based in San Francisco. But shortly thereafter, America entered World War I. My father enlisted in the U.S. Army and trained at Schofield Barracks on

Oʻahu. Later, as a second lieutenant, he was assigned to a camp in Augusta, Georgia, where he served as a machine-gun instructor. He was not sent to France, however, and when the war ended in November of 1918, he returned to Hawaiʻi.

My mother and father were married in April of 1920 in Honolulu. They had been college sweethearts and had stayed in touch by boat mail. (There was no email in those days!) My mother traveled to Hawaiʻi by ship, which took ten days at sea, and they were married the morning of her arrival (on the *S.S. Maui*, I believe). I have often wondered how she managed the trip because she was always seasick on our subsequent five-day crossings to and from Hawaiʻi and the Mainland. She was often in the cabin in bed not long after the ship sailed past Diamond Head at one end of the journey or the Golden Gate at the other end! She probably felt just great once she was on solid ground again. Or perhaps my father cured her. They had a lifetime love affair, and they always preferred each other's company to that of everything and everyone else. They spent their honeymoon at the then-upscale Haleʻiwa Hotel on Oʻahu's north shore.

My mother, Kathryn Coe, was born in Dover, New Jersey, in 1897. Her family moved to Oakland, California, when she was about four years old. My grandfather on the Coe side, Ira Judson Coe, was a civil engineer who traveled to California to work in the gold-mining industry. He could trace his family history in America back to Robert Coe, who arrived in the New World with eighty-two other passengers on a ship named the *Francis* on April 30, 1634. Ira Judson Coe was born in 1870 and married Harriet Halloway of Belleville, New Jersey.

My mother had two younger sisters, Marion and Alla. Over the years I stayed with each of them for significant periods of time when my parents were traveling to and from the East Coast. Marion married Willis Palmer, a stationery-supplies salesman, and they lived in the Westwood area of Los Angeles near the University of California (UCLA). Alla married Fred Seulberger, who had a florist shop in downtown Oakland. All were University of California graduates. Alla, the longest-surviving sister, died in 2001 at the age of ninety-one.

My father was born in 1896 in Placerville, California (El Dorado County). My grandfather, Frederick William, owned a grocery/general store in Placerville and was for some time the town postmaster, having

GRANDFATHER ROHLFING'S MEAT MARKET, PLACERVILLE, CA 1897. NOTE THE DIVERSE NEIGHBORING ACTIVITIES.

been appointed through the efforts of U. S. Senator Hiram Johnson—a Republican who had fought the large powers of the time, the railroad barons. I do not know where and when my grandfather was born, and I know nothing of his or my grandmother's earlier years. My father said that our ancestors came through Pennsylvania on the way west around 1848 (a date that fits with both the 1849 Gold Rush and a general exodus from "Deutschland"). The family roots are in Germany, of course, and it is likely that our origin was in the northwest region of that country, Westphalia, or near the border with the Netherlands, where the Rohlfing name is still prevalent today (as is Chun or Matsunaga in Hawai'i). My father also said there was a "big rift" between the Rohlfings and the Kipps (my grandmother's maiden name) over a land issue. He said that this rift caused our family to stay away from the Kipps and other relatives. Since my father was an only child (like me), all of my uncles and aunts were on the Coe side. Many clues to my family history were lost in a fire that burned most of the El Dorado County records.

In 1931 and 1932 I visited Placerville with my parents. I remember my grandmother cooking on a big wood-burning stove, and I remember being introduced to "outside plumbing" (the outhouse) for the first time. I was shown "Hangman's Tree" just on the outskirts of town, where "bad guys" in the Wild West days came to their demise. Placerville was real "Old West" country, and it gave me an appreciation for how my grandparents

lived as well as for the modern comforts we had back home on Oʻahu.

We visited the Coe grandparent side in Oakland more than the Rohlfing side because the Coe family members lived on the travel route to and from Hawaiʻi. Ira and Harriet Coe resided in a big old two-story house on Santa Clara Drive. In this house I was introduced to the use of chamber pots. This beat going down the hall (or outside, as in Placerville) when the temperature was in the forties! In those days Grandpa Coe was retired and spent most of his time at "The Club" somewhere in Oakland. He was a real gentleman and always wore a suit and hat when he went out. When World War II brought my mother and me to the Mainland, he "saved me" from Montezuma School near Los Gatos. More about that later. Suffice it to say, Ira Coe was my hero on more than one occasion.

The Great Depression and Early Travel

Although I was born in the heyday of what is now called the "Roaring Twenties," economic reality soon set in with the stock market crash of October 1929 and the prolonged economic depression that followed. Millions of Americans were out of work by the early 1930s. My father was by then working for Castle & Cooke, the "Big Five" firm that owned the Hawaiian Pineapple Company. His specialty was purchasing the materials and machines necessary to keep the pineapple cannery in operation. Nevertheless, a surplus of canned pineapple had accumulated and needed to be sold. My father and (I guess) others were sent on the road to accomplish just that.

With this mission my parents and I left Honolulu on the Matson vessel *Wilhelmina* in March 1932. We were in Placerville by June. Then we went east and spent time in places like Reading, Scranton, and Wilkes-

Barre (all in Pennsylvania), then longer periods in Philadelphia and Washington, D.C. (I know I was in the nation's capital then because I have pictures of myself with cherry trees and the Washington Monument in the background. I also have pictures of myself wearing leggings in the snow in Pennsylvania.) My father spent his days in the markets giving away samples of pineapple slices and selling the product as best he could, just as they do at Costco these days. We drove back across the country in a car that we picked up at the factory in Detroit, and we returned home to O'ahu in the late fall of 1933. We had been on the Mainland for approximately eighteen months.

As the Depression continued, we made other trips to the West Coast on Matson Line ships (the *Malolo*, the *Lurline*, and the *Monterey*). The first time that I can remember being left with my aunts and uncles in California was in 1935, when I stayed with the Seulbergers (Aunt Alla and Uncle Fred) at their home on Mandana Circle in Oakland, near Lake Merritt. This was also the year of my last encounter with Grandfather Rohlfing in Oakland. For the second grade I was sent to Miss Merriman's School, which my mother had attended when she was a little girl. It was essentially a girls-only school. This was some special dispensation in which I had no say, although I later expressed my displeasure. Several of the classes were conducted in French, and I did not have a clue as to what was going on!

In 1936 I stayed for three months in Westwood with the Palmers (Aunt Marion and Uncle Willis). I attended Fairburn Elementary School, which was my first encounter with public schools. My class of about forty-five pupils was a mixture of "upper" third and "lower" fourth graders. (I was an "upper" third grader.) It was the first time I had ever seen a playground that was covered only with gravel and dirt—no grass. It made for a lot of knee and elbow scrapes! My best friend at Fairburn was a "Kotonk" (Mainland Japanese) kid named Kiyoshi. An often-repeated family story is that I would always take off my shoes and socks after school, put them in my lunch pail, and walk home barefooted. I also dazzled the neighborhood by playing sandlot football barefooted.

My Westwood cousins, Warren and Janet Palmer, were two years older and the same age as me, respectively. They were, and still are, the closest thing for me to having a brother and sister.

In 1936 I had my first flight in an airplane. I flew unaccompanied from Burbank Airport in Los Angeles to Oakland on a two-propeller Boeing aircraft operated by United Airlines. It was a lot more fun to fly back then than it is now, as space was plentiful and passengers were treated royally. The stewardesses (not "flight attendants") wore full-length dresses! You could even see the scenery.

When my father and mother returned to California from the East Coast to take me home in November of 1936, we had to deal with a West Coast dock strike. No Matson (U.S.) ships were sailing, but the Japanese shipping line Nippon Yusha Kaisha (NYK) was unaffected by the strike. My father gained passage for us aboard the *Tatsuta Maru* for our return from San Francisco to Hawai'i. After returning home, I remember being particularly happy to be able to eat decent rice again!

I lived with the Palmers for another three months in late 1937 and early 1938, when I was ten years old and in the fifth grade. Stand-out memories of this time include the neighborhood football games, attending University of Southern California and UCLA games at the Los Angeles Coliseum, and on January 1, 1939, attending the Duke University/USC Rose Bowl game with my mother. Duke, which came into the game undefeated and unscored upon, kept the Trojans scoreless through the first three quarters. Duke's great kicker Eric Tipton kept USC bottled up and kicked a field goal. Thus Duke led 3–0 as the game came down to final minutes. USC's fourth-string quarterback, Doyle Nave, came off the bench with but two minutes left. Nave then fired four straight passes to second-team end Al Kreuger, the last pass a nineteen-yard touchdown!

The Rothwells, *Honolulu Star-Bulletin* Newspaper Routes, and Free-Form Football

On one occasion in 1939 (I think), when both of my parents went to the Mainland on one of my father's many business trips, I stayed for three months with the Rothwell family across the street from us on Hillside Avenue. For the first time I was surrounded by other kids—my close friend Nelson Rothwell, who was my age, his older sister Mary Lou, and his older cousins Frank and Bruce Burns (whose parents were in Seattle at the time). Nelson's brothers Frank and Bob were already away at college on the Mainland. This was a great experience for me. Dinners were uproarious, as Nelson's father Guy (a prominent architect) was a great fisherman and unparalleled storyteller. He had a sampan called the *Ehukai*, and I was introduced to deep-sea fishing, which I ultimately concluded was not worth the time, money, and effort—at least for me. But it made for interesting experiences and, better yet, great "fish stories."

The Burns brothers, Frank and Bruce, had substantial *Honolulu Star-Bulletin* newspaper routes, and soon I was working with one or the other as a "helper." Bruce's route extended down lower Oʻahu Avenue and into the University of Hawaiʻi campus to include pig farms on the Kaimukī side of the campus. (Today this is the East-West Center complex.) The roads back there were nothing to write home about, and snarling dogs were a daily hazard. Frank's route, on the other hand, was in a higher-class area, and it extended up the valley from somewhat mauka (toward the mountain) of Cooper Road to Lowrey Avenue. Accordingly, I was willing to help Frank for less pay!

Before delivering the daily evening newspapers, we would gather at "The Corner"—an empty lot (at that time) at the intersection of East Mānoa and Oʻahu Avenues. Wild and woolly football games ensued every afternoon with no regard for varying sizes or ages of the players. In those days no one wore protective equipment. The highly organized nature of kids' football now is in complete contrast to my experience. I'm not sure which is better, but we certainly learned how to take hard knocks. One of the older guys, Billy Barter (I will never forget him), would run with his knees up around his chin. The lot was sloped. He'd get up a head of steam, and we'd have to try to stop him. I'm lucky that I never got a concussion! One time our paper-route gang played an AJA (Americans of Japanese ancestry) team from Moʻiliʻili. We got a dirty licking!

During this period and at other times I would accompany the Rothwells for weekends at the McCarthy home at Punaluʻu. (Mrs. Louise Rothwell was from the McCarthy family that owned and operated several small hotels. Her father had been an appointed governor of Hawaiʻi in the territorial days.) In the 1930s it was a drive of one to one-and-a-half hours over the old Pali Pass Road, factoring in stops at fruit stands, gas stations, etc.

We swam, hiked, fished, and boated at Punaluʻu. The McCarthy house was a huge, two-story affair, and the boys were assigned to the second floor. One of my most vivid memories is waking up once with something crawling on my chest. I knocked it to the floor, pulled the string on the single light bulb, and discovered a scorpion of major proportions! *Quick, get one slippah and make* (kill) *da buggah!* I did.

One time at Punaluʻu, I noticed that Guy Rothwell (Nelson's father) kept referring to "umbilican fishermen." I finally asked him what he meant. He replied, "Those reef fishermen out there who walk around with those glass boxes and spear fish." (Water was up to the umbilicus—piko).

Our Mānoa Gang

My closest friends during my early years were Nelson Rothwell, David Pinkerton, and Tommy Beaumont. Nelson was the "brainy one"—he read *Popular Science* and built little engines and model planes. David, the son of a beloved Honolulu physician, lived in a big house with two full-time servants (Harry and Shizue) and a huge yard where we could play. Tommy from Puʻuhonua Street was the hiking guide for a wide swath of the mountain above our houses where we had our "clubhouses." That we managed to avoid sliding off cliffs and to survive small landslides without major injury amazes me to this day.

Our primary means of transportation was, naturally, the bicycle, and the location of our activities ranged from Mānoa Falls to Moʻiliʻili. There was a lot less traffic in those days, but the street pattern was much the same as it is today, except for the newer, upper-valley development. There were no parks like those where my grandsons Frederick and Markus played Pop Warner football while they were growing up. Instead, we played wherever we could squeeze in a game—often on the strip across from our house at Cooper Road (there were no houses there, only sugarcane stalks), or up the hill at Castle Home (a large home and grounds that was unoccupied), or even sometimes on Punahou School's fields out of view of the administration. We played baseball, too, often in the street on Hillside Avenue. We played some tennis, but since we didn't wear shoes, the experience was often unpleasant. The soles of our feet would get burned from the hot pavement at the courts by the entrance to Mānoa Valley.

Early School Days

I was fortunate to receive most of my early education at Punahou School. As mentioned earlier, I twice attended public elementary school in Westwood for three-month periods. During World War II I spent a year at David Starr Jordan Junior High School in Palo Alto, California, and three-quarters of a year at Palo Alto High School.

Punahou was then a far different school from what it is today. Classes were small. There were few cars on campus. And the student body was predominantly composed of "haoles." (Thus the inevitable slam: "Punahou for rich haoles.")

Our elementary classes were all held in Bishop Hall on the lower side of the campus. Of course, we boys liked recess and physical education the most, and we played all the usual games. The most popular was "speedball" (we called it "slaughter"), which was like soccer but you could pass the ball as well as kick it. They wouldn't allow tackle football—this was being saved for seventh grade "midget football."

One of the members of our class, Charley Bond, was always getting in trouble with the teachers—usually for "mouthing off." He lived on Rocky Hill and was often followed to school by his dog, a rather ugly, skinny, drooling German shepherd named Cassius. This didn't help Charley's situation, and he spent a lot of time in the principal's office under detention. Worse yet for him, his classmates frequently decided that Charley needed a comeuppance, and he was regularly tossed into the lily pond.

Even back then Punahou taught us about Hawaiian culture. We had music and Hawaiian culture classes with Mrs. Pukui, who later wrote the definitive Hawaiian dictionary and who was recognized as a leading Hawaiian scholar. We made music with stones, 'ukulele, and other Hawaiian instruments.

Another big thing in those days was the junior carnival—predecessor of the extravaganzas of today. It featured an E.K. Fernandez Ferris wheel, merry-go-round, and maybe one other ride like a flipping airplane. There were booths with prizes. As always, the most popular was the baseball throw to dunk some teacher or hotshot football player.

A big change at school came when we advanced to the seventh grade and classes were held in Alexander Hall. For the first time we were required to wear shoes in class, and we moved between rooms for various courses. Classes were larger, as new kids were admitted from other elementary schools such as Hanahau'oli, Lincoln, and Thomas Jefferson.

Organized sports improved. I played guard for the first time in "midget football" on a team captained by Warren Ackerman, who became an outstanding end on the Punahou varsity team and later at the University of Hawai'i. In eighth grade we played with six-man teams, which at the time were a new fad. I didn't like it as much as traditional eleven-man football.

Pearl Harbor: Hawai'i and the United States at War

I was in the eighth grade at Punahou and had just turned thirteen years old when the Japanese attacked Pearl Harbor and other Hawai'i military bases on the morning of December 7, 1941. The night before I had attended a dance at Kulumanu Studios on Farmers Road in Kāhala with my then-girlfriend Mavis Chaney. She lived in Nu'uanu Valley, and my father had driven us to and from the dance. We had arrived home at around ten p.m., so we were not in any hurry to get up early and go anywhere on Sunday morning. My father was reading the newspaper and had the radio tuned to KGU 760—one of the two Honolulu AM stations (there was no FM in those days). We heard a report that a bomb had gone off in Moʻiliʻili, and shortly thereafter Webley Edwards (later known the world over as producer/host of the *Hawaiʻi Calls* radio show) announced that Pearl Harbor was under air attack and that "this is the real McCoy." While the news that Hawaiʻi was being attacked startled us, the fact of war was not a real surprise. Japan and the United States were head-to-head on numerous issues. A special "peace delegation" from Japan had traveled to Washington, D.C., to give the (false) impression that Japan desired peace, all while planning and executing a carrier-based air attack. My father had been to the Philippines in the fall of 1940 and was particularly aware of intelligence concerning a Japanese threat, which he had previously discussed with us at the dinner table.

My father decided that he and I should go over to a naval officer friend's home on Oʻahu Avenue, about a block away, to make sure they knew about the attack. The officer was assigned to the USS Arizona, but somehow my father knew he was on liberty overnight. As we neared his home, we heard a loud whistling/screaming noise that sounded like a bomb. We ducked behind a wall and waited for the explosion, but it never occurred. It was a "dud" like many that were fired that day by our anti-aircraft batteries. We then went into the house of the naval officer and told him what was happening. He immediately dressed and left for Pearl Harbor only to find that his ship had been devastated.

The naval officer we alerted that December morning was later killed in action in the Pacific.

When we returned home, we saw a Japanese plane over Mānoa Valley and therefore had proof positive of their presence. The rest of the day was spent with radios at our sides. In the mid-afternoon there were reports of Japanese troop landings on the Waiʻanae Coast, which fortunately turned out to be false. (Perhaps some local AJAs had come ashore from their fishing boats.)

That afternoon Nelson Rothwell and I talked about taking guns—he had a pellet gun and a BB gun—and camping out in Mānoa Valley if the Japanese came ashore. If ever there was a bad plan, this was it!

After the Pearl Harbor Attack

The days that followed Pearl Harbor were pretty scary. Everyone was expecting that the Japanese would return to attack or even invade Hawai'i, particularly knowing how well their attack had succeeded in knocking out the U.S. Pacific Fleet. Martial law was declared immediately, and a blackout was ordered beginning at dusk every night. Total military control of our islands was ordered. The territorial government continued to function but was subservient to the Army authority, General Short. Military judges handled traffic and other petty violations, often requiring defendants to give pints of blood to our blood bank as well as to pay a fine. The nighttime blackout lasted for years—most every house had modified blackout windows that allowed air to get in to some extent. Right after the Pearl Harbor attack curfew was set at six p.m., but as life went on it gradually was relaxed to ten p.m. All residents (kids included) were issued gas masks, which we had to keep with us at all times. This was a pain in the neck if your chief means of transportation was an ordinary kids' bicycle.

Why the extreme reaction? The surprise of the attack and threat of another was the ostensible reason. But the underlying reason was that the military establishment did not trust the large Japanese ethnic population in Hawai'i.

The Punahou School campus was commandeered by the U.S. Army Engineers to use as a wartime headquarters. It was not returned to school use until my senior year (1945-46). It has been said that the Engineers meant to grab McKinley High School and made a mistake, but I think they knew that Punahou had better facilities! Punahou arranged for use of private homes in the Mānoa-Makiki area in the weeks after December 7, and we started school again, as I recall, just after New Year's Day, 1942. My eighth grade was located in Makiki and utilized the Henry White and Waterhouse homes, which were across the street from each other. The class of 1945 utilized homes right near our home on O'ahu Avenue. We used the Whites' dining room for social studies, and we studied Latin on the patio of the Waterhouse mansion. Organized sports were limited, so we did a lot of improvising. We also helped dig ditches for bomb shelters.

We were all fingerprinted and given identification cards, which we wore around our necks. One time we had to wear our gas masks in a basement room in Bishop Hall where they had let tear gas loose, and we had to exit after taking the masks off. Boy, did that ever burn the eyes!

During the first few months of the war my father worked part-time with the military governor's office in addition to his regular job at Hawaiian Pine, so he had to drive in the blacked-out streets. Many Island families (wives and children) left for the Mainland by ship in the weeks after Pearl Harbor, often forming "refugee" communities in select places on the West Coast and in the Rocky Mountain States. Most of the ships traveled in convoys. But one ship, the P & O's (Peninsular and Oriental Steam Navigation Company's) *Aquitania*, was deemed fast enough to outrun Japanese submarines and chanced voyages without escorts.

I completed my eighth grade classes at Punahou, but my parents felt that Hawai'i at wartime was not really the best place for a thirteen-year-old. They decided my mother would take me to the West Coast for a year. The initial plan called for my attending a boys' school called Montezuma, which was located in the Santa Cruz Mountains near Los Gatos, California. When we arrived on the Mainland, I was sent to summer camp there while my Mom looked for a place to stay in Palo Alto.

While the stay on the Mainland was being planned, we experienced the Battle of Midway on June 3 to 5, 1942. The community was aware through rumors that something big was brewing in late May, but no one knew the extent of the risks. As it turned out, these days were the turning point of the war in the Pacific, as the threat of Japanese invasion of Hawai'i was ended by the brilliance and courage of our Navy in its magnificent victory over Admiral Nagumo's Japanese fleet.

Despite the lessened pressures, my mother and I left Honolulu in mid-July 1942 on the *Honolulu Clipper*, a flying boat which departed from the Pan American pier on the Pearl City peninsula. Sixteen hours and sixteen minutes elapsed before we landed in San Francisco Bay and docked at Treasure Island. Unlike passengers on today's cramped aircraft, however, we were able to stretch out and sleep in the on-board bunks and move around freely. Even so, we were glad to see land after all those hours grinding along over water in a propeller-driven aircraft. After spending time with my grandparents in Oakland and a delightful couple of weeks at the Seulbergers' retreat at Tahoe Pines at Lake Tahoe, we traveled south. I was deposited at Montezuma School for several weeks of summer camp. It was a big change, and I did not like the place at all. My huge, cavernous dorm room didn't help, and I knew no one—very unlike Punahou. I must have made my complaints pretty clear, as my mother said I could join her in Palo Alto and go to public school.

Getting back to Palo Alto from near Los Gatos, though, presented a logistics problem—there was no train. My mother didn't have a car, and gas rationing made it a long and expensive trip. Into this breach jumped my grandfather, Ira Coe, and a friend of his who had a well-preserved Model A Ford. These two old gentlemen—dressed to "the nines"—drove all the way from Oakland, picked me up in Los Gatos, and deposited me at my mother's doorstep in Palo Alto. I have never again been more grateful to anyone!

The War Years: Public School in California

In September 1942 I enrolled in David Starr Jordan Junior High School in the ninth grade. There were a number of former Hawai'i kids there, which eased the transition to Mainland living. They included Hunter "Hunk of Manure" McClure, the son of an army officer with Hawai'i experience, also David Crabbe from the Big Island, Patsy and Barbara White, and later on Bob Faus and Peter Nottage (who continues to be a close friend to this day). We went everywhere on our bikes in this flat college town (Stanford University), and I played a lot of baseball. I was a San Francisco Seals fan and listened to and kept score on many games. I took the train alone north to San Francisco to see Seals games on several occasions. Also, of course, I was a pro-Stanford rooter when they were called the "Indians" (now not "politically correct"). We were able to attend Stanford home games free if we sat in a section way up in the upper corner of Stanford Stadium.

I joined the Boy Scouts and the YMCA, and I attended summer camps with both organizations. I liked D.S. Jordan Junior High and got good grades there. One of my daily duties was to maintain a chart of the Russian Front and to report on the war to our class at current events time. Consequently, I well remember the Battle of Stalingrad and the attempt to starve out Leningrad during its war-long siege. I think this activity may have something to do with my continuing interest in the Russian language and the Russian people.

Another experience while in Palo Alto was working on farms. Teenagers were needed to fill the manpower gap. We got paid a piece rate for picking pears, and the most I could make was about seven dollars in a day. I also picked green beans and tomatoes, which were even less productive money-wise. It was one of those experiences that led you to study harder in school!

I also picked up another small amount of spending money by writing a football newsletter, which I mailed to about fifteen subscribers. Since I read all the latest sports magazines and followed team records, I was pretty good at predicting games. My uncle Willis Palmer and others often used my newsletter predictions and background information to bet on games!

Tenth grade meant a transition to Palo Alto High School. I played guard on the junior varsity football team but didn't see much action, as I was too small (a perpetual problem!). I signed on as manager of the varsity basketball team for the late fall/winter months. At that time we had moved for several months to a small house on the beautiful Willard Griffens property in Los Altos. I had to take the City bus home after games and got home pretty late at night. Traveling with the team made me familiar with the Peninsula/South Bay area. Highlights at this location were taking the school bus in the morning and helping farm the property with its walnut and fruit orchards. This is where I got my first driving lessons at age fifteen—driving the Griffens' farm truck around the orchards. We shared a home with Marney Dearing, a friend of my Aunt Alla, in Palo Alto for the final months of our Mainland "banishment." (Marney's husband Joe was a war reporter based in London.)

By early fall of 1943 we were eager and ready to get home to Hawai'i, but the Navy didn't cooperate. All shipping for dependents was cancelled in August, and that extended until we were finally able to return to O'ahu on a converted hospital ship in April of 1944. The hospital ship was my first experience of sleeping in hammocks three high suspended between posts in a huge room. We had one small escort ship to chase away any Japanese submarines that might come our way.

End of the War Years: Punahou at the University

Punahou School had been occupying the University of Hawaiʻi's Teacher's College building on Dole Street for its upper-division classes. As a returning sophomore, I had a tough time adjusting to geometry that was far more advanced than what had been taught at Palo Alto High School, so I had to be tutored along with some other "returnees." By junior year I was up to speed, and I played junior team football. I think we lost every game, but we had a great coach named Plover Judd. Plover used to give me a ride home after some practices because he lived down near the intersection of Oʻahu and East Mānoa Avenues. I most remember the dirty licking we got from Farrington High School (64–0) on a field out in Kalihi that had no grass at all. Our varsity team that year wasn't much better. They lost to Kamehameha 64–0, and their big deal was making a touchdown against Roosevelt High School but ultimately losing the game 12–6.

I also played basketball on the junior team and baseball on the varsity. We almost beat ʻIolani High School in basketball at a gym at Palama Settlement, where I got to know Bobby Minn, Masa Yonamine, and other up-and-coming athletes of the day. My biggest claim to fame, however, was catching the entire game against Mid-Pacific Institute and driving in two winning runs with a hit over third base.

The nine p.m. curfew was still in effect in those days, so we would often stay overnight at friends' homes on the weekends. One frequent stopover was Billy Baird's in Kāhala; also Chico Hansen's on the ridge overlooking Kāhala. In Kāhala we traveled through backyards and over fences to evade the curfew patrols. We had a few close calls, as you might imagine. If the huge walls and mansions that now exist in Kāhala had been there at that time, we would have been picked up immediately! My parents wouldn't have been pleased.

Since there was a shortage of workers for agriculture, students worked in the pineapple fields about every six weeks. They would pick us up at school in big trucks and transport us to the fields in the Wahiawā area. We hoed, picked pineapples, and goofed off when we could. It was hot, dusty work that convinced all of us of the importance of an education so that we wouldn't have to do manual labor for a living! Of course, we had the card-playing gamblers on the bus and other high jinks by those who resisted hard labor. These antics enlivened our tedious days in the fields.

Return to the Campus: Class of 1946

The war with Japan ended in August 1945, after the two atomic bombs at Hiroshima and Nagasaki. We had a great party at Birdie Wilkinson's house in Kāhala. Hawai'i went nuts on VJ (Victory over Japan) Day, as we knew that four years of a highly restrained lifestyle (including martial law) would finally end.

We returned to the main Punahou campus for our senior year, and it was a great one. I played guard, as usual, on the varsity football team under Coach Tony Morse. I was backup to Beck Billson, who outweighed me by at least thirty pounds. I started only one game—against Roosevelt High School—in the regular season, but played extensively against Kaimukī and McKinley High Schools. Our team managed to win our first four games but then ran into trouble and narrowly lost to Farrington High School and Kamehameha. Our last regular season game was against St. Louis College. Had we won, we would have been champions. Punahou had not won a championship for over twenty years, and before the game an old alumnus named Fernandez came to the locker room and showed us his championship ring. This visit made us more nervous than we already were. Our right halfback went onto the field without his helmet on! St Louis's Abe Dung ran wild, and we lost 40-7. I had had a bad cold the week before the game and had to talk myself into suiting up. But Coach Morse put me in for a short time after the game was essentially over.

My very first visit to Maui occurred when we played Lahainaluna High School at the old fairgrounds in Kahului a week after our regular season ended. Our team was housed at various homes in the Wailuku/Kahului area. I started and played almost the entire game, both on offense and defense. We won 25 to 6. It was a particularly big day for me, as I made a lot of tackles and recovered three fumbles!

After the game there was a banquet for our team at the Maui Country Club, which I now visit at least three times a week for golf, swimming, or social reasons. Downstairs at the bar I was offered a drink by an alumnus who followed our team very closely, Mun Kwai Lau. When I asked for lemonade he said I had to have a real drink since I'd played so well. He bought me my first-ever gin fizz. I only had one, as it had been quite a day already!

I passed up basketball after football season, and I did conditioning with the track team until baseball season arrived. Because I had hit well in my few appearances in games as a junior, I was moved to right field for my senior-year season and only did backup catching. My hitting average wasn't so good this year, as I tended to hit long fly outs. But I enjoyed playing baseball and earned my second letter in that sport.

Graduation and the usual summer job at Hawaiian Pine came and went, and soon it was time pack up and go to college. I had applied to four universities earlier in my senior year and had taken the SATs (scholastic aptitude tests). My applications went to Duke, Stanford, and Yale Universities, and to the University of California at Los Angeles. I was accepted at all four, but Yale was always my (and, more importantly, my father's) first choice.

DAD CARRIED THE "UKE" TO THE AIRPORT WHEN I WAS OFF TO COLLEGE.

Bright College Years:
For God, for Country, and for Yale!

Bright College Years

Bright college years, with pleasure rife,
The shortest, gladdest years of life,
How swiftly are ye gliding by,
O, why doth time so quickly fly?
The seasons come, the seasons go,
The earth is green or white with snow;
But time and change shall naught avail
To break the friendships formed at Yale.

In after-years, should troubles rise
To cloud the blue of sunny skies,
How bright will seem, through mem'ry's haze,
Those happy, golden by-gone days!
So let us strive that ever we
May let these words our watch-cry be,
Where'er upon life's sea we sail:
"For God, for Country, and for Yale!"

Traveling five thousand miles away from home to attend a Main-land university in the mid-forties was a "big deal," more so than today with its jet travel. Instead of being hours away, we were days away. My initial trip to Yale in September 1946 took five days on the *Matsonia* and three days on the cross-country railroads. It ended after a drive from a New York suburb to New Haven, Connecticut. Not only was this school a long way from the sunny shores of O'ahu, but it also caused culture shock. No more aloha shirts. Have to wear a jacket, shoes, and that anti-freedom garment, a tie! This was just one of the things that changed temporarily in my lifestyle.

Our class, 1950, arrived at a time when the tradition-rich university was undergoing profound change. World War II had ended just a year earlier, and the subsequent passage of the G.I. Bill meant that veterans' educations would be subsidized. As a result, the freshman class of 1950 was the largest in Yale history.

Its eighteen hundred members doubled the school's prewar numbers. The Old Campus, which had previously accommodated eight hundred and fifty freshman, now had to oblige twelve hundred members of the class. The remaining six hundred or so freshmen—vets with wives and, often, small children—occupied rows of World War II-type Quonset huts situated out by the Yale Bowl and (hence) a bus or car-ride away from classes that we younger men reached by foot. The mix thrust us youngsters up against hardened "G.I.s" in class as well as in the gyms and athletic fields. Two-thirds of the new students were veterans, and these men were filled with purpose. Future president George H.W. Bush (Yale class of 1948) was one of those housed in a Quonset, and while there he fathered our recent president George W.

My first room at Yale was in McClellan Hall on the Old Campus next to historic Connecticut Hall. My three roommates were Nathaniel (Nat) Saltonstall, John G. Russell, and Richard Steinmetz. Nat was from Honolulu and my class at Punahou, John from Fairfield, Connecticut, and Dick from Indiana. The latter two were graduates of Choate, a New England prep school. We got along well, and we stay in touch to this day. For study time-outs, we devised a makeshift game of indoor baseball using rolled-up magazines, balls of newspaper, and various-sized windows to while away the hours of foul weather—and believe me, New Haven had plenty of that!

The academic regime at Yale was rigorous, and I had to hustle to survive Spanish taught by an Ecuadorian military officer. We read stories in *La Prensa* for homework. There was also science in the form of at least one semester each of chemistry and physics. Chemistry was an old bugaboo of mine at Punahou, but I managed 75 or C+ with some extra effort.

I had weighed playing freshman football against my need to survive academically and decided to go out for freshman swimming instead, in order to have more time in the fall to "hit the books." This worked for the grades, but eventually I wished that I had had another year of football.

My coach for frosh swimming was Delaney Kiputh, son of the legendary American Olympic coach Bob Kiputh. Both Kipuths used to walk the sides of the pool with long poles that they would use to prod swimmers caught loafing along. This was always threatening (especially for us backstrokers) since we swam nude in the days before coeds arrived on campus.

By Christmas I knew that I had made the right choice in attending Yale, as work and play fit well and I made many new friends.

For sophomore and subsequent school years Nat and I roomed at Pierson College with two new classmates, Tom Merritt from St. Charles, Illinois, and William "Bama" Nicrosi from Montgomery, Alabama. We had met Bama through the Exeter prep group in McClellan Hall and Tom through the freshman swim team, where he was a breaststroker. I still stay in touch with Bama's widow, Harold, a staunch "yellow dog" Southern Democrat who works for the Alabama State Senate and cheers for her beloved "Crimson Tide." (A "yellow dog" Democrat is one who would sooner vote for a yellow dog than for a Republican.)

Other adventures in college included ski trips to Stowe, Vermont, to Northampton, New Hampshire, and to several other areas, also visits to girls' schools, ball games in New York, and to the homes of roommates and other friends for holidays. I could afford neither the money nor the time to go home for holidays, so I stayed with school friends. A short list of these locations would include Beth Ayres, Pennsylvania, with Al Paul Lefton, Saginaw, Michigan, with Dan Toshach, Fairfield, Connecticut, with John Russell, St. Charles, Illinois, with Tom Merritt, Little Rock, Arkansas, with Tubby Phillips, Miami, Florida, with Dan Mahoney, and Falmouth, Massachusetts, with Phillip "Skip" Smith.

Memorable events along the way of four years at Yale included a spur-of-the-moment all-night drive with Tubby Phillips to Washington, D.C., when Truman was elected by surprise in 1948. We got to D.C. in time to bid the Hawaiian delegation's girls goodbye at their train station! Also, several impromptu visits to Skip Smith's place at Cape Cod stand out, including one when the lobster climbed out of the pot, scaring "Hoss" Davis (a tough punt-returning halfback) half to death.

Yes, we did have to study, too. Most of my courses were not particularly remarkable—a diet of government courses laced with some language, philosophy, history, and social studies. My favorite course came in my junior year, Mr. Ralph Turner's history course, which was a world tour of religious and cultural movements through the centuries. Christianity, Islam, Buddhism, Hinduism, you name it, they all merited attention, and he threw in some contemporary politics for intrigue. This led to some comments from the floor by famous classmate Bill Buckley, who must have been writing his first book at the time—*God and Man at Yale.*

The most memorable event of my four years at Yale took place not in the classroom but on the athletic field. Senior year began with August football camp in a small Connecticut town south of New Haven. I remember that it was very hot for our twice-a-day practices, and I remember that I hurt my ankle early on. Over time the heat passed, but the ankle was to bother me the rest of my football career. I had a very good relationship with my line coach, Harold Kopp, and with the end coach Harry Jacunski, but it didn't help with the head man, Herman Hickman, when it came to the final cut posted in the athletic department as school began. I was the only lineman on the list, and two sophomores were retained—players I had been able to push around. Clearly Coach Hickman was looking ahead rather than having a small senior guard—me, at one hundred seventy pounds soaking wet—occupy the end of the bench on game day.

What a blow this was.

Rather than try out for the junior varsity team, I moped around in our residential college, having been told by the junior varsity coach Gib Holgate to take a couple weeks off if I needed to. He then put me to work as offensive weak side guard in our single-wing attack, though I would have preferred defense.

The junior varsity had a mediocre season—only four games and, worse yet, we lost to Harvard at Cambridge. I missed the Princeton game because I had to take the law school aptitude test. My mind, however, was not too focused and, as a result, I had to retake the test in the spring. My scores were much better that time.

As the final game (Harvard, as usual) approached, the media guy from the athletic office (Charles Loftus) approached me about doing a story for the Harvard-Yale football program. Pictures of me were taken in uniform, in structured action, and with my coach. The article, "Varsity Maker," appeared on game day, so at least I had some recognition for my efforts. More recognition came at the time of the annual football banquet, when I received the Norman S. Hall award for the junior varsity player who had contributed the most to Yale football. The lesson was clear: whatever league you're in, you can achieve success and be fulfilled *provided you never quit.*

I can't leave the subject of Harvard vs. Yale without plagiarizing this story from the "Yale Alumni News" (class of '49 notes):

> "My saddest memory of 'The Game' was when two of us proudly led a young Handsome Dan (Yale bulldog mascot) out to the 50 yard line before the kickoff of the 1948 game in Cambridge. And, quickly before it even started, we knew The Game would be a disaster. The Harvard cheerleaders came to meet us with a turkey on a leash. The turkey was bigger than Dan and not the least intimidated. He (or was it she?) pecked at Dan and Dan shriveled curling up in a fetal position. We yanked on his leashes and managed to get him off the field under his own power as the jeers from the Crimson reverberated across the field. The Game ended H-20 Y-7. Ever since I've always thought of the Harvards as turkeys."

After football came intramural sports. I tied the inter-college record for the fifty-yard backstroke, and I made it to the finals in boxing in the one-hundred-sixty-five-pound weight class. The guy who won had very long arms and kept me from getting in more than a few flurries, and my previously broken nose got dangerously bent a few more times.

As we approached graduation, I passed my political science four-hour, major comprehensive test with flying colors and made the dean's list. My grades were good enough to garner invitations to four top-rated law schools—California (Boalt Hall), Michigan, Virginia, and Stanford. I chose Stanford. In retrospect, I think I would have done better in first-year law at Virginia than with the temptations of the West Coast, which included partying at Berkeley on football weekends. That frivolity led to my having to spend winter break making up assignments and trying to comprehend what the law business was all about!

VARSITY MAKER

by Charles Loftus

Last Saturday when Yale met Princeton at Palmer Stadium there was an Eli player who remained behind in New Haven. And that boy would have given almost anything to have been able to play football on that particular afternoon against the Tigers.

He had to stay behind in order to take a law school entrance examination and, let's face it, actually there wasn't a single one of the 45,000 on hand for the contest who missed him. His name was not in the program, his number wasn't listed.... In a way that's a sad commentary. Because the boy we are talking about is a football player, although he has never played in a varsity game (except in the Spring inter-squad game). As a matter of fact, he has never even had on a varsity uniform, and, yet, he, and thousands of young men just like him, furnish one of the most important cogs in the American collegiate gridiron picture.

The lad we are talking about is Frederick William Rohlfing, a Yale senior from Honolulu, five-feet, nine-inches, 170 pounds, 20 years old. He is a junior varsity player, and has been for the past (two) years.

In the junior varsity ranks you find most boys playing because they love football. Certainly there is no other reward for them. They do not become campus heroes, national football figures, no one stops them to tell them what a great game they played on a pervious Saturday, no one bothers to ask them for an autograph. We repeat, they play because they love football.

An excellent swimmer, (Fred) gave up this sport in order to play football.... He says, "there is just something about blocking and tackling that I like...our junior varsity games are just about as important to us as the varsity games are to the varsity. Probably more than that, in a way most of us feel some satisfaction in knowing that to a small degree we are helping the varsity. "Helping them, Fred? You're making them.

Yep, that's what these jayvees are, varsity makers, not in the sense that they become elevated to varsity status, but that five days a week they furnish the competition on which the varsity sharpens both its offensive and defensive

FRED ROHLFING AND J.V. COACH JAMES "G.B." HOLGATE

claws. "Sometimes," Rohlfing says, "we jayvees actually get to feeling a little sorry for the varsity. Especially when we can puncture the defenses or they have a hard time gaining against us. Then we get the full realization, man, maybe they won't be any better on Saturday, and we get frightened. Just about that time the varsity gets a spark and for the next 20 plays in a row you find yourself flat on your back."

He plays on a "different" team each week. One week he has to learn the Connecticut plays, the next week the Columbia plays, the following week he's from Dartmouth and so it goes through nine games each season. At Yale there are no cuts on the junior varsity squad....

They look forward week to week to their own games, and try to get in some preparations, although this sometimes is difficult—with the varsity making such heavy demands on their time.

We asked Rohlfing what he would take for the experience of playing jayvees football.

"Nothing," he answered. "Nothing. I wouldn't trade that experience for anything. Well, maybe for nothing except a chance to have played in a varsity game."

Bless 'em, they're wonderful kids aren't they?

(This article appeared in the official Harvard-Yale football program of Nov. 1949)

Out into the Real World

I skipped my Yale graduation ceremony in order to depart from New York for Europe on the French line ship *De Grasse* in early June 1950. My friend Philip "Skip" Smith joined me for this traditional grand tour.

It wasn't always "grand," as we tried to do it on a budget of ten dollars a day—that was for everything except rail/bus tickets to take us from town to town. We started in Paris, where Skip's ability to speak French helped us get around well. We had problems getting our return air squared away, as our "International Youth" agency failed to deliver on a promised return flight, Icelandic Air for a hundred and fifty dollars. We appealed to the American embassy, but it was all for naught. The principals had absconded with most of the money that students had paid in. Dad eventually came through with a BOAC ticket (three hundred and fifty dollars) to get me home and to law school at Stanford.

Our European adventure took us from Paris to Biarritz, to the bullfights of San Fermin in Pamplona, to Nice, Monte Carlo, Rome, Venice, Luzern, Frankfurt, the Rhine, Koln, Copenhagen, Stockholm, Bergen, Scotland, and London.

I grew up on this trip, learning to manage my money, obtain transportation, and find housing and food in strange places. I learned to engage in social relations with people other than Americans.

PART THREE

THE UNITED STATES OF AMERICA
THIS IS TO CERTIFY THAT
THE PRESIDENT OF THE UNITED STATES OF AMERICA
HAS AWARDED THE

MERITORIOUS SERVICE MEDAL

TO

CAPTAIN FREDERICK W. ROHLFING, UNITED STATES NAVAL RESERVE

FOR

OUTSTANDING MERITORIOUS SERVICE FROM OCTOBER 1985 THROUGH JUNE 1987

GIVEN THIS   26TH   DAY OF   JAN   19 89

SECRETARY OF THE NAVY

SERVICE TO COUNTRY
AND THE LAW

CHAPTER FIVE

SERVICE IN UNIFORM

Active Duty 1951-1954, Law School, Reserve Intelligence, Vietnam and the Tet Offensive

The Korean War and Naval Intelligence

When the Korean War broke out in June 1950, I was in Paris on that grand European tour with my Yale buddy Philip "Skip" Smith. Upon my return to the United States in September, I enrolled in Stanford Law School. At that time no policy had been announced regarding whether one could avoid being drafted into military service by virtue of enrollment in college or graduate school. Consequently, I was interested in exploring my options within the military.

My father said that my uncle, Willis Palmer, had a good friend in the Los Angeles area who knew about getting into Naval Intelligence. I believe his name was Chase Wanglin. Some letters went back and forth, and soon my father learned whom to contact in the San Francisco-based Twelfth Naval District. We were working on this when—the day before I was to leave Palo Alto to visit my parents in San Francisco for Christmas break—I received a letter from the draft board in Honolulu. I didn't open it. Instead, I called my father. He arranged for me to meet with the new officer recruiter, Commander George Shepherd, in San Francisco. We agreed that I would take the officer test and physical examination, continue with my first year of law school, but be available if called to go to Officer Candidate School (OCS) in Newport, Rhode Island, in the fall of 1951. The Naval Intelligence training would come after basic officer training.

I responded to the draft board letter with evidence of being enrolled in Stanford Law School and was never bothered by them again.

In order to enhance the potential of OCS acceptance, I took a course in trigonometry at the University of Hawai'i (U.H.) the following summer. This was a necessary prerequisite to an unlimited deck officer status in the event I was not selected as an intelligence candidate. I struggled to get a "C+." (It was summer in Hawai'i!) But that course, as well as later language courses I took, gave me status as a U.H. alumnus and the right to be considered a "Warrior."

Commander Shepherd came through with an intelligence specialty invitation in August, 1951. I reported to the Twelfth Naval District, San Francisco where I was sworn in as an enlisted man (Officer Candidate Seaman Recruit (OCSR) on September 17, 1951. Along with five or so others of similar status, I was issued travel orders and meal coupons and told to catch the train for a cross-country journey.

In our group was an interesting guy who had lived in Hawai'i and had attended school at 'Iolani. He was a University of California graduate and a sailing enthusiast. He, like me, wore glasses and was not able to meet the 20/20 uncorrected standard for deck officer assignment. His name was Barnaby "Barney" Farrington Smith. He was destined to become my closest friend, as our Navy careers and civilian activities ran parallel. He unfortunately died way too soon—at the young age of about fifty-seven—due to heart problems. Barney was a devoted advisor and supporter during my political campaigns, and he worked closely with another old friend, Kent "K.K." Ka'umanu'a Bowman, in ship husbandry, first for Castle & Cooke and then for the T.H. Davies Company. (Kent was a great emcee for my political fundraisers.)

Our cross-country journey to Rhode Island on the train *Gold Coast* seemed to take forever, so Barney and I had ample opportunity to share my 'ukulele and sing as many Hawaiian songs as we could remember. Our route went through the southwest, then up through Missouri to Chicago, then to New York, and finally up the East Coast to Newport. Once ensconced in our Navy barracks at Newport, we were given the traditional treatment of long lines in our "skivvies" (underwear) awaiting vaccinations, the inevitable push-ups and squat jumps on "the grinder" (parade ground), and a heavy academic schedule. Our commanding officer was a seasoned Underwater Demolition Team (UDT) qualified lieutenant, and we struggled to match his physical abilities. We marched to and from classes, after classes, and before "chow" at six p.m. We marched if it was cold and blustery, if it was pouring rain, and even if it was snowing. And we paraded in dress uniform of the day on Saturday mornings.

I was fortunate to avoid some of this all-too-frequent marching by being selected to help teach classmates to swim in the hour before dinner (always marching time). This gave a few of us an early access to dinner and a chance to get ahead on our homework assignments.

Another standout memory from OCS: during breaks between classes we all congregated in the men's room and the surrounding corridors, and a huge cloud of smoke would develop. I took up smoking there in self-defense—a bad habit that I continued for twelve years until 1963, when I quit "cold turkey."

Newport was a cold and windy place on the North Atlantic. On weekend "liberty" (out at noon Saturday and back by seven p.m. on Sunday) I usually traveled back to my earlier haunts around New Haven, and I visited former Yale roommate John Russell in Fairfield several times. I tried to get together with my summer Island girlfriend Ellen Schattenberg (who was at school in the East), but it never worked out. (She had gotten back together with her future husband, Boyd Townsley, a Merchant Marine Academy student.) My barracks buddy Larry Ornstein and I spent one weekend in and around New Bedford, Massachusetts, where we ended up in dart-throwing contests with some drunken locals at a bar.

To this day I have a close reminder of those 1951 OCS days. My golf partner here on Maui—Garner Ivey, Jr., from Georgia (Georgia Tech University)—was a fellow "OCSer." In those days he was just a Southern "good ol' boy," and we (jokingly) re-waged the Civil War. More coincidence: Garner married Mary Helen King, a classmate of mine at Punahou School (Class of 1946). He was the head of A & B Properties on Maui before his retirement.

Upon graduation from OCS and being sworn in as an Ensign United States Naval Reserve in late November, I had ten days' leave before being required to report to Naval Intelligence School in Anacostia, Maryland. I hitched a ride somehow to Westover Air Force Base near Boston and secured a (free) flight to the West Coast so I could pick up my car, which had been stored at my aunt's house in Lafayette, California. I stayed at the Bachelor Officers' Quarters (BOQ) at Westover the night before the flight, and I still remember being awakened with "Sir, you must get up now to catch your flight," and "Would you like a cup of coffee?" (Those newly earned gold bars on one's shoulders shed a whole new light on life in the service!)

Once in California, I advertised for a companion who wanted to help drive east, and I found a young man who worked out all right, although he drove too fast for my preference. We took the southern route and stopped only to sleep and eat. My companion completed his journey somewhere in the southern states (possibly Memphis), so I traveled the remaining distance alone, arriving in Washington, D.C., with time to spare on December 5, 1951.

When I checked into the BOQ Anacostia Naval Station, I was handed an envelope containing a change of orders. Instead of reporting to Intelligence school, I was ordered to report to the Chief of Naval Operations Chartroom at the Pentagon! I soon encountered my friend Barney and learned that he, too, had been ordered to a slot in the merchant-marine section of the Office of Naval Intelligence (ONI).

The Chief of Naval Operations (CNO) Chartroom

The chartroom is the briefing room for the CNO (Chief of Naval Operations). So from being a little old Officer Candidate Seaman Recruit at OCS I had, in a few short hours, risen to membership in the highest U.S. Naval official's management team! Yes, I was a behind-the-scenes "flunky" while there, but in my first week as an officer I had seen in person the top man of the Navy. It was a good start to an interesting additional career for a kid born five thousand miles from Washington, D.C., in what was at the time still a territory of the United States.

My duties required me to examine intelligence reports on the Korean War and on the French action in Vietnam (it was then called "French Indochina") and prepare briefings for high officials and the CNO. The briefer for whom I normally worked was Lieutenant Dale Everhart. We became fast friends. Even when he advanced to highly sensitive jobs, he always had time for me. I doubt I would have made the rank of captain without his help in securing and fulfilling challenging assignments while on active duty for training (ACDUTRA) in the Reserves after my active duty in Washington ended.

At least once a week, sometimes more, I would have the overnight duty in the chartroom, followed by having the next day and night off. You were allowed to sleep while on duty, but your enlisted companion was charged with waking you for obviously important news. Then it was up to you whether or not to awaken the operations officer (usually a captain) on duty in the CNO space on the fifth floor.

The good thing about overnight duty was that I could play golf the next morning at my club, Fort Belvoir. I usually played by myself on such occasions, and it helped me lower my handicap.

Initially I shared an apartment on Massachusetts Avenue Southeast with two OCS guys. The Massachusetts Avenue apartment was near the Capitol. So when I had time off, I often went over to sit in on Congressional hearings and debates. During this period I attended a lot of embassy parties at the invitation of a fellow named Johnny Parmeter. Through Johnny I met Greg Romulo, son of the famous Philippine leader Carlos Romulo. Carlos Romulo served eight Filipino presidents from Manuel Quezon to Ferdinand Marcos as a cabinet member, or as the country's representative to the United States and the United Nations. At the time I met him he was preparing to run for the position of UN Secretary General. He is well remembered for his response to criticism by Soviet Ambassador Andrei Vishinsky at the height of the Cold War. Vishinsky said that "you are just a little man from a little country," to which Romulo responded, "It is the duty of the Davids of the world to fling the pebbles of truth in the eyes of the blustering Goliaths and force them to behave." Carlos was tough and smart.

One night I met up with Greg and was introduced to Ramon Magsaysay. Magsaysay was, of course another Filipino hero. He was appointed Secretary of Defense by Quezon in 1950 and soon intensified the campaign against the communist "Hukbalahap" movement. This was one of the most successful anti-insurgent campaigns in history. He served as president but met an untimely death as the result of an air crash in 1957.

Magsaysay was a big man for a Filipino—but Romulo too was a big man by deed.

As 1951 came to an end, I was twenty-two years old, an officer assigned to an interesting position in the Navy, and resident of a town with lots of single girls who were looking for a good time (but who had their eyes on marriage).

In a drugstore at Times Square, while visiting my parents in New York City during the Christmas season, I encountered a Honolulu girl—Joan Halford, daughter of Dr. Francis "Pete" Halford and Marge Atherton Halford. Joan told me she was a student at Hood College in Frederick, Maryland, about fifty miles from D.C., so I promised to come see her or ask her to visit me. Little did I know then what would occur when this actually took place!

Getting Hitched

My first date with Joan Halford occurred in late January 1952, and it was not long before we were dating every weekend. By May we were engaged. We married on July 15, 1952, at Central Union Church at eight p.m. My father was my best man, and my ushers included Jim Wilkinson, Jack Muirhead, Peter Nottage, Kurt Johnson, Guy Rothwell, James "Fitch" Dwight, and Joan's brother Frank Halford. The majority of these guys were fellow football players at Punahou. Peter Halford, Joan's younger brother, was thirteen at the time and therefore not old enough to be an usher. But much later, as a physician, he saved my life on two occasions.

It was a big wedding—too big in my opinion—but my opinions had not been solicited. This disregard was not a very good start to our marriage, but at the time it was not terribly significant either.

Back in D.C. we lived in a one-bedroom condo at 3140 Wisconsin Avenue across from the Washington National Cathedral. Joan got a job with a bank and trust company, and we lived quite well on her salary and my ensign's pay of 350 dollars per month.

Marriage and embassy parties were not compatible. So I turned my attention to obtaining a post-graduate education. I had completed one year of law school at Stanford and could return there later, but I wasn't sure I wanted to do that. So I enrolled in night courses beginning in February at Georgetown Foreign Service School. I took Far Eastern history and a course in maritime law. I enjoyed the latter so much that I decided I wanted to go back to law school after all. I checked with the admissions offices at Georgetown and George Washington Universities and found that both the attitude and the hourly fees were better at George Washington (GWU).

In August, 1952, I began summer classes in criminal law at GWU Law School's (non-air-conditioned) Stockton Hall four nights a week. Criminal law was the one course I had not gotten at least a "C" in during my first year at Stanford, so I had to retake it. I didn't do very well in that class at GWU, either, but I did manage to squeak out a "C+."

Collateral and Fleet Support (Still on Active Duty)

After a year or so in the chartroom, I was transferred to a lieutenant junior-grade billet in the Office of Naval Intelligence Collateral Support Unit. This was a very interesting place to work, populated by some great people. The commanding officer was Commander Edward Spruance (son of famous World War II admiral Raymond Spruance) and the executive officer was Lieutenant Commander Brad Collins (for whom I named my third son, Brad). Lieutenant Gene Clark (winner of the Navy Cross for action at Inchon, Korea) and Claude Corrigan (psychological war expert) were my officemates. My assignments were diverse and challenging. I was Navy Intelligence's "Man Friday" for all evasion and escape intelligence reporting and planning. This put me in daily touch with other service representatives in this field, all of whom were higher ranking, including bird colonels (full colonels) from the Army and the Air Force. Gene Clark and I traveled to Frankfurt for a big conference in 1954, followed by my spending a week or so at CINCNELM in London. This was my only foreign duty during my three-year active duty Korean War career despite the fact that I had requested Asian-area duty.

Another of my functions was to do special Navy-related assignments for the CIA. Armed with the phone book for Navy offices, I would ferret out answers to all sorts of requests from "The Agency." One time the investigation involved construction of a special river craft for Vietnam-type riverine warfare. And there was the time I hand-delivered documents from the CIA to Navy bigwigs at a Navy facility near Norfolk, Virginia, and I rode in the back of a plush, chauffeur-driven CIA limousine!

During the last year I worked for an aggressive naval aviator/intelligence planner, Lieutenant Commander Abrams in Fleet Support. This put me in contact with force personnel planners and a new area of intelligence concerns.

But my time with Commander Ed Spruance was the most interesting and the most fun. He would gather us for a coffee session every day at 0800 (eight a.m.) to "talk story" so he could get "the scoop" on what was going on in his little command and to find out what we knew about the outside intelligence world. Our civil-service secretary (Miss Yancy) and our yeoman (Nickens) were included as well. Spruance lived his life as a small "d" democrat—he treated everyone equally—and that was unusual for a Naval Academy graduate. Psychological-warfare man Claude Corrigan and I played golf regularly with our wives on Sundays at Fort Belvoir outside Washington, D.C., I actually shot in the eighties in those days!

On one humid summer morning Joan and I drove our car to the mall entrance of the Pentagon, and I turned the car over to her. I was wearing my dress khaki uniform shirt but had hung my jacket on a hanger in the back. As I got out of the car, I slipped on the jacket with its lieutenant-junior-grade shoulder boards. I added my cap, tightened my tie, and buttoned the jacket as I mounted the front steps of the building. I walked to the escalator and got off on a floor that had a coffee spot. I was standing in a long dark hallway, pretty much alone, when I heard a gravelly voice say loudly, "Lieutenant! Young man!"

I turned to look in the direction of the voice and saw nothing but gold.

Yes, the shoulder boards of an admiral. Wow! I wasn't sure whether it was a rear admiral or higher, but that didn't matter. This was an admiral and, worse yet, he was speaking only to me.

"Yessir!" I said and came to attention.

"Don't you know there were civilians and other service personnel in the parking lot when you came in?"

I stumbled out another weak, "Yessir."

"Then why were you out of uniform?"

Now I had to come up with something. So I managed, "I won't do it again, sir."

He quite accurately said, "I'm sure you won't. Carry on." And off he went.

I managed to regroup and make it to my office, where I encountered my boss, Commander Ed Spruance. I told him my story. He told me that I had encountered the great World War II hero, Admiral Arleigh "31 Knot" Burke.

Burke had attracted national attention in late 1943. He earned his "31 Knot" title by leading a destroyer squadron in a series of striking night victories in the Solomon Islands. In the summer of 1955—a year or so after my first encounter with him—the Secretary of the Navy selected Admiral Burke over ninety-two more senior admirals to become the Navy's next Chief of Naval Operations (CNO). Burke went on to serve an unprecedented three terms as the Navy's leader. Despite a lack of formal leadership instruction, Burke led the Navy through a Cold War transition in technology, moving from an era of bullets and props to one of guided missiles and jets. On his watch nuclear propulsion became the standard for all U.S. submarines.

Somewhat later after our hallway encounter, when I was working for a different CO, I had to obtain Admiral Burke's "chop" (signature) on a policy letter. As his aide admitted me to his office, he seemed to recognize me. He affixed his signature or initials to the letter and then with a half grin inquired, "Do I know you?"

I said, "I don't know, sir," then made as speedy a retreat as I knew how.

Back to Hawai'i: The Bar

I continued to attend law school at night except for my final semester when I attended during the day after having been granted an early release from the Navy in August 1954. This enabled me to finish law school early and to graduate mid-year in 1955. (I graduated "with honors.") This also allowed Joan and me to spend several months in Europe

(March to June) before having to return to Hawai'i so I could study for the October bar exam.

Upon our return we stayed at the Atherton family's beautiful Luakaha estate off the Pali Road, where I got in some "cool" studying for the bar exam. An interesting side-note of that endeavor occurred when I took a review course offered by some local lawyers. They would review material with us on a particular field of law and then conduct a practice test. I flunked the contracts test badly, which was when I discovered that at Stanford I had taken only half the course taught by most law schools in the first year of the curriculum! This left the entire area of contract performance out of my scope of knowledge. I prevailed upon a fellow bar-taker, David Mui, to let me copy his notebook on contract performance. That quick study must have filled the void adequately, since I received notice that I had passed the bar exam in November 1955.

Law Practice

Since I had taken every course offered in labor law at GWU, I sought out a job with the attorney firm retained by the Hawai'i Employers Council while I awaited my results from the bar exam. Then called Blaisdell and Moore, this firm soon became Moore, Torkildson, and Rice (MTR). I also submitted an application to what was then the top corporate law firm in Honolulu—Anderson, Wrenn, and Jenks (now Goodsill, Anderson, and Quinn.) Attorney Sam P. King called and offered to pay me 250 dollars a month and give me a share of fees above that. But Bud Moore at MTR offered a flat salary of 325 dollars per month with the promise of an increase to 450 dollars per month when I passed the bar. There was plenty of labor law to be performed there, so I accepted the offer. I often wonder what would have happened had I accepted Sam King's invitation. Sam and I subsequently became good friends with both Navy Intelligence and politics in common, and when Sam went on to become a State Family-Court judge, I could have inherited a prosperous practice.

For the initial three years with MTR I worked mostly on the labor side of the practice—research, brief writing, and "second chair" court and arbitration work—primarily for Ernest "Bud" Moore and Ray "Tork"

Torkildson. Bud handled sugar-interest cases, and Tork handled pineapple-company and visitor-industry (hotels and restaurants) matters. As time went on, I did more and more general practice work with Tom Rice (divorce, personal injury, estate planning). He gave me more responsibility and, hence, more opportunities to appear in court. He let me take over the prosecution of a death claim by a military family for the loss of their four-year-old son, who had drowned in a water-filled hole at a construction project near Kapiʻolani Boulevard. We pursued recovery under both the wrongful death and survival statutes. The vast majority of states did not allow recovery of loss of lifetime income under that latter statute, but I found favorable authority in Pennsylvania and pre-annexation Hawaiʻi law. We lost at the Circuit-Court level but won on appeal to the Hawaiʻi Supreme Court (Rohlfing vs. Akiona, 43 Haw 373). It was the most rewarding of three Supreme Court wins in my career. The others included the Clara Kali (unemployment insurance) case, and the Save the Natatorium case in 1973 (55 Haw 677).

I began campaigning for a seat in Hawaiʻi's first State Legislature in the spring of 1959, and I was elected in July. Within a year or so I began to feel some discomfort from my attorney bosses due to feedback from corporate clients of the firm who disagreed with political positions I had taken. For example, I had taken a strong position in favor of land reform.

Shortly thereafter, I decided to open my own separate practice. Ironically, I was able to secure office space from Morris Skinner, the attorney representing the insurance company in the Akiona case, in the non-air-conditioned Stangenwald building on Merchant Street across from the Castle & Cooke building where MTR was located. So, as it turned out, I was able to continue participating in early morning attorney coffee klatches at M's Tavern attended by contemporaries Dan Case, Daral Conklin, the MTR group, along with Bill Quinn and other members of the Garner Anthony firm.

In time I moved to the Gas Company building on Bishop Street (across from the then-Alexander Young Hotel) with the Morris Skinner, Tom Bennett, and Axel Ornelles firm. In 1968, I joined up with Keith Steiner and Harold "Tex" Hughes in the Hawaiian Trust building at the corner of King and Richards. I was with them for about five years. None of these relationships were partnerships; rather, we shared expenses and, to some degree, casework. Keith Steiner (son of longtime District-Court judge Harry Steiner) had been my classmate at Punahou and Yale, and over the years we had established an even closer friendship.

Senator Kenneth Brown's legislative aide, Ann Davidson, introduced me to her brother Alex Robertson in the early seventies near the time I parted ways with Steiner and Hughes. Alex needed a place to practice, and I needed help with cases while pursuing higher office. Soon we were sharing an office in the Hawai'i building. By 1978 we had moved to the Financial Plaza, a new building with several vacant offices.

Through my Pacific contacts I learned of the move to Hawai'i of Dana Smith, who had been in Yap and other Micronesian islands with the Peace Corps. He came aboard and, in turn, introduced us to Bradley "Brad" Allen Coates—another Peace Corps lawyer who was looking for an office in Honolulu after a brief flirtation with settling on Maui. He came aboard about the time I was answering Governor Coleman's request that I help him out with his attorney general's office in American Samoa. Patty, my current wife and former secretary, tells a great story about how she pointed out the courthouse from our office window so Brad could answer a court call!

Rohlfing, Robertson, and Smith was the first name on the door. Within a year or so we became Rohlfing, Smith, and Coates, as Alex had left the firm under an ethics cloud with the Bar. This last partnership remained intact until I moved to Maui in mid-1984.

Early Drilling and ACDUTRA (Active Duty for Training)

My friend Barney Smith and I joined up with the Fourteenth Naval Reserve Intelligence Division 14-1 some time in late 1955. It was the beginning of an interesting and at times exciting third career. Meetings were held on Tuesday nights from 5:30 to 7:30 or 8:00 p.m. at the District Intelligence Office (DIO) at the Old Naval Station on Ala Moana Boulevard, where the Federal Building now stands. Initially we drilled in civilian clothes! The unit was populated with interesting people such as Commander Chuck Braden (commanding officer and also Pan American Airlines executive), Commander Don Woodrum (advertising public relations executive), Captain Wm. B. Stephenson (lawyer), Commander Samuel P. King (lawyer, judge, and politician), Lieutenant Clint "Tink" Ashford (lawyer), Captain John White (University of Hawai'i history professor), Lieutenant Joe Dacey (businessman), Lieutenant Robert Iversen (fisheries research), Lieutenant Chris Cusack (insurance), and other local luminaries. In due course we moved around to many other sites, including the Fourteenth Naval District office within Pearl Harbor, FICPAC in Makalapa, several sites on Ford Island, and the Naval Reserve Training Center near the airport. Early on we went from weekday nights to weekend drills twice a month as reserves became more deeply integrated with the active duty forces. About the time we moved to Pearl Harbor, Barney Smith was commanding officer and I was executive officer. We worked well as a team. I took over in the mid-1960s as commanding officer with Commander Dave Baker as executive officer. Baker was a manager with Hawaiian Electric at the time.

ACDUTRA was almost always more fun and challenging than our regular nighttime drills. Unlike the Army and Marine Corps, we performed annual training on an individual rather than unit basis at whatever time of year was feasible given our civilian work schedules. My first ACDUTRA (1956) was a course of instruction in amphibious intelligence held at the Naval Amphibious Base at Coronado, California. Barney Smith and I did this one then did the follow-up advanced course several years later. We soon learned where the Mexican Village was, and we "closed it" one night at two p.m. after a visit to town. The last ferry in those days was 10:30 p.m. We had had too many tequilas to drink, and we struggled to get going in the early morning. Nevertheless, we made it to class. At the end of the eight o'clock class, Barney's face was an ashen gray and he made a break to go back to the barracks. Unfortunately, as he said, not in time; so he "put the shot" (vomited) in the flowerbed adjoining the Admiral's quarters. We laughed about that for many years, but it wasn't very funny that day! (Barney later discovered he was allergic to alcohol.)

Sea Duty

In April 1958, Barney and I both requested to go aboard submarines in an anti-submarine exercise to be held off Maui. I was assigned to the *USS Cusk* (SS 348), a World War II fleet boat that had seen better days. I had barely gotten settled when we were off to sea from Pearl Harbor. We exited the narrow entrance (called "Papa Hotel"), and the captain (Lieutenant Commander Cooke) ordered "dive, dive" while I sat in the officer's wardroom. As we went down, the boat "hulied" (shifted dramatically) and plunged forward out of control. We quickly passed test depth of 750 feet and plunged on. I was braced in the passageway just forward of the wardroom and never made it to the control room until later. Needless to say, I was happy when we pulled out near the bottom at about the 1,300 foot depth, where there was substantial, if not fatal, stress on the old craft. We received no medals for this experience, but we didn't need any. Survival was enough!

Our boat was the "enemy" in the exercise, and we were sunk regularly. This was accomplished when an unarmed grenade was bounced off the hull of the *Cusk* by an opposing submarine or surface craft. We would then surface, where we got to see the world again—mostly a lot of dry, barren Kaho'olawe island.

Aboard the submarine, I prepared reports on the day's action and what little we had learned about the enemies' activities. I was assigned a four-deep bunk in the chief's quarters, in which I could barely roll over. The *Cusk* was an early snorkel-fitted boat, and when we switched power from snorkel to battery and vice versa, big suction was experienced in the boat along with a burning oil smell. To this day, I believe my hearing problems came from this colossal sucking sound that assaulted my senses while I slept on this old submarine.

A second run at the sea duty we'd previously missed (by having been intelligence specialists) occurred several years later. Barney and I were both ordered to duty aboard the *USS Radford* (DDE 446) for an exercise—but on a much bigger scale this time. We were to provide screen services for an aircraft carrier! By then Barney and I were both full lieutenants. We were given instant instruction in watch-standing, including working the maneuvering board. It was not my forte, but I gave it my best shot. One night I was on watch, acting as officer of the deck as we cruised alongside the carrier at about twenty-five knots. The message came to prepare to maneuver. I told the regular officer of the deck I was unsure of my maneuvering board solution and requested that I be relieved of being responsible for ship maneuvering, so he took command. I know I lost "points" big time at that juncture, but I felt it was better to be honest than to have a collision with an aircraft carrier! My fitness report was not as great as it might otherwise have been, but I felt "relieved."

In later years I spent another four days' duty on the *USS Constellation* to add to my minimal sea-duty career. By then I was a full commander, so I rated a stateroom just below the flight deck. Planes were taking off and landing most of the nights I was aboard, so sleep was a cherished commodity.

Vietnam

The United States had been engaged in combat in Vietnam for a number of years before I ever dreamed of going there. In fact, as far back as December 1951—when Vietnam was still called French Indo-China—I had done intelligence reporting on this war as an ensign in the Chief of Naval Operations Chartroom at the Pentagon. However, relatively early in my tour of active duty in Washington the big battle of Dien Bien Phu ended the French empire's control. The country was then divided into North and South Vietnam, with the Communists controlling the north from their capital of Hanoi and the south becoming a "free" nation with its capital in Saigon.

In late 1967 I was serving my first term in our State Senate, but I was increasingly looking towards an opportunity to run for U.S. Congress. I was curious enough about the war—and the degree to which it would be a major issue in the future—to seriously consider requesting duty there. The prior ACDUTRA (Active Duty for Training) had been at Newport, Rhode Island's Naval War College, where I had participated in the "global strategy discussions" with top military and civilian officials. This experience had whetted my appetite for major security issues. So I

asked my friend Captain Dale Everhart, who was the commanding officer of the Naval Investigative Service Pacific, if ACDUTRA in Vietnam
was possible. He said he could order me to a period of approximately
three weeks of temporary active duty at the Naval Investigative Service
Office in Vietnam (NISOV), situated in Saigon. And he proceeded to do
so. I was to perform a counter-intelligence study.

After a whole slew of shots and vaccinations, including defenses
against malaria and bubonic plague, I was ready to go. I left on a military
flight shortly before midnight January 25, 1968, and I arrived January 27
in the early afternoon, having stopped at Clark Field in the Philippines
for fuel. Arriving at Tan Son Nhut airport, I was picked up by jeep and
taken to the quarters that housed several of the NISOV staff—a "villa" in
downtown Saigon. (The usual grand "mind's eye" of a villa it was not; but
it did have a little yard and an attached servants' quarters.)

The following morning I reported to the NISOV office, located in the
suburb of Cholon. Many Chinese lived in Cholon district, and purveyors
of all sorts of agricultural and more general products lined its streets. The
NISOV office abutted Post Exchange. So between the indigenous and the
U. S. personnel, Cholon was a crowded Asian urban scene.

I began by reading reports on action in the Delta. I learned that I
would be going into the Delta either the following day or the day after. A
lot of bloody clashes had occurred in that region, many of which involved
the Swift boats of (much later) John Kerry fame.

That night was *Tet* for the Vietnamese—New Year's Eve. As I wit-
nessed the raucous festivities, I thought it might as well have been Honolulu's Moʻiliʻili. Following a barrage of fireworks at midnight, quiet
reigned at our villa in downtown Saigon.

Then that welcome quiet came to a screeching halt with a rocket
attack on the U.S. Embassy, located about two blocks away. My notes
say that this initial barrage occurred at "0250 (31 Jan 1968)." A little
farther away, mortars were pounding against the palace. The plaster on
our building was cracking from these guns. We sat in the front room
overlooking the entrance patio and the street with the only weapons we
had—my .45 pistol and a carbine of some type. Fortunately for us the
enemy and the "friendlies" were shooting at each other out on the tree-
lined boulevards.

At around seven a.m. I was issued an M16 rifle and told to hop in the back of the car assigned to our command. We then drove out to the NISOV office in Cholon. The street was utterly vacant except for the occasional military vehicle, such as ours. The native population was staring out of buildings as we passed by. Sitting in the back of that truck, I was a great target for a sharpshooter. But at that time we had very little information as to the extent of the attack. (It was countrywide.)

After arriving at the NISOV office in Cholon, we heard reports of heavy fighting between our forces and Viet Cong (VC) at the racetrack, which was less than a mile from the office. A perimeter defense of the office and the adjacent Cholon Pacex (commissary and exchange facilities) was established by Navy and Air Force personnel—the Air Force had approximately seventeen men, and we had maybe fifteen. At approximately one p.m. we were told the VC had advanced to about one and one-half blocks of our position. We installed machine guns at nearby checkpoints and prepared to fight. After approximately an hour we were advised that the VC

attack had been contained. It had consisted of two companies and had severely mauled a U.S. Marine company. We all stood guard that night. (Note: I still had not fired the M16—ever!)

At nine the next morning I left the office and returned to the villa. Again I was in the open rear of the command vehicle. We had breakfast, and I took a welcome two-hour nap. At one p.m. we were to be picked up, but our transport did not show up until four-thirty. Upon arriving at the office, we were advised that there had been mortar activity in the area that morning.

Between approximately four and five p.m. several shots ricocheted around the NISOV buildings. Apparently we were receiving fire from snipers in adjoining buildings. We took up makeshift battle stations inside and out. (Mine was near where the pet snakes were caged!)

More shots rang out. At first I was not sure whose they were. But I became sure when one bullet ricocheted off the building behind me!

Sometime in the late afternoon an Australian truck came by and disgorged four or five of their troops. They helped repel the attack we were experiencing.

An evening watch schedule was announced. I finally got some sleep (from eleven p.m. to three a.m.) until it was my turn for the "hot seat" up on the wall surrounding our compound. After I was relieved in the morning, I got a shower and lunch at a nearby Bachelor Officers' Quarters (BOQ) called "Five Oceans." A civilian guard force took over that night, so I borrowed a bunk in the same BOQ.

At seven-thirty a.m. I again reported for duty to go over intelligence reports. But at twelve-thirty p.m. Yeoman First Class Springer advised that a reservation had been made for me (an "unneeded visiting officer") on a Braniff International Airways flight scheduled for the following day.

I later stood another guard watch and slept over at the BOQ on a cot. I arose at six a.m., got a ride into downtown to pick up my gear, and made it to Ton Sun Hut by ten-thirty a.m., for my three-ten p.m. flight. On the way to the airport I noticed a lot of visible damage to buildings and vehicles. We were passing through the racetrack area where heavy fighting had occurred. The airport's roof was missing in several places. After my departure (I later learned) it suffered even more damage.

As we took off, I couldn't help breathing a sigh of relief. I was returning to a still very young family of three boys between the ages of seven and thirteen.

The flight stopped in Guam and arrived at Hickam Air Force Base the following morning. I hadn't notified anyone of my arrival since I hadn't known when it would occur. So I took a taxi and, rather than going on the freeway, I instructed the driver to take me through Waikīkī. What a contrast with Saigon! America was operating undisturbed by the war.

AUG 9 - 1968 C

U. S. NAVAL INVESTIGATIVE SERVICE OFFICE
VIETNAM
APO San Francisco 96243

NISOV/AFD:chg
1600
Ser 266
18 Feb 1968

From: Commanding Officer, U. S. Naval Investigative Service Office, Vietnam
To: Commander Fredrick W. ROHLFING, USNR-R, 462141/1635

Subj: Letter of Commendation

1. Beginning on 31 January 1968, the Viet Cong unleashed a vicious, allout attack on the city of Saigon and other major cities in the Republic of Vietnam. Several prongs of the attack on Saigon were centered in Saigon's twin city of Cholon, and some of the heaviest fighting was in the immediate area of the compound in which NISOV/NISRA Saigon is located. On two successive days, Viet Cong elements threw automatic weapons fire into the compound.

2. The attack on Saigon came at a time when defensive forces were very thin, and this factor, along with the ferocity and proximity of the attack, necessitated the utilization of every able-bodied man in the defense of this command. It was under these circumstances that you became the first Naval Investigative Service personnel to defend their command against hostile forces. The danger which you faced is best illustrated by the fact that the compound was reported as captured on two occasions. Your courage under fire, selfless devotion to duty, and eager willingness to man defensive positions over a prolonged period was clearly above and beyond the call of duty. No command could be more proud of its personnel than this one is of each of you. Your performance was not only in the finest tradition of the Naval Investigative Service but did indeed establish a tradition for others to follow.

3. It is with a sense of the deepest pride that this command commends and thanks each of you for your dedication, selflessness, and gallantry. The Naval Investigative Service can indeed be proud to have such men among its members.

4. A copy of this letter will be placed in the personnel jackets of all personnel present in the Saigon area from 31 January - 4 February 1968.

William F. Brubaker
WILLIAM F. BRUBAKER

CERTIFIED TO BE A TRUE COPY

B. F. Smith
B. F. SMITH, CDR, USNR-R
Commanding Officer, NRID 14-1

After I returned to Hawai'i, I served the rest of my planned three weeks at the Investigative Service Office at Makalapa. I received a request for an interview from Gardner Jones, a writer/editor from the *Honolulu Advertiser*. The interview appeared in the Sunday *Star-Bulletin* and *Advertiser* on February 11, 1968, and was entitled, "Rohlfing Back from

Vietnam, Tells How 'Saigon Has Gone to War.'" Since I was still on active duty, I was very careful with my words.

The essence of the interview could be captured in this exchange:

Question: "How do you assess the significance of this? Thirty-eight cities and the penetration of Saigon in a considerable force, as you said, in a way that's never been done?"

Rohlfing: "Well, I think that Saigon has gone to war. I think that, to an extent, we have been living, or the people there have been living, in another world—as an open city, presuming that it would not come under this kind of combat.

"The Viet Cong and the North Vietnamese have, in many cases, told America what to expect. They have said they will attempt to bring about a general uprising. General Giap, who is the defense minister of North Vietnam, has said that a big offensive would come, and that it would be an attempt to get the people to make a general uprising.

"Well, in that sense, if it was such an offensive—and I think that was one of the major objectives of this attack—it was unsuccessful."

As time went by, war commentators agreed with what I had said. The United States and Vietnamese (ARVN) forces actually won a great military victory as a result of the Tet Offensive. But the impact back here in the States was directly contrary—more and more people came out against the war, saying that we had been defeated.

Despite my positive reading of Tet as a victory, I was feeling pessimistic about the willingness of the U.S. to "stay the course" in the long run. That, however, I didn't want to say—at least not while in uniform.

The Long Trail in Naval Intelligence

I was awarded the Fourteenth Naval District's William B. Stephenson Memorial Award for "Outstanding Service in the Naval Reserve," no doubt on account of my volunteering to go to Vietnam. I was still a commander, and I soon succeeded to the command of our district's intelligence unit, taking over from Barney Smith. I had an excellent executive officer, David Baker, who had served aboard a carrier as an Air Intelligence Officer off Vietnam but who had left active service for a job at Hawaiian Electric Company.

Looking back over the years, in addition to my sea duty and early annual training duty stints reported heretofore, I performed two weeks of OJT (on-the-job training) at a number of naval and joint commands. These included the Hawaiʻi locations CincPacFlt (Makalapa), CINCPAC, (Camp Smith, Aiea Heights), COMASWFORPAC (Ford Island), FICPAC (Makalapa), and IPAC (Camp Smith) NavInvestServ Office (Makalapa). My assignments at these commands were usually challenging projects rather than routine performances. I also served two weeks at a number of Mainland DOD or Navy schools such as Defense Intelligence School in Washington, D.C., (two courses), Naval Amphibious Warfare School in Coronado, California (two courses), Defense University in Los Alamitos, California, and NARU in Alameda, California (two courses).

Miscellaneous active duty included four days aboard the *USS Constellation*. My OJT included service on the staff of the Naval War College in Newport, Rhode Island, where I participated in the one-week "Global Strategy Discussions" course for senior officers (even though I was still a lieutenant commander). I also participated in a two-day RIAC conference in New Orleans, where I watched on television as Nixon left the White House after his resignation.

A critical juncture in my navy career occurred when I served on active duty on the staff of CincLantFlt in Norfolk, Virginia, under the direction of my old friend and benefactor Captain Dale Everhart, head of intelligence for the fleet command as well as CINCLANT. This was a four-week, back-to-back ACDUTRA during the last two weeks of the fiscal year in June and the first two weeks of the next fiscal year (1971).

I really enjoyed the Norfolk area. The work was stimulating and at times almost over my head. But not to worry. I received an outstanding fitness report, and yet I could have provided you with a better list than Frommers' of Norfolk-area restaurants (and not a few bars).

Shortly after this duty I came before the promotion board and was selected for captain (06). This promotion was both good and bad, however, as there were no pay billets in Hawaiʻi for captains in my intelligence specialty.

So began a period of hanging out with various units, drilling here and there without getting paid (but still accumulating points toward retirement). I also took a "sabbatical" during the intense 1976 campaign for

Congress. I always found my superiors in Navy Intelligence to be sensitive to such public-service needs. As long as I lived on Oʻahu this worked well.

But when I moved to Maui in 1984, it appeared that my naval career would have to come to an end.

The Last Assignment

In the end, I got lucky. I was appointed RIAC-III (Reserve Intelligence Area Commander–Area III) as of October 1, 1985. I served in that capacity until June 1987, when I officially retired. This assignment was the pinnacle of my Navy career. I was in charge of, and responsible for, all Naval Reserve Intelligence official activities in the state of Hawaiʻi.

By then, of course, I was commuting to Oʻahu twice per month while holding down a full-time job in the County of Maui Office of Corporation Counsel. During this period I was fortunate that Mid-Pacific Airlines offered a yearly pass for inter-island travel—initially (as I recall) for $850 and later for $1,200. Today's air fares would prohibit such a frequent commute.

As RIAC- III, I reported to Rear Admiral Bob Tiernan, the DNRIP (Director, Naval Reserve Intelligence Command) at his HQ on Treasure Island. Bob was a savvy guy from the Orinda, California, area who had worked for the Nixon administration during the time of the Cost of Living Council. When my last legislative term was coming to an end, Tiernan submitted my name for the coveted Meritorious Service Medal. It was awarded via certificate signed by then-Secretary of the Navy James Webb (now a Democratic senator from Virginia).

After RIAC III, as of mid-1987, it was all over—thirty-six years of being on active duty or on call for regular active duty at any time upon twenty-four hours' notice. It had been a great ride, of which I have many happy memories. Now the retirement check is the most important thing I receive from the Navy, and it comes in very handy.

I often wonder about those guys who called it quits after the Korean War and didn't stick with the reserves. They missed out on some really interesting schools and rewarding assignments as well as the benefits. Having TRICARE may cushion the impact of the current threat to Medicare from Obama care.

CHIEF OF NAVAL OPERATIONS

The President of the United States takes pleasure in presenting the MERITORIOUS SERVICE MEDAL to

CAPTAIN FREDERICK W. ROHLFING
UNITED STATES NAVAL RESERVE

for service as set forth in the following

CITATION:

For outstanding meritorious service as Reserve Intelligence Area (RIA) Coordinator THREE from October 1985 through June 1987. Captain Rohlfing provided outstanding leadership and direction to the Naval Reserve Intelligence Program units in the state of Hawaii. He skillfully enhanced RIA THREE's mobilization readiness, training, recruiting, and retention. By virtue of his close, trusted relationships, he significantly improved upon Reserve contributions to area gaining commands. His accomplishments included a reservist-developed and implemented recruiting program, achieving an enlisted readiness of R-1 for the first time and an exemplary revision of the Mission Accomplishment Plan. He implemented intensive watchstander training for Reservists, integration of Naval Reserve personnel into the RIA THREE community, and an aggressive recognition/retention program. Captain Rohlfing's outstanding fulfillment of his tasks, mature guidance, and untiring devotion to duty reflected great credit upon himself and were in keeping with the highest traditions of the United States Naval Service.

For the President,

C. A. H. Trost

C. A. H. Trost
Admiral, United States Navy
Chief of Naval Operations

Rewards from my thirty-six years of Naval Intelligence service have been both intangible and tangible. I do miss my associations with good people such as Captains Roy Ota and Frank Embree, and many others who supported my efforts to improve the integration of reserve and active commands. My tropical white uniforms are up to speed thanks to a trip in July '09 to see my grandson, Markus A. Rohlfing, inducted into the U.S. Naval Academy Class of 2013 at Annapolis. A quick trip to the Uniform Shop at Pearl was required to get new pants—up from size 36 to 38.

CAPT. ROHLFING SWEARS IN GRANDSON, MARKUS; US NAVAL ACADEMY CLASS OF 2013.

A physical would expose some other shortcomings…what did you say? Man, is my back sore!

I am very proud of my grandson's commitment to the service of our country. I hope to revisit Annapolis for his graduation in 2013.

CHAPTER SIX

SERVICE IN THE PACIFIC

American Samoa and the South Pacific Commission

Following the brutal all-out effort to win a seat in U.S. Congress in 1976, it was time for me to take stock of my situation.

I was forty-eight years old and married with three growing boys, the eldest of whom (Fritz) was already a student at Dartmouth, while the middle son (Karl) was just beginning his matriculation at Oregon State University. My third son (Brad) was still in high school. I had neglected my law practice while seeking to be elected to Congress in two major campaigns. Was I going to remain involved in politics or be a good family provider by means of my law practice? Openings in other major public offices were few to non-existent. My Senate seat had been filled by my friend Buddy Soares, and my protégé Barbara Marumoto was a prime candidate for the House seat in my residence district following her emergence in the Constitutional Convention election. The year 1977 passed without major movement of any kind on my part.

The South Pacific Calls

I was working at my law office on a Saturday in April 1978 when I received an intriguing phone call. It was from Skip Coleman, oldest son of Governor Peter Tali Coleman of American Samoa. Skip said the governor was in Honolulu and wanted to meet with me at his Waikīkī hotel. I hadn't seen him since I attended his inauguration in Pago Pago with several business associates in 1977 after he had become the first elected governor of American Samoa. I had first met Peter when he and I passed the Hawai'i bar back in 1955 and were treated to a picnic by the Hawai'i Bar Association. That day we had a long talk by the lagoon fronting Kamokila Campbell's property out in the Nānākuli area.

Now at his modest Waikīkī hotel Peter said he wanted me to find someone to take over as his attorney general since a controversy had erupted back in Pago that he needed to resolve. I later learned that two Samoan attorneys on the attorney-general staff had actually gone "on strike" because they felt they were not being treated the same as the expatriates on the staff. I said I'd be glad to look around but I couldn't promise to find anyone to meet his immediate needs. As the conversation progressed, I thought to myself that I really needed a change of scene. So I said that I might be willing to do the job in Samoa for a couple of months, pending our finding the right person to take the job on a longer-term basis. By the next morning this became the plan and within a week I was on my way to the South Seas!

Law and Politics in "Lava-Lava" Land

Upon arriving on the main island of Tutuila, American Samoa, I was provided with a relatively new government car and a fairly comfortable one-bedroom apartment in an old government building fronting beautiful Pago Pago Bay. The building was part of the original Rainmaker Hotel. I could, and did, take a daily swim in a channel in front of my unit. (Much later I observed Edna Ta'afasau, who was then head of the government's personnel agency, carefully moving large rocks to improve the channel. She had previously been a leader in Governor Jack Burns's administration.) Housekeeping was not provided except for a weekly "once over," so it was not long before I was washing my socks by hand in the kitchen sink and, of course, doing my own shopping and cooking. Neither of these tasks was easy since stores in this unincorporated territory of the United States were not well-equipped. Before long, however, I was able to develop a workable system.

Samoan people, as well as the *palagi* (pronounced "palangi" and meaning foreigner or haole), were very socially inclined. There was a party every weekend and sometimes several during the week. There were also many *fia-fias*—events surrounding funerals that lasted for days. Until I found a good market, I ate many a meal at Soli's Restaurant, located toward the head of the bay near the village of Pago Pago.

I settled down soon enough to pull the staff back together. As the former leading palagis left, the "local boys" came back aboard. Aviata "Avi" Fa'alevao was my principal deputy, and we got along well. One of my first actions was to petition U.S. authorities on behalf of Continental Airlines and its proposal to start providing air service to the island. Pan American Airlines had long served Pago, but Pan Am was hurting financially and its services had deteriorated. At that time Pago Pago airport was more like an Ethiopian airport than a U.S. airport. Flight nights featured huge piles of luggage ("Samoan Samsonite"), beastly hot temperatures, and sweaty bodies all over the place.

Governor Coleman's agenda was, of course, my agenda. Since the governor traveled a great deal of the time, I soon got to know both Lieutenant Governor Li'amatua (Li'a) Tufele and the governor's chief of staff Lyle Richmond. Richmond had been attorney general, so I frequently consulted him on various matters. The lieutenant governor was something else! Short and stocky, Li'a was a tough and—in my view—competent leader. Although I loved and respected Peter Coleman, I was often frustrated by his deliberate ways and would wait until he was "off island" to push my projects through via the lieutenant governor's office. This became particularly true when, much later, I represented American Samoa in Honolulu.

A TREASURED AUTOGRAPHED PHOTO: "TO FRED ROHLFING, A GREAT FRIEND OF AM. SAMOA AND TO ME. IA MANUIA. PETER COLEMAN, GOVERNOR" (7/19/78)

After several weeks of a trying to solve an accumulation of immigration-related problems, I took the initiative and made contact with my

137

counterpart in Western Samoa, Neroni Slade. (Many Western Samoans worked in the fish canneries in Pago Pago Bay and, as immigrants, experienced the same problems but in a different society.) I flew over to Apia on George Wray's South Pacific Air to meet with Slade and open the door to communications. Several weeks later he returned the visit, and I hosted a dinner for him with my own funds. Unbelievably, no former American Samoa attorney general had felt such a liaison was necessary! For the rest of my time there, many problems and cases were resolved by simple phone calls from Pago to Apia or vice versa.

I also advised the American Samoan Legislature, including its committee on "status" (American Samoa's relationship with the U.S.). This interaction resulted in my joining their committee on the long flight to Washington to meet with U.S. Congress. This trip was something of a boondoggle, but we were able to present a united front in D.C. and to keep American Samoa's traditional property arrangements intact. The fine balance between individual rights under the U.S. Constitution and collective Samoan custom was thus maintained.

These arrangements arose less from law as from custom and practice. They were about *Fa'a Samoa*, the Samoan way. About ninety percent of American Samoa's principal island, Tutuila, is owned collectively. The village chief and his retinue of elders call the shots on how that land is used and by whom. Each village has a large *fale* (house) that serves as the meeting place for chiefs and visitors and as a location for funeral activities. The other ten percent of Tutuila is owned in fee simple by individuals, corporations, nonprofits, and government.

One of the things I helped fix, at least temporarily, was the ongoing lawlessness in the harbor area. A number of tuna boats from Asia and North America were tying up in Pago Harbor at various times, and a goodly amount of beer or spirits was being consumed by the off-duty crews. These inebriated sailors were then exercising their nationalistic or just inherent bad tempers to the detriment of civil order.

I managed to cure the problem by bringing all the harbor interests into a permanent organization (a harbor council) that met regularly for lunch and otherwise as needed. My pitch was that we had to comply with *Fa'a Samoa* and mediate differences if we could; otherwise, I would direct some very restricting rules and aggressive law enforcement.

Another rather unusual "accomplishment" while I was in Pago was changing the name of the government. The territory had long used the title "Government of American Samoa," which in common parlance became "GAS." The international cartoonist Gary Trudeau even created strips featuring a young Samoan government official and satirizing GAS inefficiency and bureaucratic incompetence. My proposal was to rename it "American Samoa Government" or ASG. The governor agreed, and it has been ASG ever since.

Governor Coleman had some good people working on his staff. They included P. "Brownie" Tuiasosopo, Edward Scanlan, and Anita Tolmie. I later saw Scanlan and his daughter Liz a few times in Honolulu, but I have lost contact with the others.

I accompanied Lt. Governor Li'a Tufele to the South Pacific Commission meeting in Vanuatu—an interesting place. We were given a tour that included a flight to a resort on another island. On the return to the main island a fledgling pilot gave us a real scare via a very rough landing.

My successor, Honolulu attorney Joe Dwight, was ready to take over as fulltime AG, so I returned to Honolulu to stay in early November 1978.

The America Samoa (Liaison) Office—Hawai'i

Upon my return, Governor Coleman directed me to establish an office that he and territorial leaders could use to access U.S. support as well as Hawai'i resources. I was authorized to hire a part-time secretary and a "Man Friday" type person. I picked my legal secretary, Patty Bond, for the first spot and, after conducting several interviews, hired an ex-Navy chief by the name of "Epi" Epinesa to be the "fetch it" person. We were provided a vehicle, for which I was ultimately able to obtain consular plates. The station wagon, with Epi at the wheel, made many trips to the airport, picking up and returning ASG bigwigs at all sorts of weird hours. We also obtained a teletype machine, which allowed us to have close communication with the governor and his ASG staff and department heads. Our most valuable efforts went towards securing military support from

AM. SAMOAN LIAISON OFFICE STAFF: PATTY AND EPI EPINESA.

Air Force and/or Navy sources in preparation for emergencies.

The biggest holiday of the year in Pago is "Flag Day." This is celebrated in January on what, to me, was always the hottest day of the year. A disastrous celebration of Flag Day took place April 18, 1980, when a skilled Army-Navy skydiving team traveled to Pago to put on a show over the park and bay. After making its drop of six U.S. Army skydivers over the bay, one of the planes struck the cable for the cross-bay tramway car and then crashed into a wing of the Rainmaker Hotel. It narrowly missed the main square where some 25,000 citizens were gathered. The plane, a P3 Orion, was based at Moffett Field. The crash killed a Japanese tourist at the hotel in addition to the six crewmen of the plane. A huge fire threatened the governor's home, which was situated on a rise behind the hotel. We went to "battle stations" in Honolulu and helped respond to the event the best we could. The story behind the story was that the pilots had been drinking at the Rainmaker Hotel bar long into the night and were in no shape to fly that morning. I believe that story.

Another illustration of our emergency function concerned the illness of Governor Coleman's wife, Nora. This occurred when I was in D.C. with the *faipule* (legislators) status group from Pago. Patty took charge, calling contacts in the Air Force, and was able to get an Air Force flight to divert to Pago Pago International Airport to pick up Mrs. Coleman. (In our office we referred to her as "Mrs. Governor.") We later hosted a small thank-you cocktail session with the Air Force officers who had helped us on that occasion.

Other accomplishments of the American Samoa Office in Hawai'i:

1. We convinced the Hawai'i State Legislature to invite Governor Coleman to make a speech on the role American Samoa could play, and was playing, as a center of trade and commerce in the South Pacific region. I wrote a comprehensive speech, and he delivered it almost word for word.

2. A campaign to have Canton Island (located several thousand miles south of the Hawaiian Islands) excepted from the planned turnover of U.S. occupied islands south of Hawai'i and given instead to the American Samoa administration. This turnover was a consequence of U.S.-Kiribati treaty negotiations. The U.S. had long administered Canton and several other islands in the former British Gilbert Island protectorate. Canton Island was an asset because it featured a Boeing 747-capable aircraft runway and a small harbor capable of handling imports and exports. Governor Coleman and I talked at length about creating a new tuna-fishing base, which would include a refrigeration facility just a few hours from the Honolulu market. Ultimately we failed in this effort. President Carter's State Department was determined to give Canton away.

3. Training of Samoans: We helped to create training opportunities for Samoans in Hawai'i. One example is that we helped Isalei Iuli, my secretary in American Samoa, matriculate at Kapi'olani Community College in the paralegal program. Isalei, a very intelligent lady, completed the two-year program in just one year via intense study.

The South Pacific Commission

This section is a thumbnail sketch of my service to the U.S. on the South Pacific Commission (SPC) from 1975 to 1984. Some might assume that this was a "resume-building" post that enabled me to attend fun conferences all over the Pacific region. Not so.

The South Pacific Commission, founded by the Canberra Agreement of 1947, is a technical organization headquartered in New Caledonia that provides training and assistance in social, economic, and cultural fields to all the countries and territories of the Pacific region—i.e., some five million people scattered over thirty million square kilometers of which only two percent is land.

The initial core of the organization was made up of World War II victor nations. To this core group many self-governing states have been added. The SPC has over time developed into the only multi-national organization that includes all nations and territories within the borders of the Pacific. The metropolitan members traditionally pay about ninety-two percent of the costs of this operation and for the various social and economic programs it undertakes on annually. The SPC differs from the Pacific Forum, which is headquartered in Suva, Fiji, in that the latter was formed by the independent Pacific Island states and focuses primarily on political, and to a lesser degree economic, concerns.

Regional cooperation is difficult in such a diverse and physically widespread constituency. Ethnic and cultural differences abound. Pacific people speak some thousand different languages. Resources are unevenly distributed, and tensions develop often between the rich and poor countries. The contrast between Papua New Guinea and Tuvalu is illustrative. The former is rich in natural resources of all kinds and has a population equal to sixty percent of the area's total. Tiny Tuvalu stands in marked contrast with its nine atolls and eight thousand citizens.

I received my first two-year appointment as United States alternate representative on the South Pacific Commission in 1975 from President Ford. My first conference, in October 1975, was held on the island of Nauru, close to the equator in the center of Oceania. Nauru was (and still is) quite a boom-and-bust story, as its guano reserves (phosphate) became exhausted and its investments proved to be inadequate to take the place of its exports. Delegates to the conference stayed at Nauru's only hotel, which was run by an Australian who always looked as though he'd just wandered in from Ayres Rock (in the central Australian desert).

I had a spooky experience when I went swimming alone in the early morning along the Nauru coast. I got caught in a rip and was almost pulled into heavy offshore surf that was crashing on the rugged coral heads.

Senator Porteus was the senior alternate representative. So he carried the ball at the meetings, and I spent most of my time socializing. I developed a bad cold on the final day of the conference. Too bad. I brought my miserable condition back with me to Honolulu and to the announcement of my (second) candidacy for U.S. Congress.

As my first term was ending, the U.S. finally began to give some attention to the Pacific Islands (Oceania). In 1978 an Office for Pacific Island Affairs was established in the state department, an explicit policy for the Pacific Islands was framed, and new embassies were opened in Fiji and Papua New Guinea. With the onset of the Reagan Administration the U.S. developed greater interest in regions that were vulnerable to China's economic infiltration and to the Soviet Union's then-"blue water" navy. During this period I sought consideration for appointment to the post of U.S. ambassador to Fiji. My files are filled with letters written on my behalf by prominent Republicans e.g., (Senator Stevens) and several Democratic officials, including Senator Inouye. But this was not to be, as the State department was pushing its own candidate, a foreign service officer.

Having been appointed by President Reagan to a second term as "alternate representative" at the end of 1982, my last official activity in SPC occurred when I attended the annual SPC conference in Saipan (Marianas Islands) in late 1983. Patty accompanied me, and we had a great time. I became the leader of the U.S. delegation to this substantive conference when Mr. M.M. Love, U.S. Representative to the SPC, was unable to attend. This leadership spot enabled me to unburden myself of various concerns about U.S. positions and procedures that I felt were inadequate. In a "Personal Report on the 23rd Annual SPC Conference 1-7 Oct 1983" I wrote first that the conference had dealt with "four issues which were of particular interest to the United States," namely:

a) reorganization of the SPC committees and powers of members;

b) creation of a single regional organization;

c) the Tuna Resources Management Program;

d) the South Pacific Regional Environmental Program (SPREP).

Item b. had great symbolic if not substantive significance. If the resolution were to be adopted, the Pacific territories of the United States and France, for example, would have an equal vote with their mother countries in all SPC matters. As a longtime advocate for American Samoa, this issue held great interest for me!

My report then discussed the U.S. position on the proposal and described problems of communication with the Washington office, particularly with lawyers there who were being technical (asserting the need for an inter-nation Memo of Understanding on the change) and thus could expose the U.S. as the "fly in the ointment" of greater democracy within the SPC structure.

I then discussed my views on the role of lawyers vis-a-vis political policy-makers, also on the U.S. carrying the ball for France on the environmental front (i.e., nuclear testing). I closed by recommending better conference procedures for those who, like myself, were taking responsible positions on behalf of the U.S.

I received a detailed, responsive letter from Robert A. Brand, the deputy assistant secretary of state in charge of East Asian and Pacific affairs. I didn't, however, get to see any subsequent changes, as my term ran out in early 1984.

That year, having just joined the Maui County corporation counsel's office, I was invited to speak to the Kihei-Wailea Rotary Club concerning developments in the Pacific Region. I made some controversial recommendations:

End nuclear testing.

The opposition to nuclear testing, storage, and dumping is the most strongly felt and deeply unifying issue among Pacific Islanders. Hence, we should stop our passive acceptance of French nuclear testing. (See Hawai'i legislative resolutions to this effect.) Also, we should align with Australia on nuclear policy—accept transits and visits by nuclear-powered ships, but keep our areas free of nuclear waste-dumping, storage, and testing.

Apply the Law of the Sea to tuna fishing.

The U.S. should revise its national policy on highly migratory pelagic fish species such as tuna. Specifically, it should enter into multi-lateral tuna licensing agreements and reverse its negative position on the Law of the Sea. Over time the U.S. should seek to re-negotiate provisions on deep-sea mining.

Stop over-reacting to statements by certain Island politicians.

There is not, in fact, a "commie" under every rug.

I ended the speech by noting that even in this somewhat remote area of the world substantial security issues exist. We need to keep the political support of these nations, however small they may be, in international arenas such as the UN General Assembly.

I felt particularly good about my service on the SPC when I received a copy of a letter to the editor of *Pacific Islands Report* dated May 31, 1999, from William Bodde, Jr., U.S. Ambassador, Ret. Bill was ambassador to Fiji from 1980 to 1982, and I had worked with him on a number of issues—for example, our efforts to get Canton Island turned over to American Samoa as a fishing base. In his letter Bill addressed the subject of whether future SPC representatives should be full-time government appointees, not the non-paid political type such as I had been. He wrote:

"In the past, some of the political appointees have been very knowledgeable and distinguished persons, such as George Chaplin (former editor, *Honolulu Advertiser*) and Fred Rohlfing. They were both from Hawai'i and had a keen interest in the Pacific Islands. I found that choosing alternative representatives of the caliber of Chaplin, a Democrat, and Rohlfing, a Republican, helped to build broad support for U.S. policy in the Pacific Islands."

All in all, learning more about our Pacific friends and neighbors and representing our nation in policy decisions was most fulfilling. I wonder sometimes where I would be today if I had become the ambassador to Fiji in the 1980s.

PART FOUR

SERVICE TO THE
COUNTY OF MAUI
AND VARIOUS CAUSES

HAWAIIAN LULLABY
Written by Peter Moon
& Hector Venegas

Where I live there are rainbows
With life in laughter of morning
And starry nights

Where I live there are rainbows
With flowers full of color
And birds filled with song

I can smile when it's raining
Touch the warmth of the sun
I hear children laughing
In this place that I love
Where I live there are rainbows
With life in the laughter of morning
And birds filled with song

I can smile when it's raining
Touch the warmth of the sun
I hear children laughing
In this place…in this place
In this place…that I love

CHAPTER SEVEN

MAUI NO KA ʻOI
(MAUI IS THE BEST)

As a deputy corporation counsel on Maui I took over the long-unfulfilled list of assignments of my predecessor, a young Filipino named Gus. In due course I requested, and was assigned, the planning department and other planning activities. I really enjoyed this work and was promoted to first deputy along the way. Corporation Counsel Rodger Betts was a down-to-earth guy who would give you an assignment and back up your performance if he could. The Democrat-dominated County Council, however, did not like Rodger's independent thinking (and his tendency to be tardy in response to their requests), so the council refused to confirm him for a second term. Hannibal Tavares asked me to take over but to keep Betts on the staff. I agreed.

Several months after assuming the top job I was faced with the need to replace James Takayesu, who was advising the public works department (and some lesser agencies) but who was consistently absent from the office for one reason or another and delinquent in fulfilling his assignments. A very capable attorney, Glenn Kosaka, was available for the assignment. But as a condition of taking on the public-works backlog, Kosaka demanded that he be made first deputy. I reluctantly agreed to this and, hence, had to tell Rodger that he could stay on at his existing salary but would have to give up the first deputy post. I felt bad about this. In retrospect I wish I had not agreed to doing away with Rodger's title.

My stint with the corporation counsel office included an exhaustive opinion on the land-use approval for the Kapalua Airport, which was built by Hawaiian Airlines. Other opinions are on file that I am proud to say have held up well over the passage of time. My stint also included a hard-fought jury trial over the death of a tourist at the intersection of Kala Road and Hana Highway, not to mention two Moloka'i projects, one of which brought out that island's usual raucous protestors.

The jury trial was my first in some years. I was successful in limiting the County's liability for not having suitable signage at a major intersection near the airport to ten percent of the verdict. Judge John McConnell presided over the trial.

My work in County planning law brought me into close contact with planning directors Tosh Ishikawa and, later, Chris Hart. The former was a hard taskmaster on his committee members and occasionally walked a fine line on the public-meetings laws. The latter, however, led his members with a schoolmaster's confidence and charm. He rarely stirred up a problem.

Another strong player in the planning business was Councilwoman Velma Santos, who had her own ideas for controlling growth as the head of the council's planning committee. Once set on a specific goal, she was hard to dissuade.

The first Moloka'i project of note involved a hotel proposed for Kai-aka Rock on the west end near the Kaluako'i Resort. Planning commission hearings went on for days under the expert chairmanship of Stanley Okamoto, a Wailuku insurance salesman. At the final hearing fisticuffs broke out between one of the proponent Thomas brothers and DeGray Vanderbilt, a Moloka'i environmentalist. I helped end this scrap and almost got hit in the process.

More interesting and more involved was the controversy over whether a special-use permit for a landing and picnic site on East Moloka'i should be issued for a sailing-ship cruise tour operating between Maui and East Moloka'i. The proposal was fronted by Bill Kapuni.

The council and the planning commission strongly disagreed on the appropriateness of such a permit for the use of picnic grounds on Moloka'i as a jumping-off place for the inter-island tour. I agreed with the position of the council on the issue—that a permit should not be issued—and thus kindled the ire of the planning commission and, in particular, former State Senator Toshi Ansai. The matter even led to introduction of a bill in the Legislature designed to clarify whether a new State or Existing county law would prevail. Planning Director Chris Hart was caught in the middle but eventually supported his commission's view. Ansai and the commission went to great lengths to push the Legislature's bill, sending departmental staff planner John Min to Honolulu to lobby and testify. Min's testimony and position directly contradicted the positions of Maui's mayor, its council, and myself as attorney for the County of Maui. Other legislators could only say—which Maui should we listen to?

Fortunately the bill died.

Mayor Hannibal Tavares and Howard Nakamura, his managing director, urged me to withdraw from the case in the 2nd Circuit Court despite a favorable ruling by Judge Komo that we didn't have a conflict of interest. That conflict motion, by the way, had been brought by special counsel for the Maui planning commission without prior notice or consultation with me—that special counsel being none other than my former deputy James Takayesu. In doing this Takayesu displayed a short memory. He forgot that I had found him a new job (with the prosecuting attorney's office) before terminating him from his corporation counsel position.

The case reflected tensions built over time between the council and the planning commission as those two County agencies sought control of planning decisions. After some reflection and regret I withdrew our office from the case.

Trying to satisfy two bosses (administration and the council) did not please me. After further reflection I decided it was time for me to leave government service.

Again.

I retired from the County of Maui at the end of April 1988. I filed a long report on the status of the corporation counsel's office with Mayor Tavares. My public works first deputy Glenn Kosaka succeeded me as department head. Overall it had been a good run, and my retirement compensation was now secure.

Championing a Unicameral Legislature

Among my many causes was, and still is, the adoption of a unicameral legislature in Hawai'i.

Nebraska is the only unicameral (single legislative body) state in the United States today. The Cornhuskers have enjoyed such a legislature for years. Nebraskans particularly benefit from greater accountability by their state public servants. Ordinary citizens are better able to follow bills or resolutions through the committee process if they can do so in one house only. They also can focus better on a limited number of officials. In a system like Hawai'i's whenever there is disagreement between the two houses, bills are referred to a "conference committee." This committee is composed of members from both houses, and it has the power to change any of a bill's provisions "in the dark of night."

My allies in the unicameral effort during my legislative years were Adam "Bud" Smyser, the longtime editor of the *Honolulu Star-Bulletin* and independent thinker, also Nelson Doi, Democratic senator from the Big Island who served as Governor John Waihe'e's lieutenant governor.

The idea that Congress should consist of two houses came about in 1787 when the Continental Congress was faced with vast differences in population and influence among its members—think, for example, of the contrast between New York and Rhode Island. The U.S. Constitution is based upon a compromise by which the composition of the U.S. Senate is determined by geography (two seats per state) while the number of House seats is based on population. This formula nets four seats for little Hawai'i—two senators and two representatives. California has the same number of senators (two), but its relatively huge population gives it fifty-three representatives.

As most of our states joined the Union, they copied the federal formula for their legislative bodies.

The rationale for the two-house approach came apart at the seams in 1964. That's when the U.S. Supreme Court ruled in *Reynolds v. Sims* that all state legislative bodies must be apportioned on the basis of population. As a consequence of this ruling, all bicameral state legislative bodies are now the mirror image of each other.

Here in Hawai'i *Reynolds v. Sims* and the required reapportionment caused a major shift in control away from the Neighbor Isles to O'ahu, the latter becoming all-powerful due to its more than a million population count.

Maintaining a fair balance between the islands may have been a rationale of the Kingdom of Hawai'i's leaders during the nineteenth century. In 1864, acting as one body, the 27-member House of Representatives and the 18-member House of Nobles jointly enacted legislation to restrict the power of the king over sale or other disposition of crown lands. This unicameral process continued through the remaining years of the Hawaiian Kingdom and provides a precedent that should be given weight today.

Maintenance of a two-house legislature encourages political gamesmanship and all too often a blame game. Petty personal grievances can kill good bills. Each side holds bills back to create trading leverage. The result is a session-ending logjam. If the bill does make it out of conference committee, each house must take it or leave it without amendment.

Today little ol' Hawai'i has seventy-six legislators who are each paid nearly $50,000 annual salary. The cost of every legislative session runs in the millions—too much money! It is particularly too much if you can accomplish the same goals with half as many legislators.

Though I introduced bills in successive years to achieve this major reform, the bills were killed early by a refusal even to hold a hearing. It is no surprise, of course, that current legislators will protect the status quo. Accordingly, I am convinced that this needed change in our governmental structure will only come through a constitutional convention.

I think the magic number to be elected to a one-house legislature would be about thirty-five representatives—roughly half the number of legislators we have today. This change should be a no-brainer.

The Waikīkī War Memorial Natatorium and Beach Improvement Project

There are very few citizens of O'ahu who do not have an opinion as to what should be done about the continuing sad state of the Waikīkī Natatorium ("the Nat").

Built as a World War I memorial, the Nat first opened in 1927, the year before I was born. Over the years it has hosted many an exciting swim-meet, and it has provided thousands of Hawai'i kids with a safe salt-water swimming and diving experience on the shores of Diamond Head. I went there on summer outings and also attended a night swim-meet during Hawai'i's best swimming years, when Coach Souichi Sakamoto's Maui champions prevailed. But by the 1970s the Nat was "hanging on the ropes" in a miserable state of repair.

In October of 1972, while I was campaigning for Congress for the first time, the Army Corps of Engineers announced it was working on advanced engineering and design for beach-erosion control improvements along a 3,200-foot reach of Waikīkī Beach. It was a joint plan with the Hawai'i State Department of Transportation (DOT) and the City and County of Honolulu Parks Department (CCP). The plan called for the "construction of three new groins, placement of approximately 46,000 cubic yards of beach sand, and demolition of the Natatorium." The groins were to extend out about 200 feet from the shoreline, creating beaches 150 feet wide and 500 feet long.

Upon hearing this announcement, a woman named Anne Burleigh, who was active with masters swimming groups, formed the Natatorium Preservation Committee (NPC) to fight the "big plan." She wrote letters and made calls to everyone she could think of. Early on she got the Engineering Association of Hawai'i to study the proposal and, in due course, they supported restoration of the Nat's structure along with 62,000 square feet of new beach.

Governor Burns, however, didn't seem to care about Anne or the Hawai'i Engineering Association when he wrote on April 11, 1973: "I have affirmed to the Corps of Engineers the state's position that the beach project [and demolition] should proceed." Mayor Fasi had already missed this chance to disagree with Burns (as he often did) when he also endorsed the state/federal project. But U.S. Senator Dan Inouye was of a different persuasion. At the outset of the legal battle, Inouye took a strong stand for preservation of the Nat (see May 10, 1973, Congressional Record).

I entered the picture at this time on behalf of the NPC when I submitted a formal request for a project delay of sixty days. This was denied. So we hurried to file a complaint in federal court seeking to enjoin the project as being in violation of the National Environmental Protection Act (NEPA). We contended there had been an inadequate review of the choices available to address loss of beach sand and the rationale for the beach project, much less the demolition of a historic memorial structure.

Somehow I had discovered that a study of the area was being performed by a University of Hawaiʻi oceanography department professor named Gerritsen, along with a graduate student named M. Hertel. Gerritsen was from Holland and had a long list of achievements there in his field of expertise. He brought detailed charts to court, showing that the Army's groins, when superimposed on the currents in the area, would cause the loss, rather than gain, of sand at Sans Souci Beach. In other words, the project would worsen the situation rather than fix it!

We, of course, argued that NEPA requirements would not be met if the conditions outlined in the University of Hawaiʻi study were not addressed. However, despite Gerritsen's comprehensive testimony, Judge Martin Pence held that the government had complied with NEPA, and he denied issuance of an injunction. I generally admired Pence. But being a "good old country boy" from Hilo he was prone to quick conclusions that mirrored his personal views on issues. He clearly didn't think much of the Natatorium.

Despite this setback, we did not crumble. We went across the street from the federal courthouse to our State Circuit Court, where we filed another complaint seeking to enjoin the project. We based this second legal action on our interpretation of State, rather than federal, law.

While the State's attorney general argued a complicated series of statutory expressions and administrative policies, the essence of our claim was that the State had not submitted the project to the Legislature for its possible "disapproval" as required by HRS 171-11. In this complaint I was joined by attorney Bob Dodge, a liberal Democrat who had been involved in various "do-gooder" public causes.

Unfortunately Judge Masato Doi accepted the State's convoluted argument on substantial compliance with the governing statutes, and so he denied issuance of an injunction. We went "upstairs," literally and figuratively, to the State Supreme Court and tried again.

We were able to secure an early argument before this court of five justices—four of whom were Burns's appointees and strong Democrats.

The fifth judge was the only Republican, Masaji Marumoto. Justice Abe wrote the opinion of the three justices who voted to uphold our contentions (Justices Richardson and Levinson joined him, while Marumoto and Bert Kobayashi dissented). Abe stressed a legislative analysis and realistic statutory interpretation. He wrote: "It is undisputed that no formal withdrawal of the lands not set aside in Executive Order Number 1446 was made by the governor and, therefore, there has been no opportunity for the legislature to express its disapproval pursuant to the provisions of 171-11 [which provided the power granted to the governor in this section to…withdraw public lands shall be exercised subject to the disapproval by a two-thirds vote of the Senate or House, or by a majority vote of both]."

As to the government's argument that a memorial-park purpose would be preserved under the new plan even though the Natatorium would be removed, the Court "slammed them down," pointing out that the executive order in question had set aside the lands for a "Memorial Park *and Natatorium*." The Court's order then imposed a permanent injunction on the defendant "from in any way tearing down or demolishing the Natatorium."

In looking at the situation at Sans Souci Beach today, one can only wonder why the principals did not take a more constructive and conciliatory approach back in 1973. None of the high officials concerned—governor, mayor, heads of state departments or their in-house attorneys—ever offered to discuss a compromise approach to the issues we posed. What has happened (or not happened) since is even more irresponsible. The Natatorium still stands, but is wasting away due to the ceaseless onslaught of waves, sun, and time. Mayor Jeremy Harris made an attempt to put together a restoration plan, but it died from protests such as one claiming that water quality could not be guaranteed.

Today, the mayor of Honolulu has bigger things on his mind—the giant, multi-million-dollar boondoggle train from Kapolei to Iwilei and a run for the office of governor.

One thing that the Natatorium fight in 1973 established was that I was not afraid to take on the top dogs if I believed they were wrong.

The State Legislature revisited the Natatorium issue in the late 1970s and early 1980s. Ultimately, however, nothing constructive was accom-

plished. After I re-
turned to the State
House in 1980,
I got involved in
some of the argu-
ments regarding
what to do with
the deteriorating
structure.

Represen-
tative of my ap-
proach eight years
after we had won
the case was my
testimony at a
Department of
Land and Natu-
ral Resources
(DLNR) hearing
held on October
19, 1981, at the
Waikiki Aquari-

'You too?'

um. I reviewed the history of the case and said that I had expected that
political leadership would have set up appropriate procedures to restore
the only saltwater pool in Hawai'i for use by the public, but that this
hadn't happened.

Prior to this DLNR meeting a developer, Hadley-Pruyn, had made
a proposal for an aquarium/natatorium complex in a state/private ven-
ture. While I did not agree with all of the details of the Hadley-Pruyn
scheme, I said, "It is an extremely constructive approach. We need private
sector participation to get government moving."

I went on to say that "I personally would prefer to see the Natatorium restored to its old glory and unique status as the largest saltwater
pool in the U.S., with public funds, and under public control. But in this
day one would be totally unrealistic to expect the Legislature of this state
to appropriate, and the governor to release, the necessary funds. Like-

wise, the cost of demolition—and the importation of sand—are also very high.... The Natatorium is a menace today...[and] it doesn't take much imagination to project an accident to children at the facility in its present neglected condition."

As of this writing , nothing has changed. Sadly, the Nat is no longer a fitting memorial to World War I veterans.

The Haleakalā Tramway Controversy

The tramway story probably deserves a short book in its own right. It is classic example of how an aroused citizenry can defeat even a kamaʻāina landowner's proposed development of tourism facilities.

In mid-February of 1989 brothers Gordon and Raymond Von Tempsky, owners of Erehwon ("nowhere" spelled backwards) Ranch in Upper Kula, Maui, publicly unveiled their plan for a tramway up to Haleakalā's summit from a base station on Kekaulike Avenue. The five-mile-long tram would start at the 4,000-foot elevation level and ascend to over 10,000 feet.

Beyond specific concerns about traffic noise and the other well-known ills of overcrowding, loss of open space, and scenic views, there was another compelling issue—was the peacefulness and tranquility of life on the slopes of Haleakalā about to disappear forever?

The proposal called for a base station with a gift shop and parking facilities to accommodate fifteen busses and four hundred cars. (This base station, by the way, would be located about a quarter mile from our home.) The proposal also called for a restaurant at the summit, to be made possible through a swap of fee land or an easement to be granted by Haleakalā National Park (HNP). Passengers were to ride in six-person cars suspended from forty-foot-high towers propelled by a diesel power plant. Plans predicted a minimum of one thousand passengers a day.

As we later pointed out at community meetings—and in letters to important political leaders, environmental organizations, and anyone within hearing distance—with this configuration there would be busses, supply trucks, and all sorts of vehicular traffic at all hours of the morning and evening along the main Haleakalā Highway and Kekaulike Avenue.

We also argued there would likely be an increase in downhill bicycle tours, which were already causing traffic congestion on State and local roads. HNP superintendent Don Reeser soon publicly announced his opposition to the proposal, saying that the tram scheme "would detract from the majesty of the whole mountain."

The community responded to a call to arms, and a formal No Haleakalā Tramway Committee came together as a result of meetings held at the Kula Lodge. I served as chairman pro tem of the citizen committee, and wrote a significant number of letters to legislators and public officials in Honolulu and Washington, D.C. We were successful in getting a resolution passed by the State House, and later the State Senate, opposing the project. I sought and obtained assistance from an old friend, U.S. Senator Richard Lugar of Indiana. James Ridenour, director of the National Park Service, hailed from Lugar's state. In due course Ridenour wrote to Lugar stating that the NPS "is on record as firmly opposed to the [tramway] proposal because of the adverse impacts it would have on [HNP's] unique biotic resources...[and because it] would add additional congestion at the House of the Sun Visitor Center."

Our congressional delegation at the time was composed of Senators Inouye and Matsunaga, and U.S. Representatives Akaka and Saiki. Inouye supported the proposal (mostly behind the scenes), but we were successful in causing Matsunaga to pause and drag his feet. Akaka came on board when our opposition was obviously winning, and Saiki stayed neutral. As part of the counter campaign, we printed and distributed bumper stickers and t-shirts with a tramway car in a circle with a red line through the circle.

In December 1989 in a letter to U.S. Senator Ted Stevens of Alaska I noted that: "Our community came out in force against the tram plan.... Over 2,000 people signed petitions in opposition before the Kula Community Association meeting in mid June.... Then things went quiet until just this week...when we learned of two new threats. Von Tempsky is sending multiple short form letters supporting his plan to Secretary of Interior Lujan. The second threat comes from...our senior U.S. Senator [Inouye] who has prepared, but temporarily delayed, introduction of some sort of an amendment to an appropriations bill permitting a change in the Haleakalā Park Master Plan and, thereby, allowing the access to the summit sought by Von Tempsky. We're told that he held off because of opposition from an unnamed colleague."

As to this unnamed colleague, I either didn't know or else have since forgotten his name. It could have been Lugar, but I can't say for a fact. The "hot" war of the spring, summer, and fall became a wait-and-see game in early 1990. Ultimately the tram project died along with its sponsor—a good guy—Gordon Von Tempsky.

The Fagan Campaign:
End of an Up-and-Down Alliance with D.G. "Andy" Anderson

It was 1990 and Andy was chairman of the Republican Party of Hawai'i. He was targeting selected Republican Party candidates for special support statewide. I was living on Maui in retirement, having left government employment. My friend Paul Fagan from Hana (grandson of Hotel Hana-Maui's builder Paul Fagan, Sr.) and I had talked about the possibilities of his running for office. We had met in the early summer for coffee with Andy. Andy said he wanted me to oversee the party's campaign on Maui, and he offered compensation therefor. I subsequently declined his offer.

Discussion of Fagan running for the House (7th District) came up, but Fagan declined because he was friendly with incumbent Democrat Mark Andrews. In late June Orley Paxton, who had run against Andrews in 1988, indicated that he was again interested in the seat.

A week later Andrews let it be known that he would not run for reelection. Fagan indicated to me that he was now interested in going for the Upcountry House seat, so we commissioned a poll on his name recognition. It turned out most favorable, and on July 22 he decided he would run. I agreed to be his campaign manager. I then learned from Maui Republican activist Jim Wagoner that he had gotten Andy's state party's targeting committee to endorse and commit support to Orley Paxton.

Three days later I wrote to advise Andy of this decision and to request "even distribution of all party funds through the primary, and no in-kind services unless equally available to my candidate." I concluded, "Simple, eh? And the only fair way to handle it." Andy did not respond.

We commenced a major grassroots (house-to-house and sign-holding) campaign. On September 12 I sent another note to Anderson saying that I'd heard a rumor about a letter to be sent from GOP headquarters urging members of the party to vote for Paxton. I asked Andy "as a personal favor"—based on thirty years of working for the (Republican) cause together—not to send that letter.

Later I talked to Andy on the phone. He attempted to get me to just "go through the motions only" for Fagan since he was "going to lose badly." Andy wanted me to take over the management of former Maui fire chief Herb Campos's council campaign instead. While Herb was a friend and a good candidate, I was already fully engaged—which apparently Andy couldn't (or wouldn't) understand. He claimed he had a poll showing Paxton beating Fagan 51 percent to 17 percent. I directly asked him about the rumor of an all-out party endorsement for Paxton, and he said he had "seen something like that pass through" (i.e., pass through his office).

On Sunday, September 16, Paul Fagan, Chris Halford, and I met at my Kula home. We had learned that the Maui County Republican executive committee, of which I was a member, had approved without notice to me a Paxton-endorsement direct-mail brochure that would contain party-leader statements of support for Paxton—in short, a "Republican team" brochure.

We decided to respond by going "public" with an open-letter ad in the mid-week *Maui News*.

The following day Fagan reported that he'd received a political piece in the mail entitled "the Republican Choice" ostensibly issued by "Paxton for State House" but noting "production *paid for by Republican Party of Hawai'i.*" It contained endorsements of Paxton by two County party individuals and D.G. Anderson. We changed our responsive ads accordingly and went on the counter-attack, charging an interference with Maui's choice of representation by Honolulu bosses. We also held a press conference and recorded some new radio spots. Andy held a press conference and predicted that his candidate would not only win the primary but also the general election.

His feel for the Maui electorate proved to be non-existent, as Fagan swept to a primary victory with 58 percent of the vote.

Unfortunately in the final analysis it was all for naught, as Fagan lost in the general election to David Morihara, Kula grocery-store owner, a Democrat.

I later called publicly for a party investigation and audit of the entire targeting committee process under Anderson's leadership, arguing that it violated party rules. I added, for "those who do not care about legal or moral niceties there is another indictment—the effort was unsuccessful and turned off more people than we can afford to lose." (Undated letter to Jerry Kane, GOP Kaua'i chair. See also Letters to the Editor, *Honolulu Advertiser*, December 7, 1990.)

Five years later Andy announced that he was leaving the GOP to join the Democrat Party.

As far as I was concerned that was just fine.

Colon Cancer and Parkinson's

Before taking on the task of campaign manager for the Fagan campaign in mid-1990, I took a test for blood in the digestive system at the Kaiser Permanente clinic in Wailuku just as my contract with them was coming to an end at the end of June. The test showed traces of blood, and I resolved to get it checked out further. As I was transitioning between medical plans at the time, I didn't get tests right away. I moved to HMSA before the year ended but still did not do anything about the warning signal. After all, until election day I was running Paul Fagan's campaign full-time.

In late January, 1991, when the campaign was all over, I experienced a major blood episode during a bowel movement. After a series of tests over the next four weeks, I was admitted to Queen's Hospital for major surgery performed by Dr. Peter Halford (my former wife's younger brother). On March 10 Dr. Halford removed two feet of my colon along with seven lymph glands in the cecum area of my abdomen.

Upon leaving the hospital ten days later (and after a relapse caused by drinking too much water that had been urged upon me by my night nurse), I commenced weekly chemotherapy. This was administered under the guidance of Dr. Curtis Andrew here on Maui (and Dr. Kevin Loh in Honolulu), and it continued for a year. Patty and I went on several cruises, working around the chemo treatments by having them en route. I particularly remember having one on Cape Cod, and another in Maine when we stayed with the Nat Saltonstalls (my college roommate).

The onset of this cancer was, of course, a wakeup call as to my lack of immortality. I believe that a lifetime habit of attempting to stay in reasonably good shape was a major plus in fighting this deadly disease. I also believe that my mental state was equally important. Several books were most helpful. Tri-athlete Ruth Heidrich's book entitled *A Race for Life* and Paul Tsongas's *Journey of Purpose* provided me with valuable attitude guidelines. I stressed the lessons of conditioning, both physically and mentally, in a talk to my classmates at the Yale class of 1950 reunion in 2000.

Fortunately the cancer has not (as far as I know) come back. Some say it never is gone, rather that it is in remission. I have had numerous colonoscopies since, and will be due for another soon.

Then in 2005 I was diagnosed with Parkinson's disease. This is a neurologically debilitating disease that, so far, I have been able cope with under the care of my Maui physician, Dr. George Powell. (George is a strong conservative, so we talk politics as well as medicine.) At this writing I can still swim some and play golf reasonably well for an eighty-year-old. But I experience tremors in my left hand and arm and some imbalance in movement. A back problem has forced me to ride in a golf cart rather than walk the eighteen holes, but at least I'm still out there, usually twice a week trying valiantly to break 100!

We strongly support the Michael J. Fox Foundation for Parkinson's Research. This group is working effectively to find a cure—or at least to find ways to prolong movement without the effects of Parkinson's. Support this foundation!

United States Magistrate Judge

One of the best decisions I made in the early 1990s was to apply for a vacancy in the part-time position of U.S. Magistrate Judge (USMJ) for Maui. My predecessor was Larry Ing, a busy Wailuku attorney. He described my duties as being relatively innocuous, mostly misdemeanor hearings every couple of months. Someone else—an administering agency in Denver, Colorado—would do the secretarial work and deal with fines and so on. Ing said that I would be called occasionally to fill in for full-time magistrate judges in Honolulu.

My first assignment was a week in Washington D.C., August 1991—an orientation seminar for all the new magistrate judges. We stayed at the Hay Adams Hotel, located in Lafayette Park across the street from the White House (where President-elect Obama stayed for a few days before his inauguration).

Due to our alphabetical proximity in seat assignments, I got to know a fellow new USMJ by the name of James "Jim" Robb from Grand Junction, Colorado. We had several dinners together in Washington, and later we both attended a seminar in Chicago. Jim had worked in Washington for Senator Dominick, and he had a good handle on Colorado politics. Unfortunately Jim passed away a year or so ago before he and his wife Maggie could visit us on Maui. Jim was held over at the end of his term and made the necessary time requirements for ultimate retirement. Jim was honored by the Colorado Legislature for his hard work in the land-preservation field. He was a great storyteller and a fine judge. I only wish he and his wife could have made it to Maui while he was alive.

In my Maui hearings as a USMJ I became familiar for the first, but not last, time with rule violations by commercial bike-tour firms in Haleakalā National Park. This exposure to the issue provoked my current voluntary involvement on the same subject with the Kula Community Association. These guided and unguided tour groups, which operate on State and County roads, are only minimally regulated. The County of Maui has authorized a formal study of the operations of these tours. That study is currently underway and will lead, I hope, to the required actions.

As time passed, I became more and more familiar with USMJ duties by way of Honolulu assignments. I handled initial hearings, grand
jury returns, settlement conferences, non-jury trials, immigration ceremonies, and other miscellaneous matters. Criminal law was never my
"thing" while I was in private practice, so it was refreshing to learn "new
stuff." I particular enjoyed presiding over the new-citizen immigration
ceremonies, and I strongly urged these new Americans to become fluent
in the English language.

When my term came to an end in 1996, the court announced it
would not fill the three neighbor island part-time positions. Rather, it
would convert to a half-time post in Honolulu. So I applied for that position. I proposed to commute several times a week.

Fortunately this didn't happen. I think my marriage, as well as my
equanimity, would have greatly suffered.

And yet as a consequence I fell just short of the five years of service
required that would have made me a quadruple "dipper" by way of the
retirement fund for USMJs (in addition to my State retirement, Navy
retirement, and social security). My ski buddies always teased me about
my "dippership," but this never bothered me as I felt I'd earned it! In any
event, the stipend would have been very modest, since part-time magis-
trates work for practically nothing. One year, when I did a lot of work in
Honolulu, I earned close to $15,000. As a consequence, I forfeited some
of my social security. Fortunately that happened only once.

So now whenever some form calls for "occupation," I have a choice.
I usually write "retired." But I don't think I will ever truly retire.

The Maui Open Space Trust

While in the Legislature in the 1970s and 1980s, I was often involved
in environmental issues. On Maui my first effort to preserve open space
and agriculture was through a formalized land trust. In this effort I
worked with Isaac Hall and his wife Dana, Jeff Stark, Dr. Rick Sands,
Mary Evanson, Bonnie Newman, Leslie Kululoio, Mark Sheehan, Hugh
Starr, and others prominent in the environmental movement. I attended
several conferences and schools, and these studies qualified me as a "land

counselor." (One of these schools was located a few miles north of San Francisco, and I was worried I was going to turn green and revert to the hippie days!) I even knew a lot about conservation easements and other ways to preserve open space while taking advantage of the U.S. Tax Code. For several years I was the executive director of MOST (Maui Open Space Trust).

During the time I held this position, Jeff Stark and I tried to convince our Legislature to pass a law permitting County governments to adopt regulations that would allow residential "cluster developments" in rural and agriculture zoned areas. We were working according to the same anti-sprawl principle that is currently gaining popularity—allow growth only within existing urban-developed areas.

We failed, despite numerous trips to Honolulu. The Senate committee chair Randy Iwase (Democratic candidate for governor in 2006) refused to hear our bill. He wanted a wholesale revision of the land-use zoning law and would not act without one.

With this setback, we tired of the game. A few years later we turned our projects over to a newly formed land trust, the Maui Coastal Land Trust, which is doing an excellent job.

Righting a "Grave Injustice": The Story Behind HB 860 and the Maui Vets

Initially I became aware of HB 860 while reading a story in the *Maui News* of March 9, 2001. This bill provided for State retirement credits for active military service by World War II, Korean, and Vietnam veterans employed by the State of Hawai'i or its counties who were members of the Hawai'i Employees Retirement System (ERS) before 1989. Previously these credits were provided to veterans who served after 1989 (Act 385 S.L. 1989). Thus, HB 860 was designed to provide equality between the earlier veterans and the post-1989 veterans. I soon discovered that several Maui vets had been working to accomplish this goal for a number of years. I got in touch with the leaders of the group and said I would be glad to help them. Of course, I had a selfish as well as public-service motive on this one in that I fell into the class of people who would benefit if the bill were to pass and become law. I had retired from the U.S. Naval Reserve a year or so before the effective date of the earlier ACT 385 and hence received no military-based benefit in my legislative-based retirement pay.

The group of Maui vets lobbying for HB 860 included the following gentlemen: Masaru Abe, Alvin Soares, Itsuo Hashiro, Joseph Medeiros, Abel Cravalho, Rafael Acoba, Noah Ah Ling Leong, and me. Most of these vets were U.S. Army-affiliated, but Cravalho had been a Marine, and I think Acoba had served in the Coast Guard. The ethnic diversity was obvious—AJA, Portuguese, Filipino, Chinese, and haole.

MASARU ABE'S MAUI VETS GROUP; SIGNING OF HB 860

The Cayetano Administration had taken a firm position against the bill on the grounds that it was retrospective, and that it would cost too much. Accordingly, I wrote letters to various legislative leaders arguing against the administration's position. In these letters I made the following statements:

"With regard to (alleged) retrospective application, first note that the bill is not 'retroactive.' All benefits would be paid in the future; no going back is provided for. Secondly, note that any retroactiveness [a newly coined Rohlfing word that should have been "retroactivity"] results from HB 860's statutory redefinition of the class of ERS members who will qualify for benefits from past military service. The Legislature already decided in 1989 that as a matter of principle and state policy, retirement system credits (and hence benefits) should be granted to a class of people—members of the ERS who had rendered active military service—but in so doing they imposed an arbitrary date for the qualifying service, thus discriminating against veteran ERS members with relevant service prior to 1989." We also argued that this discrimination might be tantamount to constitutional denial of Equal Protection of the Law and hence contrary to the 14th Amendment to the U.S. Constitution.

As for the lack of money, the claim that $37 million unfunded liability would be created was challenged not only by our group but by attentive senators. Republican Minority Leader Sen. Fred Hemmings in a policy statement entitled "Grave Injustice" (March 30, 2001) pointed out that "ERS is awash in money with $9 billion in reserve. It has enough money to pay additional benefits to those who retired before 1989 without making a dent in its massive account."

Our group's leader was Masaru Abe, a retired Maui County Parks and Recreation Superintendent and still active "makule (old) league" baseball player. Co-chair was Alvin Soares, a retired State Department of Education principal. Our "secret weapon" was Itsuo Hashiro, now deceased, then a State Department of Transportation Highway Division retiree who had earned a Bronze Star in combat. Though he was legally blind, hard of hearing, and wheelchair-bound, Hashiro traveled to Honolulu to testify on his "own nickel" (just as all the rest of us did). With Noah's assistance he made three trips in style, including the one for bill-signing by the governor. (Senator Hemmings's statement noted that "it was heart-wrenching to see a blind veteran in a wheelchair as he testified on the need for this bill.")

Masaru Abe demonstrated real leadership in keeping this diverse group together and in making contact with Democratic legislators, in particular with Senator Jan Buen from Maui who put her shoulder to the wheel. My job was to convince wavering Republicans that this was not the time to be stingy, that the ERS could afford it. In the end the bill passed unanimously in both houses. Buen wrote a *Maui News* "Viewpoint" piece entitled "Veterans victorious with a never-say-die attitude," published July 16, 2001, right after the bill was signed by Governor Cayetano. Our group attended the signing. Senator Buen concluded her op-ed piece this way: "It took twelve years to pass this law. The eight Maui veterans are to be saluted for their dogged persistence. Because of them, 2,000 veterans who were left out will now reap the same benefits. They shall not be forgotten."

In my case the amount of the actual benefit increase worked out to a relatively small amount, but for many vets the benefit was substantial.

I was proud to be a member of this dedicated group of men.

Maui Apportionment Advisory Council to the State Reapportionment Commission of 2001

The Al-Qaeda terrorist attacks in New York and on the Pentagon were not the only things that occurred in 2001. Here in Hawai'i our State constitution provides for a review of apportionment of seats in the State Legislature every ten years. The constitution requires that this review be conducted by a State commission assisted by advisory councils from each of the four counties. I was appointed by the State House to the Maui council along with friends Mark Andrews, Madge Schaefer, and Manuel "Junior" Moniz. I had served with Mark in the Legislature and had played golf for a number of years with his father, Dr. Joe Andrews. Junior Moniz was my wife Patty's distant cousin, and had been a Maui councilman. Before retirement he was Hawaiian Air's Maui manager.

With a twinkle in her eye Madge would smile and describe herself as just a "Wailea housewife." In fact, she was a savvy political operator with a strong will and equally strong voice. It turned out she had been council chair (or mayor) of the huge Ventura County in Southern California before "retiring" in Hawai'i. We were to work well as a team. Most of the commission meetings that we attended were held in Honolulu, beginning on June 14, 2001. There were eight meetings altogether, the last of which took place on November 30, 2001. Reapportionment matters can be very esoteric and convoluted, but in this instance our concerns were pretty basic.

The commission's proposed plan employed a population base that included aliens and non-resident military dependents (NRMDs). We estimated there were as many as 80,000 resident aliens in Hawai'i who were ineligible to vote, most of them concentrated on O'ahu. The bulk of these were Filipinos concentrated in the Waipahu, Kalihi, and Liliha areas. Likewise, an undetermined number of military wives resided on O'ahu at or near the many facilities at Pearl Harbor, Schofield, and Kāne'ohe.

Controversy arose over the question whether or not to include alien and NRMD numbers in the overall base population tally. This question had consequences for the state's two leading political parties. Political insiders knew that the higher the base population numbers on O'ahu, the less chance that the neighbor islands would receive additional legislative seats despite marked neighbor island population growth since the previous reapportionment. The areas in question on O'ahu were solid Democratic Party territory. The neighbor island populations, however— although dominated by Democrats—had gained a lot of newcomers from the continental states who would sometimes vote for good Republican candidates.

The commission felt that it couldn't exclude aliens from the tally for the simple reason that they were uncountable—the Immigration and Naturalization Service had no population figures. But the commission did have numbers and locations of NRMDs, as statistical data thereon had been supplied by the military. Nevertheless, the commission's intent was to include NRMDs in the total despite the fact that all prior Hawai'i legislative reapportionments had excluded them.

The majority Democrats explained their position as follows: NRMDs should be included in the population count because—unlike students or military personnel, who declare a home of record elsewhere—no one can be sure that the dependents of military personnel do not qualify as residents. Thus they argued that the NRMDs had a "right to be represented" in the Legislature.

I responded to this argument at the October 3, 2001, hearing at Maui Waena Intermediate School as follows: "[The majority argument] puts the cart before the horse. It assumes that to exclude NRMDs we have to prove a negative, when there is a legal presumption that dependents' residency follows that of the military serviceman or woman. It ignores the fact that our statutory elections code specifically says that dependents are not to be deemed residents merely by being stationed in our state. It ignores the state constitution's 'permanent residents' test for the apportionment base. It erroneously confuses the duty of legislators to represent all persons physically present in their districts with the formula and mechanics of obtaining fair and equitable representation for our taxpaying and voting citizens throughout the entire state. It ignores the Supreme Court redistricting case of Reynolds v. Sims, and subsequent cases...and, last but not least, it is simply incompatible with the rationale of 'one person, one vote' since it dilutes our votes here on Maui, thereby inhibiting our input on crucial issues."

Madge and I had indicated early on that we would attempt to fight the commission in the courts if necessary. The Maui Advisory Council official report summed up this activity as follows: "A...picture of the participation by advisory council members in the overall process...would not be complete without a mention of preparations made by Schaefer and Rohlfing for a legal challenge to the commission's inclusion of NRMDs in the base. These actions included: 1. building a bipartisan, several-county coalition committed as plaintiffs; 2. retaining former State Attorney General Margery Bronster to bring action in federal court; and 3. raising sufficient funds for attorneys fees and costs."

Much of the lawsuit funds were returned after Chairman Wayne Minami announced his decision that he would vote with the minority members to exclude NRMDs. He also swung the balance on the issue of ending Maui's "canoe districts" (where legislators were to be elected from more than one island).

Best of all, applying the changed population base brought Maui a new representative, this one from the Lahaina (West Maui) area. So our struggle had borne fruit!

Shortly thereafter we received some recognition for our efforts. Madge and I were pictured on the front page of the *Maui News* on December 30, 2001, as designees for its "People Who Made a Difference" recognition during the past year.

Fred Rohlfing, Madge Schaefer
Two Who Made a Difference

from the *Maui News* Sunday, December 30, 2001

Start trying to explain the intricacies of reapportionment to someone and watch their eyes glaze over.

The process of redrawing district lines for legislative seats in the state is a complicated one, involving jargon like "base population" and "census blocks" and "allowable population deviations."

It also involves canoes—at least it used to—as in the canoe districts that see a single legislator representing islands in two different counties.

Two members of the Maui Advisory Council to the Hawaii Reapportionment Commission distinguished themselves this year as they led the fight to end the practice of making counties share a lawmaker—a practice that often gives short shrift to voters and waters down Neighbor Island representation in the state Legislature.

Fred Rohlfing and Madge Schaefer took the term "advisory" in Maui Advisory Council to new heights, constantly pushing the case of Neighbor Islands during the meetings of the Reapportionment Commission.

Neither of them are strangers to politics.

Rohlfing, an attorney who lives in Kula, is a former state legislator who has also served as the county corporation counsel, the top civil attorney representing county government.

Schaefer is a Maui Meadows resident who has lived on Maui as a permanent resident for five years after being a part-time resident for 20 years.

She is a former mayor of the city of Thousand Oaks in California, and also served on the Ventura County Board of Supervisors in that state.

As soon as the reapportionment process began, Schaefer and Rohlfing sounded the alarm—the method being used to count the state's population was being unfairly weighted in Oahu's favor.

Rohlfing took on the issue of counting resident aliens, pointing out that tens of thousands of aliens who can't vote are being included in the state's population. Schaefer hammered on the issue of nonresident military dependents, people who live in Hawaii because a spouse is stationed here but who report that their permanent home is somewhere else.

In both cases, since most aliens and nonresident military dependents live on Oahu, that island's population was being unfairly inflated by counting people who can't vote in a Hawaii election.

The net effect when legislative districts of equal size are drawn gives Oahu more senators and representatives than it should have at the expense of the Neighbor Islands. Voters on Maui, the Big Island and Kauai also protested at having their counties sharing legislators with districts in other counties. After a long debate lasting months, the tenacity of Schaefer and Rohlfing and the outcry of Neighbor Island residents paid off.

The commission changed its plan, dropping nonresident military dependents from the population count and keeping each county in the state whole, sinking the plan for legislative canoe districts.

The Maui duo said they couldn't have pulled it off without lots of support from many areas, and say they're just pleased the commission did the right thing.

The end result gives Maui County six full House seats and three full Senate seats, an increase of a full seat over the current divided representation.

"I'm stunned that we were able to make such a monumental change," Schaefer said of the commission's change of heart. "There was a giant wave moving forward, and Maui was going to get left in the lurch again."

Schaefer and Rohlfing were able to stop that wave, to the benefit of Neighbor Island voters who will see their voices strengthened on Oahu as decisions area made on the future of the state.

"We have to feel good about what we did," Rohlfing said. "But clearly it was the people on the commission who saw the light—they did a great job. It's a very fair and reasonable plan."

Without a canoe in sight.
—Mark Adams, staff writer

Encore: Three Years on the County Salary Commission

I was on a roll with the reapportionment plan victory and figured I could put in some additional volunteer time for the County. I applied for a seat on either the Police Commission or the Planning Commission but was offered neither. However, in April of 2005 I accepted Mayor Alan Arakawa's appointment to the Salary Commission, which under the Maui County Charter is a very important body. Unlike most such governmental institutions, the County of Maui's Salary Commission has more than just advisory power—it makes the final decisions on salaries for all directors and deputy directors as well as all nine councilpersons.

It took a while to learn the routine and the bureaucratic terminology, but after several meetings I began to participate in decision-making. One of my causes, having served as corporation counsel, was to see that the two principal lawyer positions (corporation counsel and prosecuting attorney) in the county were being adequately compensated. I found that the prosecuting attorney at the time had been placed in a higher "tier" than the corporation counsel and earned a few thousand dollars more annually. That led me to study the tier system, which ranks departments in four groups.

I couldn't find a substantive rationale for these divisions. Instead I found expert opinion from people who had served in the County personnel office against the tier setup (Ken Taira, for one). So I proposed to equate the salaries of the two legal officials, and the commission so agreed. I also proposed that, when we acted upon the full schedule of adjustments for all directors and their deputies, we abolish tiers altogether. For this proposal I had the support of a key adviser to the commission—Lynn Krieg, the director of personnel. When the new salary "model" was developed, we succeeded in creating a single schedule for all positions.

The incumbent corporation counsel, Brian Moto, had, prior to my appointment, already prepared comprehensive arguments for considering higher pay for his position. Such an increase would enable higher salaries for staff attorneys and thus provide an opportunity for recruitment of better personnel for litigation and advisory roles. Moto tied his arguments to those of the State Judicial Commission by advocating that his job be compensated at a rate equal to ninety percent of the salary of a State District Court judge ($110,486 as of 2007). He argued that the County salary should track that of the District Court judge in future years as well. Unfortunately, my colleagues would not agree to anything beyond a one-time tie to the District Court judge's salary. However, the precedent was established for measuring pay for the office with a comparable level of legal status and training.

The "salary model" developed under the leadership of certified Public accountant and chair of the commission Doug Levin during my tenure was a major accomplishment. It established a framework for equitable treatment of the various departmental leaders while taking into objective consideration factors such as their budgets, number of personnel, professional requirements, cost of living indices, salary inversions, neighbor island comparisons, and departmental interface.

We spent a great deal of time determining a fair salary for Maui's County Council members. This work involved researching salaries for similar offices—both in Hawai'i and across the country—as well as hearing from a number of citizens and several council members. Former Mayor Alan Arakawa testified against salary increases of any amount, saying that council members were micromanaging where they didn't belong and wasting enormous amounts of time. On the other side of the issue was his former executive assistant Dave DeLeon, who had moved on to work for the Realtors Association of Maui and who testified that he favored an increase. When I questioned him on his former boss's opinion, however, DeLeon supported Arakawa's view that council members interfered with administration procedures.

In due course the commission approved a very substantial salary increase for the County Council (to $66,000 per year), which was more than I could support, so I cast a negative vote. Despite the fact that the increase was a substantial raise, there was surprisingly little "bitching" from the public. My experience consistently supports the view that no matter what amount politicians are paid, most voters feel they are overpaid!

In three years I only missed one commission meeting. Most of my colleagues on the commission were conscientious public servants who contributed time and brainpower to the issues at hand. I particularly enjoyed working with Michael Westfall and Andy Herrera, but all of the members contributed under Doug Levin's leadership. We had good staff support on this commission from Dave DeLeon under Mayor Arakawa and Don Couch under Mayor Tavares. Shelley Pellegrino was most helpful on several of my initiatives.

Fritz Rohlfing's Federal Judgeship Nomination

My most frustrating cause stemmed from my eldest son's nomination to the United States District Court for the District of Hawai'i. "Fritz" (Frederick W. Rohlfing III), a graduate of Punahou, Dartmouth College, and the University of Chicago Law School, submitted his name for a U.S. District Court vacancy in May 2001 via an Internet form. At the time another candidate had the endorsement of the Hawai'i 2000 Bush for President Campaign Chair, who was State Representative Barbara Marumoto. Nonetheless, in October 2001 Fritz was vetted by the White House Counsel's office, and in January 2002 he was nominated to the federal bench by President Bush.

The U.S. Senate confirmation process then commenced. At the time of his nomination, Fritz had been practicing law in Hawai'i for over eighteen years, mostly as a business litigator. Although litigators of Fritz's generation rarely have the opportunity to try cases because of the strenuous efforts made by today's judges to broker pre-trial settlements, Fritz had been lead trial counsel in three jury trials to verdict and in three bench (judge-only) trials. He had represented clients in contested-case hearings before County and State agencies, successfully argued innumerable motions before federal and state courts, and had ten nationally reported appellate cases to his credit. So it was no wonder that the Hawai'i State Bar Association announced in February 2002 it had found Fritz to be "highly qualified for the position of U.S. District Judge" and that he met "our very highest level of standards for recommendation to the Bench." This rating was the assessment of Fritz's fellow members of the Hawai'i bar, those who had practiced with him and who knew him best.

A separate review was conducted by the Standing Committee on the Federal Judiciary (FJC) of the American Bar Association, which had been consulted in advance of all proposed federal judicial nominations since the Eisenhower administration. Upon taking office in 2001, President

Bush announced that he would no longer consult with the FJC prior to nominating individuals for the federal judiciary. The Senate Judiciary Committee (SJC), however, requested the FJC to continue to evaluate the President's judicial nominees.

In March the FJC dispatched Mainland attorney Jane Barrett, who was then a partner in the Los Angeles office of mega-firm Preston Gates & Ellis and was designated as the FJC's ninth circuit member. Barrett's assignment was to evaluate Fritz's integrity, professional competence, and judicial temperament by examining Fritz's legal writing and by conducting interviews of Fritz, federal and State judges, and practicing members of the Hawaiʻi bar. She was then to prepare a written recommendation to the full FJC as to whether Fritz should be found "well qualified," "qualified," or "not qualified."

During the interview Barrett told Fritz that he met the ABA standards of integrity and judicial temperament and displayed excellent writing skills. She told him, however, that she did not think he had sufficient trial experience and that his law firm was "a political law firm." She did not explain to Fritz how she had arrived at this conclusion. I suspect it may have resulted from Fritz's filing of an amicus curiae brief a few years earlier on behalf of the LDS Church in the same-sex marriage case then being considered by the Hawaiʻi Supreme Court. In any event, Barrett subsequently submitted a written report recommending the FJC give Fritz a "not qualified" rating, and the FJC wrote to the Senate Judiciary Committee stating that Fritz was "not qualified for the position of U.S. District Judge."

Despite the inevitable and considerable negative consequences flowing from Barrett's FJC report, neither Fritz nor the public at large have ever been permitted to see the report. Consequently, neither Fritz nor the public at large were ever given the opportunity to respond or counter whatever basis there was for that disparaging report.

Fritz's nomination was thus pending before the SJC with two diametrically opposing recommendations from outside legal organizations. The guys on the ground (the Hawaiʻi bar) rating him highly qualified against a cabal of entirely Mainland-based lawyers (the FJC) rating him not qualified. Pursuant to a quaint (read undemocratic) senatorial tradition of the SJC, it was time for Hawaiʻi's two senators to submit their "blue slips" to the SJC. A positive blue-slip submission would mean the senator favored confirmation of the nominee. Sadly, neither of our senators submitted those slips. Both stated that as long as the ABA opposed the nomination, they would not support it. Without at least one positive blue slip from our senators, SJC Chairman Orrin Hatch would not schedule an SJC hearing. Without an SJC hearing, Fritz's nomination could not proceed to the full Senate for a confirmation vote.

Fritz and his supporters then initiated an extensive letter-writing campaign in an attempt to change the ABA recommendation or to counter it with endorsements from other organizations. Honolulu labor lawyer Lowell Chun-Hoon helped organize a petition of thirty-four members of the Hawai'i bar that included a reference to Fritz's "AV" rating from the Martindale-Hubbell organization, a rating that "identifies a lawyer with very high to preeminent legal ability." Fritz was also endorsed by the Consumer Lawyers of Hawai'i, the Hawai'i Chapter of the National Employment Lawyers Association (NELA), and Local 142 of the International Longshore & Warehouse Union. The Hawai'i NELA Chapter pointedly noted in its letter to Senator Inouye that "other sitting judges in Hawai'i had less trial experience than Mr. Rohlfing, yet were found to be qualified by the ABA."

Congressman Neil Abercrombie informed one of Fritz's supporters that he had lent his "assistance to the extent allowed by my position as a Member of the U.S. House of Representatives," while recognizing that "the U.S. Constitution places the confirmation of judges entirely within the Senate's jurisdiction."

As the process dragged on, Senator Inouye responded to a letter from Lowell Chun-Hoon by stating that he would "not stand in the way of the Judiciary Committee should it decide that a hearing is appropriate," thereby giving us a ray of hope that we might see a breakthrough. A hearing would have had the salutary effect of forcing the FJC to publicly state its reasons for opposing the nomination, thus providing Fritz with an opportunity to refute Barrett's charge that he did not have substantial courtroom experience. But when we attempted to get Senator Akaka to take the same position as Inouye, he flatly refused. Had he not so refused, I believe there would have been a hearing. I believe Fritz would have overcome the FJC's opposition and been approved on the floor of the Senate, and he would be on the bench today.

Haleakalā Downhill Bicycle Tours

This is a classic case of problem-solving that requires the interaction of private business, the public at large acting through community organizations, and elected and appointed public officials. These tours—the product of the commercial vision of a certain "Cruiser Bob"—started in the early eighties. Numerous competitors joined in over time.

In the early days these bicycle tours always started at ten thousand feet, e.g., at the Haleakalā summit, then rolled down through the national park onto State and County roads until they reached Paʻia on the coast. Sunrise was always the main attraction, which meant that the tourists had to wake at three or four a.m. Having breathed the cold air at this elevation and gotten their bathroom break, tourists of all ages, sizes, and bike-riding abilities would put on appropriate gear and clamber onto bicycles. After a parking lot spin they would line up behind their tour leaders and commence their ride down the side of the mountain on the federally owned road. National park authorities required a ten-minute interval between each launch of these commercially led groups. (As a magistrate judge I enforced those rules for four years).

The trip was no picnic. The summit road is often wet, windy, foggy— even icy. (It snows on Haleakalā every couple of years.) Turns are sharp, and the constant pull of gravity encourages speed. After leaving the park, the bikers would continue on a State road for miles until hitting an abrupt stop-signed intersection at the end of Crater Road, where they would make a right turn. Frequently the leader of these tours would ignore the stop sign and swish his group out in front of downhill traffic.

From here the group would travel five miles of State highway that has no pullouts, narrow shoulders, and even narrower bridges on turns. All this time the group was followed closely by the van that had driven them to the summit. The van served to block traffic, which would stack up behind the caravan. Unhappy drivers often attempted to pass the caravan—a high-risk maneuver on a fast and curvy two-lane highway. The situation invited catastrophe.

After reaching the polo field in upper Makawao the traditional tour would then move onto County roads across to Olinda Road and then

Baldwin Avenue down to the main highway (Route 36) that goes to Hana.

There is another type of bike rider on this mountain every day—the unguided type. These thrill seekers take the same route without the protection of the professional service provider. These groups set their own pace, in groups of up to twenty bicycles. Their bikes often come from visitor-oriented cycle shops that, for fear of lawsuits, prefer not to rent their bikes. Instead these shops sell the bicycles to customers and buy them back at the end of the tour. This stratagem has yet to be proven effective in protecting the provider from liability.

My involvement in matters relating to these bike tours began when I received a telephone call from Paula Holroyde, a neighbor of mine. She told me she was the chair of a Kula Community Association (KCA) subcommittee on the bike issue. She wanted me to read her book of notes on the issue and decide whether to join her subcommittee, which included Camille Lyons, former State Rep. Mark Andrews, Harriette Holt, Rici Conger, Elliott Krasch, and Monica Loui. I read the material and decided to get involved. We were later joined by Gina Flammer, who in turn became KCA president.

The Haleakalā Downhill Bicycle Subcommittee had done a lot of work before I came aboard. They had studied the tour operations, obtained material concerning the regulatory schemes for the Waikīkī Beachboys as a potential model, and had prepared a list of suggested new rules for operation of the tours. The assumption was that the County of Maui would enact these rules or create concessions as a supplement to its very limited permitting statute for bike tours. Around this same time an important event was taking place. The Maui Police Department assigned an officer, Jeffrey Mahoney, to study the bike tours. In his comprehensive report dated June 26, 2006, he states the following:

"In summary, the current volume of bicycle tour operations, both guided and unguided, and sheer number of riders poses a concern for all using the highways and subsequent roadways. Additionally, age and rider experience are potential risks for this type of activity. The current highways and roadways being used for this activity have design limitations and inherent problems not conducive to this type of activity." Mahoney's report goes on to make a number of specific recommendations relating to tour operations. It concludes: "The combination of expanded rural residential communities and increased traffic on antiquated roadways has led to the conflict of today…. This problem will not go away and…changes need to be made."

I raised issues of jurisdiction. Although the County had begun to express concern, much of the conflict between the tours and local motorists was occurring on roads that belong to the State. The committee agreed that we should test the County's jurisdictional power. We asked Representative Joe Souki to send a letter requesting an opinion from the State attorney general whether the County of Maui could regulate bike tours under section 291C, 163 (14) HRS or any other provision of existing law. Souki made the request, and the answer came back that we would have to amend State statutes to enable this action to be taken by the County. Soon thereafter I prepared a draft bill which Mark Andrews, of our committee, took to Rep. Souki for introduction in the 2007 legislative session. The bill was designated HB 349. A companion Senate Bill 1058 was introduced by Senator Kalani English. We provided in-person testimony on these bills, and at the end of the session we were pleased to see the House bill pass final reading as Act 181 SL 2007.

While this was going on, another issue was pending in the Maui council—namely, consideration of increased insurance liability limits for bicycle tour companies. Bill 84 was introduced to the council at the request of Corporation Counsel Brian Moto. He first proposed a requirement of five million dollars in coverage, but in the end that figure was reduced to three million dollars.

The Tavares County administration then included an item in the '07 budget for a comprehensive study of the downhill bike industry, in the sum of $250,000. After a substantial review the contract was let to Kimura International Inc. of Honolulu, and they will shortly render their report.

As early fall hit the mountain, a tough, intelligent lady by the name of Marilyn Parris, the superintendent of Haleakalā National Park, played her winning hand. After a fatal cycling accident occurred in the park, she ordered a "safety stand-down" beginning October 10, 2007. All bike tours were suspended for sixty days. Parris said that "with three fatalities and several serious accidents within a year it is important to stop and critically analyze this commercial activity in the park." She then extended the stand-down indefinitely while undertaking a comprehensive review of all park commercial activities. Her park plan combined with the County's study should provide the County Council and Tavares administration with ample information upon which legislation can be based to regulate all bicycle tours, unguided as well as guided.

My hope is that legislation will be prepared to establish a "Haleakalā Recreational Authority," which will provide for a limited number of bike operator concessions. The County could then exact reasonable fees from these concessions. The total sum derived from the franchised operations should be enough to cover an administrator, a secretary, at least one field officer with arrest powers, and appropriate vehicles and communications equipment. (In the heyday of these tours the industry as a whole made over $20 million a year.) This County office would be authorized to work closely with the National Park Service, in particular with new superintendent Sarah Creachbaum.

This is still a work in progress. Gina Flammer and I, along with our fellow subcommittee members, will be hard at work on the bike-tour issue even as you are reading the last lines of this account.

Looking Back:
Perspectives on the Hawaiʻi GOP

My own political successes and failures need to be seen in the context of my party's successes and failures. Unfortunately my party has grown accustomed to failure. But it wasn't always so. In my early years on the stump, starting with 1957 and my Oʻahu Young Republican presidency, Hawaiʻi Republicans appeared to be in pretty good shape. In the statehood election of 1959 we produced a governor, a lieutenant governor, fourteen State senators (majority control), and eighteen State representatives (enough to sustain a veto). We also elected a popular U.S. senator, Hiram L. Fong, who held the office until retiring in 1974.

But not long after those ballots had been counted, trouble began to stir. Lieutenant Governor Jimmy Kealoha, convinced that he was responsible for Bill Quinn's gubernatorial success, began his own unannounced campaign for that office. Meanwhile the Republican senatorial group splintered badly as the neighbor-isle "barons" got selfish. In 1962 we began to hemorrhage with the loss of the governorship and control of the Senate. We never regained the latter. It took fifty years before we won the governorship again—with Linda Lingle and her running mate Duke Aiona victorious in 2002 and 2006. Legislative seats remained beyond our grasp, with the exception of the twenty House seats Lingle was able to win in 2000 as state party chairperson.

The years in between were very dry. In 1986 Pat Saiki was able to win the First District Congressional seat that I had failed to secure in '76, but she was sidetracked when she sought to move to the U.S. Senate in 1990. Now it is even drier—you might say the land is parched—as we hold no seats in U.S. Congress,* a measly two seats in the State Senate, six seats in the House, and the lame duck governor/lieutenant governor slots.

Some of this failure can be attributed to the grandstanding of the "Religious Right" during the late eighties.

As I was retiring from my Maui County job in early spring of 1988, I gave some thought to running again for the County Council. I talked with Linda Lingle, who was a councilperson at that time, and she encouraged me to run. As a first step I decided to participate in my party's annual convention, at which delegates are elected to state and national conventions. Attending the Upcountry Maui organizational caucus, we received a rude awakening. The room was stacked with conservative "born again" Christians and other religiously inclined people, most of whom I had never seen before. Mayor Hannibal Tavares was there as well, and Patty and I sat near him in the back of the room. One after the other the delegate slots to the state convention were filled by the newcomers. Hannibal finally was elected on the third ballot, and I made it on the fifth. Patty was elected an alternate. A straw poll was taken on the GOP candidates who would be contending for the presidency, and this new Christian crowd picked Pat Robertson overwhelmingly. Patty and I were the only people present to vote for George H.W. Bush, who became the eventual winner of the nomination and of the presidency that November!

In July of that same year, 1988, the *Honolulu Star-Bulletin* carried a story entitled "Maui Republican Calls For Building A New Party."

---

* But see page 209 re special election of 2010.

The story opened with my announcement that I would not run for office in '88 and went on to state that I had called Hawai'i's new GOP members "'Sunday School Republicans' bent on an ideological purge of mainstream party members, [and that] the state of the Republican Party of Hawai'i is so disturbing that I can no longer conscientiously carry its banner into an election battle." The article went on to say that I suggested creation of a new party to be called the "Home Rule & Freedom Party" whose major planks would call for bringing decision-making back from Honolulu and the State Capitol to the County governments.

Before it passed from the scene, Rev. Robertson's movement caused us to lose the following Republican incumbents to the Democrat Party: Senators Donna Ikeda and Ann Kobayashi and House Members Kinau Kamali'i and Virginia Isbell. All cited their support of free choice as the reason.

So, overall, why have the Democrats had the edge for these many years?

In a nutshell, they have identified better with the non-Caucasian majority of our citizenry. Democrats have won elections over the years by running hard against the Big Five, corporations that ran the sugar and pineapple plantations throughout the islands. These firms were dominated by haoles, as was the business community. But we have seen the breakup of Big Five power and the rise of multi-ethnic control of the business and social communities. So why hasn't the political equation corrected itself?

I believe the answer is that images change slowly in politics. Not only that, Republicans have projected a lot of negative images. Democrats have taken advantage of the Republican Party's extreme expressions—e.g., the "Religious Right" and other boomlets by overly vocal conservatives.

Then there is Senator Inouye—the second most senior U.S. senator and head of the appropriations committee. Money is the mother's milk of politics, and Senator Inouye is the key to "Big Bucks" for the Democrats. His recent contribution of $100,000 to the Democrat Congressional Committee to be used on behalf of Senator Hanabusa is a sample of how the pros play the game and an example of what we as Republicans must overcome. (Inouye has been in Congress since 1959 and in the Senate since 1962!)

Hawai'i Democrats traditionally close their statewide political campaigns with a big, emotional rally in Hilo, on the Big Island, far from the urban colossus of Honolulu. That strategy would sound "dumb" to a Mainland political consultant. But it is shrewd. While listening to the event on radio or watching it on television, the minds of the descendants of Hawai'i's plantation workers fill with images of earlier, tougher days. They remember how their parents and grandparents sacrificed for them—day after day in the hot sun, if you will. Who're they going to vote for? You guessed it—the Democrats. In a minute.

CHAPTER EIGHT

LOOKING DOWN THE ROAD

A New Beginning

"A New Beginning" was the slogan for the successful Linda Lingle campaign in 2002. That campaign broke the stranglehold on the governorship exercised by Hawai'i's Democratic Party *for ten consecutive gubernatorial elections.*

The slogan would be appropriate today for the Hawai'i GOP if applied to its national status or our own legislators and councilmen. A young person interested in political issues and contemplating running for office might very well ask GOP leaders: "Why should I run as a Republican? You have only two State Senators and only six House members. So I could never serve in the majority, and I couldn't get my bills passed." Indeed, I am hard pressed to come up with an honest answer that would persuade the questioner to join our party.

Yet there is so much one can accomplish as a part of needed political change when it finally is achieved! Think about what it meant for Hawai'i Democrats to have been a part of the breakthrough in 1954. My decision to run as a Republican in 1959 naturally followed my activities as chairman of the O'ahu Young Republicans. The GOP did well in the first statehood elections, achieving a high tide of eighteen Republicans in the House, control of the Senate by a whisker, and control of the governorship. It is most disappointing to report that in the fifty years since Hawai'i attained statehood only two Republicans—Hiram Fong (U.S. Senate) and Pat Saiki (U.S. House from District 1, part of O'ahu)—have been elected to national office from this state.* My party's record in State Legislatures and Island County Councils has not been much better. For many years the GOP has failed to enter any candidate at all in many districts. If it has run someone, that person has been relatively unknown in his or her community. Consequently, we get crushed in places like Wahiawā, Kalihi, ʻAiea, Waipahu, and many a neighbor-isle district. Republicans tend to rear their heads successfully in East Oʻahu, Windward Oʻahu, Kona, and Kihei.

One of our mistakes as Republicans is our failure to engage on the issues that result from Hawaiʻi's many vulnerabilities. Finding answers to these critical problems is hard work, but it can be done.

Clearly we are the most vulnerable state in the nation. We are situated some 2,400 miles off the U.S West Coast in the most remote archipelago in the world. Consequently, we are susceptible to the following troubles:

1. Shipping Disruptions

    Hawaiʻi is heavily dependent upon ocean shipping for nearly all of its supplies, be they building or consumer goods. Maritime labor stoppages may occur when any one or more of a variety of unions so chooses. These stoppages can be caused by on-board ship unions like the Sailors Union of the Pacific (SUP) or longshore unions such as the ILWU. The major issue in my 1972 campaign against Rep. Spark Matsunaga was his failure to lead Congress to a better way of handling these stoppages instead of relying on a declaration of National Emergency under the Taft-Hartley Act— Is the health and safety of one state such an emergency?—and the weak provisions of the Railway Labor Act. My proposal was to create a separate new federal agency to oversee labor relations with the non-contiguous states and the island possessions of the United States (Puerto Rico, Virgin Is., Guam, Marianas, American Samoa, Alaska, and Hawaiʻi). New provisions would require early action by federal conciliators and, ultimately, binding arbitration of the dispute. While I believe in collective bargaining, certain broad public interests require that the parties be aided in their negotiations so that disputes come to quick resolutions.

---

* Charles Djou became the third one on May 22, 2010.

2. Natural Disasters

   Hawai'i is particularly exposed to natural disasters—e.g., hurricanes, tsunamis, earthquakes, and storms of all varieties. A recent lightning storm on O'ahu knocked out power for the entire island, just like that. A State cabinet leader argued that we need to establish a "smart grid" that has "self healing" features. I am not a technocrat, so I'm not sure what he means. But one thing is for sure—we can't run away in the family van to San Francisco. The State of Hawai'i has amassed a Hurricane Relief Fund of around $185 million in the event that casualty insurance companies decide not to cover hurricanes. Our solons and others want to apply these funds to the current deficit and/or to any number of politically attractive purposes. That is a no-no in my book. The next hurricane is likely soon.

3. Water Shortages

   We have plenty of water most of the time. But we do not have plenty of storage. Year after year here in Kula, Maui, we suffer from drought. We need to build reservoirs, and we need to share resources across our regional systems. Upcountry Maui residents whose names are on the "slower than molasses" water-meter wait list must unify and lobby for equal treatment with other County water users, including obtaining funds for pumping. An effort of this nature can be reached through website www.umla.ws.

4. Oil Dependence

   We must find alternative sources of energy and not continue to rely on processed fossil fuel for ninety percent of our energy needs. Most of this oil comes from Indonesia and some from Alaska. We need to continue efforts to establish ocean gradient, solar, geothermal, bio-fuel, and wind power.

Other Major Areas of Concern

O'ahu Mass Transit

For a long time Hawai'i has indulged in a love affair with the automobile. There's never been enough money to match Southern California in building freeways, however. In 1960 and 1961 I offered legislative initiatives for mass transit in East O'ahu. State transportation officials laughed and said, "Hawai'i commuters would never ride trains." Yet now the successors of those same bureaucrats are actively seeking to build a multi-BILLION-dollar train system from Kapolei to downtown Honolulu. It is now late in the game, and revenues from the special 0.5 percent add-on to the general excise tax are lagging badly. The project needs federal money, too, and who knows how much of that is left after the recent bailouts and the Obama/Democrat-led congressional spending spree. The price tag of this project is enormous, and it leaves most of O'ahu's commuters without service.

Its biggest supporter seems to be Honolulu Mayor Mufi Hannemann, who also is running for governor. You can surely guess which of these efforts will receive priority attention.

The Hawai'i Superferry

Since the early days of the automobile the people of our islands have visualized a ferry system that would enable them to transport cars (and people and goods) across our sea channels. In the late fifties the Hawai'i Democratic party argued in favor of a government-owned and -operated ferry system similar to that of Washington and Alaska. Democrat John Hulten made it his major issue and rode it into the presidency of the State Senate.

Our House transportation committee in the early sixties looked into the Hulten plan (and others) in detail and concluded that such a system was too expensive and "too rough" on passengers. The latter conclusion refers of course to our notorious Moloka'i and Alenuihaha Channels. The only time I have ever experienced seasickness was as a boy of twelve aboard a sampan called the *Ehukai* while crossing the Moloka'i Channel.

Seaflight operated high-speed hydrofoils in Hawaiian waters during the seventies. These vessels were oriented toward tourists. They didn't carry cars.

But the Hawai'i Superferry, which burst upon the inter-island scene in the early 2000s, was a new kind of "cat"—a huge catamaran with twin hulls, each one the length of a football field and a half. It could carry 866 passengers and 282 vehicles. It had been built and was later operated by a private enterprise, but from start to finish Superferry was engaged with government at many levels.

The vessel offered for this service, programmed for Kaua'i and Maui initially, was the *Alaka'i*. (A second vessel, the *Huakai*, was scheduled for completion in 2009 but succumbed to the ultimate blow delivered by Hawai'i's Supreme Court against Superferry operations). John F. Lehman, who had served as Secretary of the Navy during the Reagan administration, was the biggest single investor in the system. Opponents of the ferry complained about Lehman's military connections and potential use of the ferries for Stryker forces. Senator Dan Inouye's chairmanship of the Senate defense appropriations committee also received criticism for funding facilities that aided the ferry system. A former Hawaiian Air executive, John Garibaldi, led the initial effort to establish the Superferry, but he was ultimately replaced by former CINCPAC Admiral Thomas Fargo. The presence of Fargo helped stir the anti-military opposition.

Three major fronts developed in the fight to establish this interisland service—the public relations front, the operational front, and the legal front.

The State Supreme Court announced its first ruling on the Superferry August 23, 2007. The court said that the state must conduct an environmental study on its state harbor improvement. Writing for the unanimous court, Associate Justice James Duffy said in part: "The exemption [to an environmental study] was erroneously granted as the State Department of Transportation (DOT) considered only the physical improvements to Kahului Harbor in isolation and *did not consider the secondary impacts on the environment that may result from the use of the Hawai'i Superferry.*" Attorney Isaac Hall, representing Maui environmental protection organizations, asserted that "This means that the State has to look at a project as a whole, and not just at the isolated parts." But should the requirement for environmental study extend that far? The State was merely *improving a pier facility*, not operating the ferry itself. Moreover, commercial water carriers such as Young Brothers Tug & Barge have plied waters of all the islands without an environmental impact study (EIS) for years. Given these facts, one could hardly find fault with Governor Lingle for "guessing wrong" and allowing the Superferry to go forward without an EIS. Protesting groups alleged that the State's decision to waive the EIS requirement had in fact been made by the Governor's chief of staff, Bob Awana, and by the Superferry executives.

The public relations and operational issues came into play just three days after the Hawai'i Supreme Court's ruling, triggered by a massive protest at Nawiliwili Harbor as the *Alaka'i* sought to make its first landing with passengers and vehicles. Observers assert that at least 1,500 Kaua'i residents deployed to the area. A number of them went into the water on surfboards, boogie boards, canoes, and various other watercraft, and some as swimmers. The U.S. Coast Guard attempted to control these protestors and made many arrests, but they were overwhelmed. The *Alaka'i* made port late in the evening, and passengers were abused verbally as they disembarked.

The greeting on Maui was nowhere near as aggressive. Superferry operations for our island, after a few traffic adjustments, proceeded normally.

Not long after the Kaua'i protests the issue was stirred again by Maui Circuit Judge Joseph Cardoza when he ruled that the Superferry could not operate while the EIS was being prepared.

This obstruction caused Governor Lingle to call the Legislature into special session, during which the legislators passed a statute that allowed ferry operations to proceed even though the EIS was still being prepared. In identifying the Superferry the drafters of the legislation (called "Act 2") spoke of a "large capacity ferry vessel." With this language they were hoping to create statutory provisions sufficiently broad in scope—in other words, provisions that would not seem to be exclusive and "special" only to the Superferry.

Polls taken around this time showed that more than eighty percent

of the population of the state favored the ferry. This support was less on the neighbor islands than on Oʻahu.

But public support carried no weight at the Hawaiʻi Supreme Court. As soon as they could get their hands on the matter, the justices shot down Act 2. They ruled that the bill was unconstitutional in that it called for special rather than general legislation—e.g., it was designed for the benefit of one ferry company and not all ferry companies. The decision came out while the Legislature was in session, so ferry supporters hurried to save the company from this potentially fatal blow. A former attorney general under Governor Ariyoshi, Michael Lilly, was the most prominent in this effort. In an article in *Building Industry Magazine* March 29, 2009, Lilly said: "The legislature could enact simple language making clear that environmental laws do not extend to secondary impacts as follows: 'Significant Effect' does not include or require consideration of 'secondary impacts' on the environment that may result from governmental action. The latter provision is retroactive to enactment of this chapter."

Lilly engaged in discussion with Senate President Colleen Hanabusa and other key legislators but was unable to obtain support for his proposal. Lilly notes in his article that Attorney General Mark Bennett agreed that his proposal was one of five or more solutions to the Superferry dilemma that would have fixed the problem. Despite being so advised, Hanabusa failed to act. Voters might remember this failure when they consider her quest to go to Washington, D.C., as Abercrombie's successor in the U.S. House.

What did all this push-pull and legal mumbo-jumbo mean to "Joe Sixpack"—a.k.a. Mr. Average Hawaiʻi resident?

The demise of the Superferry was a financial disaster for the average Island family. Take an O'ahu family of four desirous of a week's vacation on Maui. Doing the numbers roughly: round trip on the Superferry for four people at $49 each would have cost $196 RT. The vehicle would have cost $114 RT. Thus, the entire trip would have totaled $300 plus taxes. The family could have loaded its vehicle with "stuff"—surfboards, boogie boards, fishing gear, cooking supplies, food, Christmas gifts, you name it. But now the same family of four has to fly Hawaiian Airlines, our major air carrier. One-way fares range between $58 to $120 each person under current practices. Estimating on the low side, let's say airfares to and from Maui would cost Joe and his family $60 each segment, or $240 times two, a total of $480. Now add the cost of a rental car—an average $38 per day for seven days, costing $266. Add fees for the check-in bags, an estimated $40. Mr. Consumer Sixpack, read it and weep. Superferry: under $400. By air: over $700.

And the TV pundits wonder why blue-collar people have little use for environmentalists and their lawyers!

Overall, the scoreboard reads: For those who view the Superferry through the prisms of anti-militarism, aggressive environmental protectionism, and nativism—a major victory. For those who want to travel with their families and friends and their cars for vacations on other islands, thus avoid increasing costs of air travel, luggage fees, and rental car expense—a major defeat.

The polls showed that an overwhelming number of our citizens were in the second group, losers once again.

I would therefore recommend a state policy that supports the creation of a modern interisland ferry system by private enterprise in partnership with public agencies (and adoption of Mike Lilly's proposed EIS statutory change). In the absence of private-enterprise interest in such a system, the State would explore a State-funded and operated interisland ferry system. Thus it would provide a marine highway in lieu of an exclusively on-land state highway system.

Throughout the battle for the Hawai'i Superferry, Governor Lingle remained strongly in favor of its operations. Had she agreed in the beginning to delay operation until an EIS was prepared, the end might have been different. Then again the Superferry was able to prove itself through actual operations. Projects such as these require steadfast leadership and commitment. It is clear that the legislative majority also recognized that the ferry was a step forward for bringing the people our state closer together.

Education

Among the fifty U.S. states only Hawai'i has a single public school system for children K-12 statewide. The system was founded during territorial days and survived review in early statehood days. The results from this system are both good and bad.

Everyone is supposed to be treated equally, no favorites allowed. But it doesn't work that way in practice. The better public schools are located—surprise!—in wealthy residential districts. And poorly performing schools are in poorer districts. The system has a way of pulling students down to a common denominator. Certain schools receive more money than others as a result of the efforts of legislators.

The State school board is elected and made up of dedicated people, but they are not responsible for *raising* the money for the system, only for *spending* it. They must beg the legislators for appropriations. Thus, educational accountability is split between the Legislature, the school board, and the governor. As a consequence, most national surveys of school systems rank Hawai'i near the lowest of all states. The federal No Child Left Behind Act responses in Hawai'i are miserable. School after school reports that its goals are not met. The Democrat-controlled Legislature's answer is always to throw money at the system rather than reform it. As a result, improvement is insignificant.

In her first successful gubernatorial campaign (2002) Linda Lingle proposed decentralization through the establishment of locally elected school boards that would replace the statewide Board of Education. She ran into a Democrat-led legislative stone wall. She rarely talks about this issue today.

One hopeful sign is the interest being shown in charter schools. Regions that have charter schools like them.

Vouchers (to be used to purchase enrollment at private schools) have yet to be tried due to the massive opposition they generate with the politically powerful teachers union (HSTA). Yet it would make sense to utilize the resources of the many very good private schools on all islands and give kids from poorer areas a shot at a first-class education.

When I was in the Legislature, I introduced a bill that would have decentralized control by transforming existing "school complexes"— regional combinations of elementary, middle, and high schools—to formal school districts. The bill provided each complex with an elected school board, and it gave these boards the power to impose a school tax to be billed along with property taxes. This would have given district residents a means of contributing financially to the goal of better education for their children. Some bright legislator should look up this bill and reintroduce it.

Health

Our state is known for its concern for its citizens. It has not waited for Hillary Care, Obama Care, or any other federal care. Early on our Legislature passed a bill requiring that Hawai'i's businesses carry health insurance for their employees who work twenty or more hours a week (the Hawai'i Prepaid Healthcare Act of 1974). I voted for this bill and would do so again today.

Among those implementing this bill and paying for or providing health care have been two large health firms, HMSA and the Kaiser Permanente organization. HMSA is a community-based nonprofit organization that pays a major portion of the bill from the doctor of your choice. Kaiser provides its own doctors, and you pay for their services through membership fees.

Our state also has a comprehensive governmental hospital health care delivery system. There are State hospitals on all of the major islands. Maui Memorial Medical Center is one of the biggest and most profitable of these institutions, and it has therefore sought and received more autonomy. However, the State system is in major financial deficit at this writing.

I am currently a member of a State commission that plays a key role within our state's health system. It is called the Statewide Health Coordinating Council. We review applications from a myriad of health providers seeking to meet explicit written criteria. Our recommendations for approval or disapproval go to the last step in the process—an executive in the State health department who sits in our hearings.

The debate on Obama Care is taking place as this is written. I am satisfied with the medical coverage that I have and fear that it will be taken away by the programs being proposed in Washington. So I say— leave my health care alone! A moderate bipartisan bill focusing on tort reform, medical savings accounts, and incentives for young people and the poor to obtain health insurance might get my support.

Karl Rove, former deputy chief of staff to President George Bush summed it up this way: the Democrats "are scaring voters by proposing a takeover of health care that spends too much money, creates too much debt, gives Washington too much power, and takes too much decision-making away from doctors and patients."

Native Hawaiian Issues

The Hawaiian Renaissance is a touchy, albeit important issue for our people. We who were born and reared in these beautiful islands often question the award of special benefits and privileges to fellow citizens simply because they have Hawaiian blood. I will not attempt to cover the Hawaiian Renaissance story comprehensively, but a book that deals with politics of Hawai'i today would be incomplete without some reference to the events of recent years in the Hawaiian community and the impact thereof on the broader population of these islands.

I feel fortunate to have had close friends of Hawaiian ancestry while growing up and attending Punahou School and thereafter. My classmate and lifelong friend Kurt Johnson was one of a kind. His mother, Rachael Johnson, introduced me to matters Hawaiian, as she taught me songs on the 'ukulele and spoke of earlier days. She was a wonderfully warm and caring lady who lived the aloha spirit and demonstrated down-to-earth wisdom.

Another part-Hawaiian friend in Punahou football and politics was James K. (Jimmy) Clark, whose switch to the Democratic Party in the late sixties inspired one of my major speeches in 1969. I was also close to James "Fitch" Dwight, who was our quarterback at Punahou in 1945. When I injured my leg during a summer break from college, Fitch was always available to provide both transportation and friendship. He and Kurt were ushers in my first wedding in 1952.

Modern pro-Hawaiian reforms first took shape with the creation of the Office of Hawaiian Affairs (OHA) by the 1978 State Constitutional Convention. Part-Hawaiian politicians such as John Waihe'e were active in this process. Waihe'e went on to win election as governor over my old nemesis "Cec" Heftel in 1986. I hardly had time to give a cheer from Maui before political activists in the Hawaiian cause raised new issues at Washington Place.

As former Governor Cayetano describes it: "When I became governor in December 1994, Hawaiian political activism was in full stride, stronger and more militant than ever. There was obviously great pride among Hawaiians, especially among the young, as they wielded their growing political power in trying to shape issues important to them. But by then, hubris, arrogance, hypocrisy and racism had made inroads into the Hawaiian movement and would take a toll in eroding the once widespread pool of support expressed by non-Hawaiians on Hawaiian issues in the 1978 election.... Most of the major changes Hawaiian activists sought were not possible without the support of the local community, a point many would soon ignore" (*Ben*, page 366).

Even before this more aggressive period, I often received criticism from part-Hawaiians for my efforts to protect residential lessees from the excesses of lessors. I was a land-reform activist, and Bishop Estate (benefactor of native Hawaiians) was a big lessor in my political district, leasing many thousands of acres for home sites. My critics sought to perpetuate Bishop Estate's residential leasehold land program and the financial contributions that lessees were inadvertently making to Kamehameha Schools. Hence, the critics opposed my efforts to democratize home ownership.

Ironically, the Land Reform Act of 1967, which provided for sales in fee to residential lessees in a "development tract" under various conditions, brought millions of dollars to Bishop Estate. This windfall enabled the Bishop Estate trustees, chosen in those days by the Hawai'i Supreme Court, to construct branch schools on the neighbor isles while also modernizing the earlier Kamehameha schools and expanding their outreach programs on Oʻahu.

In 1995 the *Wall Street Journal* estimated the Bishop Estate's endowment at ten billion dollars, greater than the endowments of Harvard and Yale!

Not all of the politically influenced trustee appointments were bad. Former Honolulu councilman and political boss "Matsy" Takabuki invested in Goldman Sachs and made big bucks for the Estate. However, politically appointed trustees used some of these same proceeds for their own purposes.

Trustee appointments reflected the strength of the Democratic political machine that extended into the State Supreme Court. Appointments made by the 1990s Supreme Court included Democrat powerhouses Speaker Henry Peters, Senate President Dickie Wong, Department of Education Superintendent Lokelani Lindsay (from Maui), Governor John Waiheʻe's close associate Gerard Jervis, and Honolulu City Councilman Matsuo Takabuki. (For the full story of the politicization of the Bishop Estate and its redemption, see Sam P. King and Randall Roth's book *Broken Trust*.) Fortunately, the Cayetano administration tackled this insider corruption and ultimately succeeded in deposing the offending trustees. By 1999 the Supreme Court was stripped of its incestuous powers over the selection of these trustees.

The Hawaiian sovereignty movement rests on the claim that the overthrow of Queen Liliʻuokalani in 1893 was illegal and, therefore, native Hawaiians are entitled to restitution. Extreme elements of this movement demand independence for Hawaiʻi and an entirely new governmental structure. Moderate elements want to protect existing programs for native Hawaiians and take control of the crown lands. The Office of Hawaiian Affairs has demanded the authority to levy taxes, write ordinances, control national parks, administer justice, and impose rents on military uses. But a new Hawaiian nation would demand a lot more. Thus, a brief look at the "overthrow" and pending legislation to further native Hawaiian goals is in order.

While I have read a fair amount of Hawaiian history (mostly Daws and Kuykendall), I don't claim expertise in the subject. However, recently I read a privately published book by my friend and former distinguished law colleague James S. Campbell, who (I believe) does a particularly good job recounting the lead-up to, and the circumstances of, the "overthrow" of Queen Liliʻuokalani by the haole-dominated Annexation Club, which was led by those Campbell aptly calls "the missionary boys." (See pages 65-80 of *Country of Origin, the Sandwich Islands* (ISBN 1-4196-6438-. Order from www.booksurge.com.)

At page 74 Campbell gets to the crux of the overthrow issue: "Very few people (either native or foreign) had any idea of what was going on in Honolulu…. The whole thing happened so rapidly that it was over before the Hawaiians had a chance to protest. Had they voted on the change of government there is no doubt in my mind that the queen would have been retained anyway. I think almost everyone feels great sorrow for the Hawaiians but no one can figure out what to do that would favor them without running into the equal protection clause of the 14th amendment to the Constitution."

Campbell adds: "When Liliʻuokalani took the crown, the party was almost over [i.e., for the Kingdom of Hawaiʻi]. The only source of new revenue she could think of was to regulate and tax opium and gambling. When she renounced the Constitution of 1887 and got only Sam Parker and one other minister to adopt her absolute monarchy, the kingdom collapsed from within because it was no longer real." He adds, "Today our Hawaiian community believes the kingdom was overthrown by the United States, [but] I have found no evidence that [U.S.] Minister Stevens actively conspired in any way with any annexationist to overthrow the kingdom. In hindsight, I personally think [Stevens's] recognition of the provisional government was too hasty, but one would have had to have been there to make such a judgment…. A constitutional monarchy could have survived as an independent nation, just as the Kingdom of Hawaiʻi and the Republic survived, but not an absolute monarchy" (Campbell pages 78-79).

Campbell's analysis of the overthrow differs sharply from that of Jon Van Dyke in his weighty tome *Who Owns the Crown Lands of Hawaiʻi?* Van Dyke and his team of researchers/writers do a superior job tracing the history of the crown lands through various stages of the Hawaiian monarchy of the nineteenth century, a period when Hawaiʻi increasingly reflected the influence of expatriate Americans and immigrants from Europe and Asia. Van Dyke argues that native Hawaiians were still in political control of their nation during this period. He cites their voting control right up to the end of their monarchy despite a threefold increase in non-native population in the last half of that century. Of course, the bulk of that population influx, originating in Asia, was not allowed to vote. This latter period also reflected the increased influence of agriculturists and businesspeople from the United States. Van Dyke details the Hawai'i Supreme Court decision in 1864—translated into a statute in 1865 by the kingdom's unicameral Legislature—declaring that the crown lands were inalienable and that they belonged to the office, not the person, of the monarchy. When the Republic of Hawai'i was created in 1894, it assumed title to approximately 971,463 acres of crown lands, valued at that time at approximately 2.3 million dollars. These same lands have since been owned in succession by the Territory of Hawai'i, the United States, and since statehood by the State of Hawai'i.

As for the overthrow of the queen in 1893, Van Dyke clearly believes U.S. actions—particularly the landing of troops from the *USS Boston*—tipped the scale toward the revolutionists and against Lili'uokalani. He quotes U.S. Secretary of State W.Q. Gresham's statement that "There is no doubt that their presence [i.e., American armed forces] provided a psychological support for the revolutionists." Van Dyke also notes the early recognition given the provisional government of the revolutionists by American officials.

With a totally different view Malia Hill, in a Grassroots Institute of Hawai'i release of November 12, 2008, debunks many of the factual representations made by Van Dyke. She charges that he depended on "highly biased reports of the Hawaiian revolution that have since been discredited," that he "ignor[ed] the democratic concerns that led to the revolution and annexation," and that he placed "unwarranted" stress on the legal weight of the Apology Resolution of 1993. She also charges Van Dyke with "a willful attempt to avoid the inescapable truth that no continuing and recognized [native Hawaiian] government has existed since Lili'uokalani." She emphasizes that there were many non-native citizens of the kingdom (Asians and others who could not vote and others with no Hawaiian blood) who were born and raised in the Kingdom of Hawai'i.

The Akaka Bill
(a.k.a. Native Hawaiian Government Reorganization Act)

The Akaka Bill (S. 1011) now pending in U.S. Congress attempts to equate Hawaiians with Indian tribes in order to allow them to establish their own "nation." The bill envisions that this new Hawaiian nation, once established, would then negotiate with the State government for the transfer to it of the crown lands and funds to meet its goals.

The attempt to mesh American citizenship with a nation-within-a-nation concept is a lawyers' dream. Never-ending litigation will ensue.

The main objective of the Akaka Bill, according to U.S. Congressman Neil Abercrombie, is the transfer of land and money from the ownership of the State, where it benefits all Hawaiʻi's people, to ownership by the Akaka Bill's newly established Hawaiian nation governing body. There it will benefit only qualified native Hawaiians. Transfer of the crown lands to the restored Hawaiian nation would be a predictable consequence if the Akaka Bill is enacted. Unbelievably, there are no provisions for a referendum by the voters of Hawaiʻi on the concept of the Akaka Bill before congressional action is taken. Nor is there provision for such a referendum on ultimately negotiated agreements between the State and the Hawaiian nation.

Looking at the legal issues of Akaka, one runs smack into the 14th Amendment equal protection clause. This clause makes it illegal for any U.S. state to "deny to any person within its jurisdiction the equal protection of the laws." The Supreme Court has also ruled that the 5th Amendment makes it illegal for the federal government to deny equal protection as well. "Equal protection" can be defined in a number of ways, but no matter how it is defined, it always applies to situations in which people are treated differently because of race or ethnicity.

Rice v. Cayetano 528 U.S. 495 (2000) contains a specific ruling by the U.S. Supreme Court that native Hawaiians are an ethnic group, and that preferential treatment due to membership in that group is unlawful. *Rice's* main holding was that restricting voting in OHA elections to native Hawaiians violates the 15th Amendment's prohibition against race-based voting qualifications. (The Court did not rule on the 14th Amendment arguments raised by counsel.)

So, if one matches the constitutional provisions with the rulings to date, it appears that Congress cannot pass a law that gives native Hawaiians the right to organize a nation that then claims additional special rights and privileges. As the Akaka Bill attempts to do this, it is clearly unconstitutional.

A counter argument has been advanced that rests upon some painfully stretched legal analysis. Its proponents argue that since Congress has the power to regulate commerce with foreign nations and the states "and with the Indian tribes," it therefore has the power to create new tribes—the native Hawaiians, for example. Why tribes can be created but not foreign nations or states (which are also mentioned in the commerce clause) is a question that is not resolved by the advocates for this position).

Other attempts to put a legal foundation under the Akaka Bill rest on soft sand. The definition of "native Hawaiian" in the bill is extremely broad. A single tribe would have to include 400,000 native Hawaiians spread out in Hawai'i (250,000) California (60,000) and the rest of states (100,000). This would be larger than any previously recognized tribe. Moreover, native Hawaiians have a far more mixed ethnicity than do Indian tribes. The majority of people who claim Hawaiian ancestry have a very low quantum of Hawaiian blood. Large numbers of them have never even visited Hawai'i!

Of late, advocates for the Akaka Bill have heavily emphasized the 1993 U.S. Congressional Apology Resolution (apologizing for the overthrow of Lili'uokalani). But that resolution ignores the facts recounted in Jim Campbell's careful analysis. The Apology Resolution, moreover, completely ignores the findings of the Native Hawaiian Study Commission of 1983, which found no basis for reparations.

Significantly, the Apology Resolution has been diminished by the recent case of *Hawai'i v. Office of Hawaiian Affairs* 129 S.Ct 1436, in which the U.S. Supreme Court vacated an injunction issued by the Hawai'i Supreme Court against the sale of any ceded lands until the claims of the Native Hawaiians had been resolved. Our Hawai'i court had relied upon the "whereas clauses" of the Apology Resolution as the basis for its injunction. But the U.S. Supreme Court would have none of that argument and held that "whereas clauses" could not bear that kind of decisive weight and did not therefore alter the provisions of the Admissions Act regarding such lands.

Accordingly, attorneys on the negative side of the Akaka issue believe that this recent OHA case is as much a landmark as *Rice v. Cayetano*. The court in OHA ruled that the Republic of Hawai'i ceded absolute title to government and crown lands "free and clear from any trust of or concerning the same, and from all claims of any nature whatsoever, upon the rents, issues, and profits thereof that arose before 1898." It is clear that the 1.4 million acres of ceded lands are held in trust for all of the people of Hawai'i.

Akaka advocates claim that the bill will protect existing race-based programs and hence Hawaiian culture. But how does one fail to give recognition to the contributions of non-native Hawaiian residents to that culture over the past two hundred years? The missionaries put the Hawaiian language into writing. Celestial navigation was reintroduced by non-Hawaiians. One need not be of Hawaiian blood to play the 'ukulele like Ohta-San. Do these non-Hawaiians deserve some lands because they contributed to Hawai'i's culture? The Akaka Bill falls short again.

Also noteworthy, the United States Commission on Civil Rights voiced its views to U.S. Senate and House leaders by letter dated August 28, 2009. The letter includes the following statement:

"We do not believe Congress has the constitutional authority to 'reorganize' racial or ethnic groups into dependent sovereign nations unless those groups have a long and continuous history of separate self-governance."

The commission adds: "In essence it [the Akaka Bill] is an attempted end-run around the Supreme Court's decisions in *Rice v. Cayetano* and *City of Richmond v. J.A. Croson Co.* The Constitution, however, cannot be circumvented so easily."

Although the legal arguments that it is unconstitutional are persuasive, I also think the Akaka Bill fails on broader grounds. Akaka fails on the basis of policy.

Hawai'i is a special place where people from all over the world have come together. Some come to visit and only learn a bit of our culture. Over time, though, these visitors constitute a huge number of people. We who were born here without Hawaiian blood are integrated into a common culture—a mix of the customs and practices of the Polynesian, the Asian, the non-Polynesian Pacific Islander, and the haole/palagi (white American).

My extended family is typical of Hawai'i's families. My grandchildren are half haole and half Japanese. My wife is pure Portuguese. Her ancestors emigrated to Hawai'i from the Madeira islands in the late 1800s. My two sons are partly of missionary stock and can trace their heritage on their mother's side back to Amos Starr Cooke. My in-laws are a mix of Chinese, Japanese, Hawaiian, haole, and Portuguese. Would I dare to treat those with the Hawaiian blood differently from the others? Do they have special rights in our American community? Remember that race is often a divisive and destructive concept. Would you want to apply "affirmative action" in Hawai'i? Could you?

The bottom line is that Akaka's bill is race based, and we have never subscribed to legally enforceable special advantages to any race before. We are one people—an 'ohana made up of fathers, mothers, sisters, brothers, brothers-in-law, sisters-in-law, uncles and aunties (some by blood and countless others), cousins, and nephews. Our races are "all mix 'em up." This great 'ohana is thoroughly imbued with the aloha spirit and a deep love of these islands and all who live here.

Akaka advocates say their bill is necessary to protect some 180 federal programs that currently provide for native Hawaiian benefits. Yet it is very unlikely that the new government created under Akaka will include due process or equal protection provisions. The new native Hawaiian entity could discriminate at will among its own citizens!

When Hawai'i's citizens voted in favor of statehood in 1959, they approved Congress's Admission Act by a margin of 94 percent. The Admission Act guaranteed that the State of Hawai'i would consist of all the major islands and that its constitution would always be republican in form and not repugnant to the U.S. Constitution and the principles of the Declaration of Independence. There are some who say that the vote wasn't "pono" [proper] since there was no place on the ballot to vote for independence or commonwealth. These objectors have a point. But with fifty years of statehood behind us, it is a little late for this type of second-guessing.

Lastly, with respect to the crown lands issue, I could support using income from crown lands leases or sales for State social projects, economic assistance, and other existing programs which have the most likelihood of aiding the most needy of our citizens. Such assistance would automatically reach substantial numbers of native Hawaiians but not exclude other similarly impacted races. This approach would not engender opposition from the broad community.

On the other hand, if Congress enacts Akaka, it would divide the state without the consent of the people of Hawai'i. It would hand parts of the state to a new government of native Hawaiians, an unknown body, without any effort to obtain their consent, or ours, in advance.

The Akaka Bill, moreover, holds out false hopes to native Hawaiians. If enacted after years of claiming that it will create a promised land of taro and wine, what will be the reaction when it is shot down on constitutional grounds?*

I would favor bringing the Akaka Bill to a vote by our state electorate in a statewide referendum. The Akaka Bill should be submitted to a vote by U.S. Congress only after approval by the voters of Hawai'i.

Pacific Issues

Hawai'i's degree of involvement in Pacific Island issues over the years has fluctuated markedly. Hawaiian King David Kalākaua, egged on by his prime minister, Walter Murray Gibson, sent the Hawaiian warship *Kamiloa* into Micronesian waters in 1887 in an attempt to unify the then-non-colonized archipelagos under the Kingdom of Hawai'i. The expedition quickly flopped, and the fiasco led to the "Bayonet Constitution," which forced restraints on the behavior of the "Merry Monarch." That affair symbolizes the go-stop of Hawai'i-based interest in Micronesia, Melanesia, and Polynesia.

---

* As this book was being put to bed, word leaked out that the Obama administration had amended the bill to give the new governing Hawaiian authority *sovereignty* **before** negotiations similar to Indian tribes. This caused the governor and her attorney general to oppose the bill. That changed to support again through the adoption of amendments preserving the State's regulatory and criminal powers during negotiations. The odds thereupon switched in favor of overcoming the 60-vote procedural barrier. The bad news is the bill may pass. The good news is that the odds of a court victory by opponents haven't changed.

With encouragement from the late George Chaplain, editor of the *Honolulu Advertiser* (who preceded me on the South Pacific Commission), editorialist John Griffen wrote many a story about Pacific nations, their leaders, and their policies. We miss Griffen today, as the Pacific Islands coconut wireless is largely silent. Our national leaders have done little for Oceania and mostly have focused upon a policy of military "denial" of the area to other nations. The Japanese were our first major competitors in the Pacific; now they have been joined by the Koreans, the Chinese, and their Taiwan cousins in seeking economic expansion in the Pacific.

One constructive thing we could do to help Pacific Islanders would be to support establishment of tuna canneries in the areas where the migratory fish are actually being harvested by purse seiners. Today the fish are taken to Thailand or American Samoa to be canned. My friend and Punahou classmate Peter Wilson—long-time tuna guru, former head of fisheries for the Trust Territory, fisheries advisor to the Papua New Guinea government, and tuna cannery builder in the Maldives—will be glad to enlighten anyone desiring information on this prospect.

The National Scene

I supported Senator McCain in 2008 by acting as his Maui coordinator. Our efforts were primarily directed at raising money for expenditure in battleground states on the Mainland, as Hawai'i's four electoral votes had been pretty much written off for election purposes. Obama was born in Hawai'i and graduated from the same private prep school that I attended (Punahou School), so we had to buck local affinity. In my fundraising letter to Maui residents I warned of what we might expect with an Obama presidency—big spending, higher taxes, reduced security, recognition of radical regimes, liberal take-over of the Supreme Court, and investigation/rehash of various post-9/11 security actions by the Bush administration. But it was all for naught. We are now experiencing all of those things big-time, along with a comprehensive health care bill that reminds one of "Hillary Care" in the early nineties.

But there is hope for the Republican cause.

Increasingly polls are showing that support for Obama is slipping. Scott Brown's victory in Massachusetts is a bellwether of change in national politics.

The Republicans

Nationally, some of my party's leaders seem to be asserting themselves after an initial post-inauguration restraint on criticism of the new president. Sarah Palin's resignation from the governorship of Alaska received major media attention. She is bright and a strong campaigner. I believe she will run for president. Mitt Romney still looks strong. Huckabee is a good showman. Maybe Rudy Giuliani will re-surface. The GOP has roughly two years to build a standout contender.

Here at home the GOP challenge is even greater than it is nationally. To retain any semblance of political power, the Hawai'i GOP must retain the governorship now held by Linda Lingle. She will step down at the end of her term in November of 2010. Our leading candidate, Lieutenant Governor Duke Aiona, is already in the field raising money and setting up his organization. I would urge the party to concentrate on seeking seats in the State Senate to support and complement Aiona. He cannot be seen to be a loner down at the capitol. Both Duke and the GOP Senate candidates should develop a package of plans and policies which would build upon the record of the Lingle/Aiona Administration and, in particular, be responsive to the economic recession that is occurring in our state and to the various vulnerabilities discussed above. Viable alternatives are needed to the "big rat hole" (Mufi's train), and a renewed effort for an inter-island ferry should be promised. Duke needs to show that he was intimately involved in the Lingle Administration for the past eight years and that he knows how to govern. He must develop answers to our vulnerabilities and the broad issues stated above.

Our state party, like the national Republican Party, spends a lot of time arguing within itself. Conservatives bash moderates and vice versa to the applause of the Democrats and the mainstream media. The average voter could care less as to charges back and forth. I am still a moderate on social policy but have over time adopted views that are more conservative than those I held in my legislative days. For example, I oppose the "public option," the reduction of Medicare benefits, and other coercive and expensive aspects of the healthcare reform measure, and I support a "surge"—and with it a lot more troops—in Afghanistan. I believe the states must assert themselves when dealing with the federal government. I supported Senator McCain in 2008 and am even more convinced today than I was on election day that he would be a leader far superior to President Obama.

I am very concerned about the rapid slide into socialism and lack of fiscal restraint being exhibited by U.S. Congress and the White House. We need to protect our freedoms, reduce taxes, and encourage free enterprise. We should not kowtow to dictators nor allow radical nations such as Iran and North Korea to have nuclear weapons.

Some things in politics don't change very much, not fundamentally. So the GOP should look around in its files for Glenn Hudson's "Victory in 1970" plan and bring it up to date. On a swing through the Islands over a year ago Governor Lingle herself identified potential candidates. Party officials need to contact those people early on.

Special Congressional Election
(May 22, 2010)

As this book was in the final rewrite/design phase Hawai'i's First Congressional District (Waipahu to Makapu'u Pt. on O'ahu) was the site of a major winner-take-all, mail-in election that received national attention. The vacancy to be filled was that of Democrat Neil Abercrombie, who has represented the district since 1990. Abercrombie has had enough of Washington, D.C., and wants instead, to run the state when Republican incumbent governor Linda Lingle's term comes to an end at the end of 2010. The term at stake in the May 2010 special was only the unfilled term of Rep. Abercrombie, so the long term election to fill the seat for the usual two-year term will still occur in the fall of this year. Only one Republican since statehood has been elected to Congress in this district, Patricia F. Saiki. Pat served two terms (1986-1990) before taking on Dan Akaka for one of our Senate seats. The Republican candidate for the special election was young Honolulu attorney Charles Djou. Djou has served as a Honolulu City Councilman for eight years. His competitors were Democrats, State Senate President Colleen Hanabusa and former legislator and 2nd district Congressman, Ed Case. 317,000 ballots were mailed out and 170,312 cast for a 53.7% participation rate.

The results: Charles Djou 67, 610 votes (39.4%): Colleen Hanabusa 52,802 votes (30.8%), and Ed Case 47,391 votes (27.6%).

A lot of money was raised and spent. Djou raised $1.2 million. Hanabusa was second with a collection of over a million, while Case raised around $700,000. Djou ran a strong campaign and consistently cited his record as a no-tax-increase fiscal conservative who would vote that way in Congress. The two Democrats took different roads...with Hanabusa being the more traditional machine candidate (endorsed by Senator Inouye and leading Isle Democrats) and Case the more moderate, independent. As Case had bucked the machine several years ago when he ran against Akaka for the Senate, he did not have access to the union voters that his fellow Democrat had. Senator Inouye took personal umbrage when Case challenged his colleague Akaka, and has shown no signs of moderation since. Hawai'i's three surviving former governors, Ariyoshi, Waihe'e, and Cayetano, held a press conference in the final week in which they urged the electorate to vote for one of the Democrats while demonizing Djou. Negative ads appeared on TV from all sides, but more were run by the Democrat candidates and their Washington Congressional Campaign Committee, until the latter pulled out of the race after spending $314,000.

What all of this means won't be clear until the regular election for this seat is held in just a few months. But it is clear that Djou's sparkling victory has stimulated and inspired the Hawai'i Republican Party. It indicates, also, that Djou's message of fiscal concern at the national level hit home with Hawai'i's independent voters...a potent force. Hanabusa, by coming in a surprise second, has some momentum of her own to go with her support from the Inouye/union machine. That momentum increased markedly when Case announced the withdrawal of his candidacy at the State Democratic Party Convention May 30th. Arguably, Case put his party first and chose to fight another day. Meanwhile, Djou will probably put in more hours in a jet seat than the average fulltime pilot for United does during the next five months. Fortunately, he is young! By winning in November Djou could be the poster boy of a longer-term revival for our party. Hopefully, his success has improved the odds for gubernatorial candidate Duke Aiona, as well.

EPILOGUE

Our time capsule has come to the end of its journey. All that's left are appendices.

The first question I have for you, my reader, is this: Do we learn from history? The famous English poet Samuel Taylor Coleridge didn't think so. He said that experience is a "lantern on the stern, which shines only on the waves behind us." I disagree. I believe that an understanding of past events provides a framework within which new issues can be faced, issues that determine future courses of action.

I hope that the experiences I have described in prior pages will help to guide my grandchildren in meeting the challenges of modern life. It is those grandchildren who inspired me to write this book, which started out with a file title "Opa Reminisces" or "Grandfather Remembers."

My list of those who should receive thanks for their help in making this book happen begins with Paul Wood of Kula, Maui, an award-winning freelance writer. (You've often seen his articles about Hawai'i in the Hawaiian Airlines inflight magazine.) He also writes books (*False Confessions*, for one, is both funny and poignant) and teaches writing at our local campus of the University of Hawai'i. Paul has been my source of expertise on editing, presentation, and production. Without his kokua (help) I never would have made it.

Another irreplaceable person is Karen Bacon, a former islander who now lives in Ashland, Oregon. Karen designed the book piece by piece in preparation for Watermark's publication.

In 2006 my lifelong friend Keith J. Steiner of Honolulu wrote and published a quality coffee-table book (entitled *Hawai'i's Early Territorial Days*) that examined the relationship between Hawaiian postcards and Hawaiian history. I pestered him for information about the prospects of publishing my own story, and he responded with a wealth of data. As soon as Keith stepped in, my memoir-writing endeavor began to get serious.

Needless to say, nothing would have been accomplished on this project (or anything else) without the support, patience, and understanding of my loving wife Patty. We have much to be thankful for in our home high on Mt. Haleakalā, where no one can take away our fabulous view of four Hawaiian islands—West Maui, East Moloka'i, Lana'i, and (though partially blocked by a huge eucalyptus tree) Kaho'olawe.

So many people have assisted me in achieving positive results in my life that it is impossible to list them all, much less explain their individual contributions. I am, nevertheless, dedicating this book to the following individuals, without whose drive, determination, and constructive examples I wouldn't have achieved much of anything on the political scene or in my practice of law.

As to my law practice, I will always be grateful for the mentoring of V. Thomas Rice and Raymond "Tork" Torkildson during my years (1955 to 1960) with Moore, Torkildson, and Rice. Both have passed away. Tom gave me meaningful control over general practice cases and let me go for the gold with cases like the Survival Statute action, which I won in the Supreme Court over sizable odds (*Rohlfing v. Akiona*). Tork was a Harvard Law perfectionist who taught me how to write effective briefs. He was at heart a country boy from the Dakotas and had a wonderful sense of humor. After a martini or two he would put a bowl over his head to resemble a combat helmet and then regale his guests with stories from his days in the U.S. cavalry in France during World War II.

For their guidance during my work in American Samoa and the Pacific region I am deeply indebted to the late governor of American Samoa Peter Tali Coleman, his former lieutenant governor Li'a Tufele from the Manu'a Islands, and press representative Edward Scanlan.

Were it not for the challenging active-duty training provided by Captain Dale Everhart U.S.N., I would probably not have risen to the rank of captain (06). Dale and my last N.R.I.P. boss Rear Admiral Bob Tiernan,

Captains "Stu" Kuhn and E.C. Grayson of the San Francisco Bay region, and (of course) Barney Smith will always be my favorite naval-intelligence colleagues.

In Hawai'i politics one of the first individuals who helped me immensely was Henry K. Ho, a retired Navy civilian clerk. Together Henry and I walked the streets of Kaimukī, Pālolo, Maunalani Heights, 'Āina Haina, Niu, Hawai'i Kai, Kahala, and other places day in and day out in the early years of my political endeavors. When I was first elected in 1959, he served as my first office clerk in a makeshift office in the old National Guard armory.

Also on board every time I needed him in both civilian and military life was my dear friend Barnaby "Barney" Farrington Smith, captain in the U.S. Naval Reserve, who died prematurely at age fifty-seven during open-heart surgery. I wonder whether he gave me too much of his heart as my campaign manager, fundraiser, fellow Naval Reserve officer, and just plain longtime loyal friend dating back to our entry into the Navy in San Francisco and Officer Candidate School at Newport, Rhode Island.

Then there is Dan Ichinose, a life insurance specialist with Occidental Life. Pat Saiki, a Hilo native and wife of Dr. Stanley Saiki who later became Hawai'i's only Republican congresswoman—for two terms—recruited Dan to my cause when she helped me run for the State Senate in 1966. Dan was a "rock" in my two congressional and two Senate campaigns. He was the brother of well-known sports promoter "Sad Sam" Ichinose. Dan once decided he would turn the most Democratic precinct in my district in my favor. By election time he knew every voter in that district by first name! He was tireless and constantly upbeat.

Tom Nekota from the Farrington High School athletic department was my entree to heavily Democratic Kalihi in the all-out second congressional campaign. He will remain memorable as the leader of my "ground forces." He went on to serve a term on the Honolulu City Council before drowning near Ala Moana Park in 2008.

I will long be grateful for the sound advice and counsel I received from Ed Brennan, head of Gold Bond Stamps and former campaign manager for Mayor Neal S. Blaisdell. Likewise for the fundraising leadership of Frank Manaut, who retired as Bank of Hawai'i president, for Castle & Cooke executive George Miyasaka, and for "Sig" Kagawa of Occidental Life Insurance.

High on my short list is Barbara Marumoto-Coons, who still serves Hawai'i as a state representative. Barbara recruited a volunteer group of *akamai* (savvy) women who, in time, filled various positions in my Senate office and campaigns. She played the role of "Sparky" Matsunaga with skill and humor when we rehearsed for the debate with him on public television in 1972, and she provided necessary leadership when I terminated our paid consultant from Seattle very late in the '76 campaign for Congress. She was at my side in various leadership positions during my last four years in the House. She does everything well and, as I like to brag, still carries a taste of the "Rohlfing brand" in the Legislature today.

I also acknowledge my debt to the late Hannibal Tavares, who as mayor of Maui County hired me to serve as his corporation counsel after Patty and I had moved to Maui. Hannibal was a big man in body, word, and deed—all of which he matched with a big heart.

Last but not by any means least, I honor my parents. Ted and Kathryn Rohlfing, immigrants from Placerville and Oakland, California, to faraway Hawai'i in the early 1900s, were hardworking, down-to-basics, good citizens. As parents they were firm but fair. They expected me to achieve academically and to be a civilized person. Early on they discussed worldly affairs with me, and they taught me important fundamentals about service to family, state, and nation. They set high moral standards by example through the way they lived. I have had much to live up to.

Who could have asked for anything more?

Aloha pumehana,
Frederick W. Rohlfing
Kula, Maui, Hawai'i 2010

APPENDIX ONE

A SUMMARY ANALYSIS:

THE ROHLFING
1976 CONGRESSIONAL CAMPAIGN

Alf Pratte was a *Honolulu Star-Bulletin* reporter for a number of years. In the early 1970s he was hired to head the Senate Republican Office. That office provided staff support to all Republican State senators. I asked him to take leave from this job and to "moonlight" for me in my second congressional campaign in 1976, for which I offered to pay him the paltry monthly sum of one thousand dollars.

A month after the campaign ended, Pratte produced a fifteen-page memorandum reviewing the campaign. Pratte, who was a member of the LDS (Mormon) church, went on to become a professor at Brigham Young University in Provo, Utah.

Highlights from Pratte's comprehensive evaluation follow. I have edited Pratte's text extensively. Where I have something to add, I have placed my own comments inside [square brackets].

Pratte begins thus:

> This memo is designed simply to outline some of the
> good and bad points of the most successful campaign ever
> waged by a Republican candidate for congressional office in
> the State of Hawai'i. [Pat Saiki was to take over this title a few
> years later by winning the seat, which she held only for two
> years before attempting unsuccessfully to move up to the U.S.
> Senate.]
> Overview: The Rohlfing 1976 campaign can be described
> as a congressional race in which a Republican with modest

funding "did as well as might be expected" against a wealthy and exposed Democrat businessman in a predominantly Democrat state in the face of a state and national Democrat landslide…. With a little more money and some luck [and a better decision-making structure] Rohlfing might have won. There is strong evidence had the Rohlfing campaign maintained the aggressive and hard-hitting theme it had utilized throughout the primary, Rohlfing could have defeated Cecil Heftel. From the beginning, however, the Rohlfing campaign was characterized by inconsistent decision-making, shifting of strategy and lack of funds. *It ended by being engulfed in one of the largest media blitzes ever seen in Hawai'i.* Heftel's campaign, meanwhile, has been described as the most expensive ever conducted in the U.S. [for congressional office].

Decision-Making

[Pratte describes the interplay in campaigns between amateur volunteers, professional media people, and candidates. He notes that an outside consultant was hired early on to overcome the "problem of objectivity."]

The consultant hired by the Rohlfing campaign was C. Montgomery ("Gummie") Johnson of Olympia, Washington. [Johnson was Ed Brennan's choice, and Brennan was my chief fundraiser. We paid Johnson three thousand dollars a month plus expenses. His fees totaled approximately forty thousand dollars in all.] Johnson and Rohlfing had a relationship of trust and confidence [for most of the primary campaign period], but Johnson's relationship with campaign coordinator Barbara Marumoto and many volunteers deteriorated progressively over time. Decision-making gradually shifted to a strategy committee headed by State senator Mary George and including Rohlfing, Luann Seigle of the advertising agency, Pratte, and campaign manager Dan Ichinose. [The makeup of this committee evolved in the final days with the addition of Walter Dods as new chair, Stuart Ho, Stan Hong, and Jack Kellner.]

The turning point in the decision-making process came following the primary, when Johnson proposed a newspaper tabloid for distribution to 185,000 homes which contrasted Rohlfing and Heftel as part of Johnson's "positive-negative" campaign plan. No member of the strategy committee liked the mock-up. There was particular sensitivity that we were making the same error Doi had made in his run for mayor against Fasi—being aggressively negative. The committee scrapped the tabloid and opted for a number of positive ads to be developed by a subcommittee made up of George, Pratte, and Seigle. From this point on, Johnson lost nearly all influence in decision-making. [I terminated Johnson shortly after the aforesaid meeting.]

Decisions were made [thereafter] with a minimum of objective factual data. The strongest personality—usually George, Rohlfing, or Dods—prevailed. Ironically, we saw the committee phoning Dods on vacation in Mexico City for input while ignoring the retained expert, Johnson, completely.

General Theme of the Campaign

The key problem [was] "schizophrenia" over the theme of the campaign.

It was determined by Johnson and agreed by Rohlfing ["acquiesced in" would be better terminology] that he would run a "positive-negative" campaign. No Republican could possibly win in a Democrat state unless he conducted an aggressive campaign, hitting Heftel on what Johnson's survey showed—namely, that the electorate did not approve of Heftel's money, power, and abrasive TV personality. Rohlfing had already criticized Heftel for not living up to statements [made on television] by Heftel that he wouldn't run for Congress unless he sold his TV stations. Rohlfing opened his campaign headquarters across from Ala Moana Shopping Center under a mock TV tower attached to his headquarters. He made a full financial disclosure and challenged Heftel to do likewise. Heftel responded that he couldn't understand why he was challenged for being successful. The numerous news releases and impromptu speeches prepared by Pratte and Mary George received much less coverage than Rohlfing's challenge to the millionaire Democrat's powerful communications position. Rohlfing's campaign workers—such as

Ichinose, Nekota, and Luke—however, began to complain that the local vote was "being turned off" by the attacks on Heftel's wealth and broadcast holdings.

On the Friday before the [general] election Pratte reported that he had had a conversation with Frank Fasi. Fasi claimed he had seen polls showing Rohlfing trailing Heftel by ten points with independent Hoshijo starting to take votes from Heftel. Fasi praised the early [Rohlfing] campaign and said, "You cannot win without an aggressive attack." Fasi hooted at Rohlfing's person-to-person campaign. He said he had to laugh at candidates who get up at the break of dawn to meet workers in the fields [and rely on house-to-house contacts]. "I never did that. I stayed in bed. I had breakfast downtown [with his cronies]. But I made sure I was on the six o'clock news. And I made sure I had TV advertising. That's the only way to win nowadays."

Media Advertising

Rohlfing never had much of a chance against a millionaire candidate who literally bought the office by spending three times as much on advertising. Heftel also had the advantage of using his station [Channel 9] for a number of years to his own personal advantage. Even so, Rohlfing's TV advertising could have been more effective. Three of the four ads showed Rohlfing carrying out legislative duties [walking through corridors in the State Capitol in one of them.] Another showed a meeting with people at a backyard luʻau. Rohlfing was not shown speaking. The ads were too short and too sterile when they needed to communicate with local voters [In TV spots Heftel was the guy on the beach—and I was the guy in the Capitol in a suit.] Rohlfing's "negative" radio advertisements were also replaced in October by a series of positive advertisements after the primary panic. This weak thrust in advertising may have been due to the lack of input from other decision-makers and the free hand that Seigle and Margo Wood had in the campaign while under Gummie Johnson's direction. At least two of the strategy committee members had no idea whatsoever about the visual or spoken content of the work until it was a *fait accompli.*

Rohlfing's [Gummie-created] thematic catch line—"He doesn't have to change what he is to become the man you can trust"—was, to some, complex and hard to understand. But the city editor of the *Star-Bulletin* thought the slogan was "brilliant."

News Media

Still another area where the Rohlfing campaign failed to achieve the coverage it should have was in the area of positive news coverage. Part of the problem was due to the candidate himself...who declined to meet the demands of the press as effectively as Heftel. Though receiving close to a hundred releases, the news media had only a superficial understanding of the candidate or the issues while being obsessed with Rohlfing's comments about Heftel's TV holdings. [When we "switched gears" in October, we tried to put the TV ownership issue off the front of our effort.]

Field Operations

Had there been more money, field operations could have been more effective. [Money was not a field-op problem.] But Tom Nekota did an admirable job in directing this phase of the campaign. [Nekota was assisted ably by my son Fritz and a longtime supporter, Ken Luke.] Inroads from these efforts in the west Honolulu districts were not enough.

Where Rohlfing Lost

Even before the election [Campaign] it was known that the [west Honolulu districts—'Aiea, Kalihi, Nu'uanu, downtown Honolulu, and Mo'ili'ili] would hold the key to victory or defeat. Rohlfing managed to carry Hawai'i Kai, 7th district, Kāhala, 8th district, Waikīkī 11th district, and Mānoa, 13th district. But these [more upscale] districts do not an election win even when a candidate has been walking for thirteen months and has help from nearly every union in town. In the words of the *Star-Bulletin's* city editor, "Elections in this district are won by the Kalihi housewife—and she believed the Heftel TV ads." It is the impression of the author that there was no detailed game plan for breaking into this important area.

The Hoshijo Factor

Hoshijo's campaign featured a last-week media blitz and an attack on Rohlfing for representing Hawaiian Electric Company in a case involving eviction of tenants who had overstayed their residential leases in Kāne'ohe.

Hoshijo polled 23,699 votes—16.9 percent of the total cast. Heftel received 59,690—42.4 percent—and Rohlfing 53,406—38 percent. It was the general feeling of those associated with both campaigns that Hoshijo hurt Heftel more than Rohlfing by taking Democratic and [hence] AJA votes from the Democrat. [But Hoshijo took two thousand votes from me in my strong areas in east O'ahu and in Mānoa, where she took 3,449 to my 6,965.]

Union Factor

Still one more factor that had some bearing on the Rohlfing for Congress campaign was Rohlfing's overwhelming number of endorsements from major Hawai'i unions. These endorsements were effective, as Rohlfing received real campaign help from many of the unions. ILWU, HGEA, HSTA, and UPW all provided walkers and/or phone-bank support.

[Unions that endorsed me were the United Public Workers, Hawai'i State Teachers, Hawai'i Government Employees Association, ILWU, Hawai'i State Federation of Labor AFL-CIO, United Brotherhood of Carpenters & Joiners, International Brotherhood of Electrical Workers, Fire Fighters Association, American Federation of Government Employees Local 882, Hawai'i Teamsters and Allied Workers, Hawai'i Restaurant Employees and Bartenders Union, all ten of Hawai'i's maritime-oriented unions via the Honolulu Port Council, and the Service Employees International Union.

Heftel was endorsed by the Laborers Union. A number of these endorsements came too late to enable us to exploit our advantage, and we were dependent upon the union to get the word out. After the election I learned that Van Diamond of the AFL-CIO had prepared a strong letter on my behalf to union supporters and for publication. But he was, strangely, turned down on financing. Had I known about it, I would've mortgaged the store and every other asset I had in order to get that letter out.]

Conclusions and Recommendations

1. The value of outside consultants is questionable in Hawai'i today. Fees paid to Johnson [$40,000] constituted twenty percent of the campaign expenditures. Johnson was unable to provide the basic day-to-day direction that was needed in a major campaign. Furthermore, the Rohlfing congressional team did not follow Johnson's counsel even when it was given.

2. Eliminate the Mainland consultant and use that money for mass media. The Rohlfing '76 campaign is a classic example that money speaks louder than smiles and handshakes at the door. As Fasi said, "Elections are won on the six o'clock news and in TV advertising." Hoshijo spent thirty thousand dollars in just two weeks. Heftel spent four hundred thousand.

3. TV content. Present the candidate in a warmer manner. Use at least the voice of the candidate. Involve a diverse group in the decision-making on TV ad content.

4. Overall decision-making must be consistent with the campaign theme. Instead of following through with the "positive-negative" approach, the campaign shifted to an almost entirely positive approach. This shift was pleasing to decision-makers but unsuccessful in capturing the much-needed Democrat and independent vote. The rejection of the Johnson tabloid was probably the key strategic error in the campaign. It was a safe and easy choice to make.

5. Another factor leading to poor decision-making was the lack of reliable polling material. BMI was Johnson's source. But Dods and Pratte would have preferred Dan Tuttle's group.

6. There needed to be closer liaison with the National Republican Party. The (GOP) field rep indicated to Pratte that the national headquarters had no idea how close Rohlfing was to beating Heftel. Too much party emphasis and money went to Quinn against Matsunaga—an unwinnable race from the outset.

Friends and Foes

Insights on a Few of Hawai'i's
Leading Politicians Since Statehood

Voicing one's views about other people is always touchy, and even more so in print. So this appendix is a cruise through the rose bushes.

Bill Quinn

I became initially involved in Hawai'i with Republicans and the Republican Party when I supported Bill Quinn for the territorial Senate in 1956. He lost, but there was more to come. In 1957 I was elected chairman of the O'ahu Young Republicans. In 1958 Quinn was appointed governor of the Territory of Hawai'i by President Eisenhower, replacing Samuel Wilder King. I supported this move at the time, as I was contemplating a run for State office in the event we achieved statehood. We did in 1959, and Quinn became Hawai'i's first elected governor by defeating delegate John A. Burns.

Quinn was a very smart attorney—he delivered great speeches—and had much personal talent and charm. His weakness was his tendency to rely too heavily on political advice from "Merchant Street," otherwise known as the Big Five (Hawai'i's sugar factors and agricultural corporations). Another description of the "Big Five" would be "Haole Big Business."

Quinn's lieutenant governor, Jimmy Kealoha, soon split off from the Quinn administration and heavily emphasized his local roots and his Island style of doing things. Kealoha thought he was responsible for Quinn beating Jack Burns in the first statehood election. He wasn't, but he had helped with the Hawaiian vote in particular. It was a lot easier to get in to see Jimmy than the governor, but he pushed himself into the administration of agencies and was not privy to Quinn's inner circle. Kealoha ran unsuccessfully for governor in 1962.

The Democrats countered Quinn's PR machine with a lineup of talented lawyers and other professionals, particularly in the Senate where the likes of Nelson Doi, Sakae Takahashi, George Ariyoshi, and Nadao Yoshinaga held sway. They were merciless in working over Mary Noonan, Quinn's appointee with jurisdiction over the prison system. His personnel and transportation department people were similarly treated.

The fact that Republicans (dominated by neighbor isle "old barons") controlled the Senate led Quinn to ignore the eighteen (mostly younger) Republicans in the House—including me. We were not brought into discussions on such controversial proposals as Quinn's "Second Mahele," also known as "J. Akuhead Pupule's" land program. (Hal Lewis, a.k.a. "Akuhead," was a top disc jockey at the time). That exclusion colors my evaluation of Quinn who was otherwise an outgoing, colorful campaigner and a good governor.

In 1959 it looked as though the Republicans would have an opportunity to lead the new island state. But there was too much "me first" in the Senate and not enough teamwork between our House minority and Governor Quinn. Quinn's overwhelming defeat in 1962 at the hands of the Burns-Inouye machine was cataclysmic for Hawai'i Republicans, who have struggled ever since with only minorities in the Legislature and only two gubernatorial victories since 1959 (Linda Lingle in 2002 and 2006). As I have indicated in another portion of these comments, if Quinn had not run against Senator Spark Matsunaga in 1976, I would probably have raised an additional $100,000 for my race against Cec Heftel. I could have used that money for media advertising. But then, Heftel might have just gone ahead and spent even more of his own money!

Jack Burns

John A. Burns was elected in the fifties as our last territorial delegate to Congress—with much help from the ILWU—and to the governorship in 1962. His legislative strategy was responsible for Hawai'i obtaining statehood in 1959, as he deferred to Alaska becoming the first non-contiguous state in 1949. He worked closely with AJAs who had returned from heroic service in World War II. With them he built a new Democratic Party that took over the territorial Legislature in 1954.

I did not get to know him personally until quite late in his gubernatorial career, which lasted from 1962 to 1973. As minority spokesman on policy, I was very critical of Burns's administration. For example, in a speech to the Honolulu Lions Club on April 13, 1966, at the old Armed Services YMCA (a gathering attended by Burns himself) I outlined nearly a dozen areas where his Democratic administration and the Legislature had run into troubles, including traffic safety, traffic congestion, Magic Island, Koke'e's proposed national park, school system disputes, and the Maui prison site (*Honolulu Star-Bulletin* 4/13/66). I then characterized his administration's response to these problems as a political "Disneyland"—equating various Disney "lands" with State departments, e.g., "Fantasy Land," "Frontier Land," and others.

Later, however, I appreciated Burns's off-the-record contacts with our Senate caucus on judicial nominations, particularly so when I was a member of the judiciary committee. On one occasion he tried to give us a Republican on the State Supreme Court—Betty Vitousek, a well-respected Family-Court judge and wife of Roy Vitousek, Jr., a prominent attorney and lobbyist whose father was a longtime Republican stalwart and superb fundraiser. (My dad was on his fundraising target list!) Under "guidance" from Sen. Hebden Porteus, our minority leader, we Republican senators sought instead to have former State senator Yasutaka Fukushima nominated instead of Vitousek. Burns went ahead with Vitousek, and she was voted down by the judiciary committee. I regret that negative vote today.

Burns's speeches were stiff, and that's how he appeared in public. The lack of applause by his own party members when he delivered the annual "state of the state" address to joint sessions of the Legislature was nothing short of embarrassing. I used to feel genuinely sorry for him. But he worked hand-in-hand with the AJAs and labor unions, which were the strength of the Democratic Party, and together they accomplished a lot of good things in the field of labor, land, and social legislation. As a staunch Catholic he passed his "moment of truth" with flying colors when he allowed the abortion-reform bill to become law without his signature. (I voted for it.) After Burns became ill, I frequently saw him while he was practicing his short game and his putting at Waiʻalae Golf Course. On such occasions we would often have friendly small-talk on current subjects. During his reign I was critical of the way powerful unions in particular exerted excessive influence over administration actions, and I worried about the overdevelopment of our most valuable lands by cronies of the governor. In retrospect, though, the Burns record was quite good when measured against that of other Democrat governors.

Elmer Cravalho

Elmer was something of an enigma as far as I was concerned, but he is a very smart and respected politician. Elected speaker—initially with Republican support—in territorial days as part of an ILWU-brokered process, Cravalho treated our eighteen-member minority with fairness at the outset of statehood. This may have been because our minority leader, Joe Garcia, had a good working relationship with Cravalho. Later, though, we were to feel the sting of his power as he "fired" all three Republicans (Representatives Devereux, Dwight, and myself) from the Maui Special Investigative Committee after we filed a minority report that he didn't like.

When Amby Rosehill as minority leader and I as minority floor leader had an open disagreement on the floor of the House, he moved in and sought to make the disagreement fatal to our efforts. However, we patched up our differences soon after and kept our eleven-member Republican caucus together. As I was not living on Maui during his years as mayor, I did not personally observe his successes and failures in that office. But overall the community on his watch was well-balanced, with new tourist hotels and condos supplanting many a failing plantation. Elmer's reputation for exercising his authority and getting things done

is still strong on Maui. No major Maui developer escaped without giving up land for beach access or agreeing to provide substantial employee
housing as prescribed by Elmer. Maui is a better place due to these efforts
by Cravalho.

Tom Gill

I served with Tom for three years while we both were in the House.
Tom was a dedicated liberal who could win you over with logic or lose
you with caustic comments. He was a leader in the Esposito faction that
lost out to the Cravalho-ILWU group in the bipartisan organization of
the 1958 territorial Legislature. Gill was a labor lawyer who represented
AFL and teamsters unions, so occasionally we were on opposite sides on
arbitrations or other labor cases. I frequently agreed with his positions on
transportation issues (e.g., for mass transit and against the cross-island
H-3 highway). He was for major land reform, as was I, though I was not
as radical or outspoken as he. I often wonder what would have happened
to Hawai'i if Tom had beaten Burns in 1970. One thing for sure is that
we would have had a far cheaper and more effective mass transit system
on O'ahu than that which is now being undertaken by Mufi—and maybe
a State-operated ferry system! Growth generally would have been slowed
and taxes increased.

David McClung

Chair of the House lands committee after the statehood election,
Dave made a name for himself with many land-reform measures. He also
exposed a number of problems in the administration of the Hawaiian
Homes programs. In the early days of statehood he was focused on writ-
ing the rules for the management of lands acquired by the state via the
Statehood Admissions Act. Anyone interested in the legislative history of
this topic should read *Land and Politics in Hawai'i* by Robert H. Horwitz
(Michigan State University) and Norman Meller (University of Hawai'i).
It features a blow-by-blow account of the contest in the conference

committee (of which I was a member) between the House reformers and the more traditional Senate delegation led by Francis Ching, Republican senator from Kaua'i. Dave led the charge for greater control of government leases and against the sale of State land. This was, of course, the exact opposite of what he proposed to do (under the "Maryland Land Law") to privately held lands—i.e., to give homeowners the right to purchase their homesites from the big estates who were leasing the parcels for a period of years (usually 55 years).

Dave was more gregarious than his fellow reformer Tom Gill. He enjoyed having a drink or two at a Korean (or other) bar after the session. Some of his union friends (seafarer's union types in particular) and clients would often join him and mix business with pleasure. The bill was defeated in the Senate by one vote (Senator Ariyoshi's) after colorful torchlight anti-reform protests were staged by Hawaiian groups in their best parade-going regalia.

But McClung persevered and went back to the statutory drawing board. He took my "Lessee's Bill of Rights" (a regulatory statute for residential leaseholds) and incorporated it with his provisions for condemnation by the government of "development tracts." The resulting land reform bill was ultimately approved in 1967 (Act 307 S.L. 1967). In return for his inclusion of my comprehensive regulative proposal, I was able to bring along some of my fellow Republicans on the final Senate vote. (I think we had seven in all.) Before the bill was finalized, Dave arranged for us to meet with various officials in Washington, D.C., We also met with former Columbia Law School dean William Warren, whose fee was underwritten by the Bishop Estate. He then accompanied us to a decisive meeting with IRS officials. The objective was to devise a scheme that would protect the Estate and other charitable trust landowners from losing their charitable tax exemption by being deemed to be in the "business of selling land." Accordingly, we mandated the State's intervention as a "straw man" purchaser through condemnation (a forced sale) on behalf of the individual homeowners. When the concept was challenged later, the U.S. Supreme Court upheld it. I believe that my role in the development and passage of this bill was the most important accomplishment of my legislative career.

Not surprisingly, I remember Dave McClung with fondness.

Donald Ching

Donald Ching was a young lawyer with whom I served first on the junior bar association board of directors and thereafter in both the House and Senate. He was a low-key, get-the-work-out kind of person. In the early seventies—I think after my first run for Congress against Sparky— Don asked me if I'd be interested in the State Supreme Court, even if it meant the end of my political career. After due consideration I told him I would accept such an appointment. Time passed and nothing happened. Don then told me that it was going well with Governor Burns but some of his advisors, including son Jimmy, thought I'd been too critical of his father and too outspoken against Democrats generally to be "rewarded." True or not, I hold no grudges. I admire the service that Jim has rendered as a State appellate judge.

Sam P. King

Given that Sam possesses a great intellect, one can only marvel at his other qualifications and accomplishments, which are often disguised by his modesty and his down-to-earth sense of humor. When I first returned home after my active service with the Navy (in 1955), Sam was the first person to offer me employment. He said he'd pay me $250 a month and split the proceeds 50/50 on any business that I brought in. As I thought I wanted to practice labor law pretty exclusively, I turned him down and accepted a flat salary of $325/month (and upon Bar passage $450) from E.C. "Bud" Moore, whose firm represented the Hawai'i Employers Council. The survivor firm name is Torkildson, Katz, Moore & Hetherington.

I got to know Sam well at our Naval intelligence reserve meetings in the old H.A.S.P (military police)/14th Naval District complex on Ala Moana Boulevard and later at various other Pearl Harbor sites. In addition to his legal skills, Sam is an accomplished storyteller and public speaker. And he is a consummate intelligence officer. In due course he was appointed to the State Family Court, then (via Hiram Fong and President

Nixon) to the federal bench, where he has further distinguished himself. Between the state and federal jobs he ran a good race for governor. Not only that, he never held it against me that I was a Quinn advocate when his dad, Samuel Wilder King, was territorial governor. The book *Broken Trust*, of which he is a co-author, testifies to Sam's scholarly but brutally frank style on public issues.

One of my bigger disappointments in life was my son Fritz's inability to get confirmed as a U.S. district judge. One of the consequences of that was not seeing more of Sam!

Dan Akaka

I considered Dan Akaka to be overshadowed by his colleague in the U.S. Senate, but I also considered him to be a fair person. My wife and I visited him while he was in the House, and we enjoyed a pleasant breakfast in the House dining room. My view changed with his actions in regard to my son Fritz's federal judicial appointment. It was Akaka who denied Fritz a last-chance opportunity to appear before the Senate Judiciary Committee. Had Akaka agreed not to oppose it, as had Senator Inouye, Chairman Hatch from Utah would have proceeded with a hearing on the nomination. Then Fritz would have been given a chance to learn what had led the ABA to oppose him and the opportunity to rebut same. I am almost certain he would have gotten committee approval and thereafter, a Senate floor vote.

As a consequence of this misjudgment, I supported Ed Case with modest contributions in his challenge to Akaka in 2006. Unfortunately, the emotional appeal to preserve a "kupuna" in office—and Democrat power politics—enabled Akaka to defeat Case.

Walter Heen

In early years in the house I worked well with Walter Heen. He was willing to introduce bills that I had drafted on community problems. Included were a series of bills related to the silting of Paiko Lagoon, a condition which threatened the value of a number of my constituents' properties. "Scotty" Koga was also helpful with "pork barrel" type bills. Both of these legislators represented the 16th Rep. District, the neighbor to our 17th. Heen and I were together in the Senate for two years. Then he went off to the City Council and later the judiciary. I was sorry he didn't stick around longer in the Senate. He was an outstanding judge.

Ambrose "Amby" Rosehill

My Republican colleague from the 17th District, Amby was always colorful and a good friend. He was a graduate of Kamehameha and proud of his Hawaiian ancestry. He was a fine orator, and he possessed more political and common sense than most of his colleagues, including me.

In the very first special session of the Legislature in 1959 he gave me a taste of that shrewd practicality. In that first session we attempted to pass a major bill setting up the essential form of the State government. This bill was to condense numerous territorial agencies into not more than twenty departments as required by the newly effective State constitution. But the House (controlled by the Democrats 33-18) tangled with the Senate (controlled by Republicans) on details in conference. As a result the special statehood session was adjourned without agreement on a bill. The media went wild—that was not the way to start a new state, they naturally opined, and in this instance they were right.

On the Sunday afternoon following the Saturday adjournment I received a phone call from a *Honolulu Advertiser* political reporter. "Some legislators are promising to waive their salaries ($750) if a special session can be called," he said. "Will you be willing to do that?"

Being young (31) and naive I brightly said, "Yes, sure I would." Without thinking about it, I thereby incurred the wrath of those who couldn't afford to waive their compensation and pandered to the conservative anti-government types.

When Rosehill got the same question, he said, "Yes, I will—if the majority members waive theirs, too!" Of course, no Democrat was willing to waive the $750 salary. So Amby ended up with the best of both worlds, appealing to the public watchdogs while at the same time not implying criticism of those unwilling to make the sacrifice. Smart man, Rosehill.

Early on he led me to vote consistently for home rule. You can go back and check our votes on bills which took functions or duties away from the counties. You'll find the "R" boys, Rohlfing and Rosehill, consistently in the negative column. Amby often quoted our senior colleague in the Senate, Hardy "Doc" Hill: "If in doubt, vote no."

Rosehill had a wonderful sense of humor. One night during campaign season he approached a house on Sierra Drive to solicit a vote. It was later than normal for house-to-house campaigning. So when he knocked, he got an angry blast from the back bedroom. The male occupant shouted "Whatdaya want? Beat it!"

Rosehill responded, "I just wanted to talk to you about my candidate in the election."

The occupant yelled, "Who the hell is that?"

Rosehill responded, "I'm here for Anna Kahanamoku"—a Democrat who was running in our district. "I'll send you a brochure. Good night!"

Daniel Inouye

No discussion of Hawai'i politics would be complete without mention of our senior United States senator, Daniel K. Inouye. I first met Dan when he was in the final days of his attendance at George Washington University Law School, in the summer of 1952. He was with a group of Hawai'i law students having a snack at the basement store opposite the university's Stockton Hall in the Foggy Bottom area of D.C. Others in his group included Kats Miho, Epi Yadao from Hilo, and Alvin Shim. I was in my Navy uniform, as I had not changed after work at the Pentagon. We had a brief non-memorable exchange.

Shortly thereafter Dan returned to Hawai'i, and in 1954 he led the Democratic ticket to its revolutionary sweep over the Republicans. With statehood he successfully ran for our only seat in U.S. Congress. Then in the 1962 second big sweep by the Democrats he won the seat he now continues to hold. Yes, he has been a U.S. senator for 47 years and in D.C. for 50!

I remember an early exchange in "Letters to the Editor" that we had while Dan was still in our territorial Legislature. It had to do with his support of the ILWU leadership, which was said to be pro-communist (the details of the exchange I've long since forgotten).

In 1973 Dan came to our support almost immediately when we sought to save the Waikīkī Natatorium. He must have done so on instinct.

It was not until I served in American Samoa and as director of that territory's liaison office in Honolulu that our acquaintance became more personal. I was helping Governor Coleman with the perennial Samoan problem with air transportation, then still affected heavily by federal regulation. Dan helped us with the CAB matter, and we succeeded in getting Continental Airlines to replace Pan Am.

Later I traveled to Washington with a committee of *faipules* (Samoan legislators), and we had briefings and informal meetings with Dan at his office.

Again we went to Dan when Governor Coleman came up with his imaginative scheme to convert Canton Island to a fishing base governed by American Samoa. We attempted to turn the State Department away from its plan to give the island to the Kiribati Republic. Coleman's plan envisioned the repair of the harbor, updating a 747-capable airfield, and adding refrigeration capacity. Such a fishing base would have meant direct short flights in to the Honolulu fish market for purse seine fishermen.

As I was the liaison guy for Governor Coleman in Honolulu, there were other issues that brought us to Senator Inouye's number-one aide in his Honolulu office, Col. David Peters. Dave never failed to assist us. Transporting Samoans to Honolulu for emergency medical care was one of those shared efforts.

All of this interaction with the senator, however, paled in importance when compared with our communication on the issue of my son Fritz's confirmation when he was appointed by President George W. Bush to the U.S. District Court for the District of Hawai'i.

The U.S. Senate has some weird practices. One of them is the "blue slip" process for judicial nominations. If a senator from the nominee's state turns in his blue slip to the judiciary chairman, that means he approves of that candidate. If both senators from that state turn in their blue slips, normally the candidate will receive a hearing before the judiciary committee and—depending on the committee's reaction—will have his name sent to the floor for final approval. The story of what happened to my son when he encountered the blue slip process is contained in Chapter 7.

Dan has since supported the Rohlfings in other ways. He gave Markus Rohlfing, my grandson, meaningful endorsements to the U.S. Naval Academy and the Merchant Marine Academy. Markus was inducted to the USNA on July 1, 2009.

Inouye doesn't need any endorsements from me. But he has been a great provider for Hawai'i and is highly respected by his peers. He is now the most senior senator, chairs the powerful appropriations committee, and is third in line to succeed to the presidency. Politics aside, he is my friend.

Hiram Fong

United States Senator Hiram Fong was a one-of-a-kind individual. He fought his way up from modest circumstances, was a graduate of McKinley High school and University of Hawai'i, and for years was a prominent Republican leader in the territorial house. I did not come to know him until he was elected America's first Asian senator in 1959. Thereafter, I worked with him on many projects. When I visited him in Washington, he always provided me with a desk and support staff, often his press guy Larry Nakatsuka.

As a State House member I worked with the senator to get the federal government to return beach park property in Wailupe, East O'ahu, that had once been a Coast Guard facility. Later, when I was a State senator, we worked together on other federal land transfers for educational purposes. I never felt uncomfortable or nervous talking with him, as he was a genuinely humble person. Hawai'i lost a great public servant when Senator Fong passed on.

Nelson Doi

Hilo's Nelson Doi was always open and friendly. I liked his forth-right style and admired his oratory—particularly when he was taking on his Democrat rival, Senator Nadao Yoshinaga, on the floor of the Senate in 'Iolani Palace in the early statehood days. He was a good lieutenant governor and a fair and reasonable judge. I worked together with Doi and "Bud" Smyser on enacting a constitutional amendment that would provide for a unicameral legislature. We didn't get very far with the idea, but it still makes sense to me (see Chapter 7).

George Ariyoshi

Ariyoshi didn't quite fill the shoes of Jack Burns at the outset, but he grew a lot in office. He ended up having spent a lot of time in offices on the 5th floor of the capitol, first as lieutenant governor with Burns, then as governor for two terms.

While we were in the Senate together (before he moved upstairs) George once chastised me on the floor in a session-ending speech for criticizing Governor Burns's annual budget. Notwithstanding, I have always liked George. Not many people truly fit their campaign slogan, but George fit his to a "T"—the slogan was "quiet but effective." He was fiscally conservative and saved us from overspending on a number of occasions. He more than once showed real political courage, including when he was the deciding vote against the Maryland Land Law (that I supported). The bill was prominent in the Democrat Party's platform.

I appreciated the fact that he granted my request to be succeeded by Rep. "Buddy" Soares when I resigned to run for U.S. Congress in 1975. In 1984, when I resigned a second time to move to Maui, he appointed Lowell Dillingham to my House seat.

Ariyoshi is still active with businesses who utilize his knowledge of important people in Asian nations and Hawai'i.

D.G. "Andy" Anderson

It is a challenge for me to write about my longtime colleague D.G. "Andy" Anderson.

The many ups and downs we experienced over the years began when he was first elected to the house from the windward district in 1962. Most of the younger members of our Republican minority of twelve (sharply down from the 1959-62 total of eighteen) wanted to elect new leadership. For the first three years of statehood we'd been led by Joe Garcia, a plantation labor relations/personnel man from the Big Island, as minority leader and Webley (*Hawai'i Calls*) Edwards, also from my east O'ahu district, as minority floor leader. The younger GOP members had been frustrated in presenting alternative solutions to those offered by the Democrats, and we wanted to hire stronger research people. We argued that such staff changes should take the place of good ol' boys who were good with coffee service and personal errands primarily.

We approached Andy to support our slate, which comprised Rosehill for minority leader, me for minority floor leader, and I believe Kats Miho as minority whip. Andy played both sides against each other for commitments to committee assignments and other perks. But ultimately he voted with us. As a consequence we called him "the swingman." It was an early revelation of things to come.

With Rosehill's decision to run for the Senate in 1964, the minority leadership went to Kats Miho. Miho was generally satisfied with the status quo, so we clashed. By 1965 others in the caucus joined me, and Miho was removed as leader. I was elected as minority leader. Andy was elected floor leader. Jim Clark, another windward representative, was chosen as whip. This combination worked well. We hired a good research staff, and we developed a sensible legislative program.

In 1966 all three GOP leaders were elected to the Senate. So were Representatives Percy Mirikitani, Web Edwards, and Eureka Forbes. Andy opted for the Ways & Means committee and developed into a first-class legislator.

As indicated earlier, my focus was on land reform in my first years in the Senate. Andy worked with Senator Nelson Doi on a highly publicized Department of Education program called "2 on 1," which was supposed to cure our education problems. It didn't.

In 1968, with the untimely death of our capable Republican Mayor Neal Blaisdell, the mayor's office came into play. Frank Fasi was the Democrat candidate to beat. Wadsworth "Wads" Yee, Andy, and I were all mentioned by the press as Fasi's potential opponents, and we met on several occasions to try to pick our candidate. Ultimately, Wads and I pledged our support to Andy. For me this endorsement was a major commitment of time and energy, and my law practice suffered. I spoke for Andy at schools, luncheon/dinner/coffee-hour groups, and before the media. I even wrote up a transportation policy for him and delivered it as a major plank in his campaign. By the time the contest was over, I felt that I'd almost been the candidate myself.

But we lost.

Indicative of future communication breakdowns, I did not receive a call or letter or other indication of appreciation for my efforts from Anderson. In 1970, as earlier described, we chose different candidates against Jack Burns for governor. Andy backed Senator Porteus, and I backed Sam King. King defeated Porteus but then lost to Burns.

As time rolled on in the Senate, Andy and I (as floor leader and policy leader respectively) inaugurated a multi-year effort to repeal the four-percent gross income tax on food and medical bills. I prepared most of the research materials as well as other projects and positions. Andy handled the PR presentations. Andy had little to do with my congressional campaigns.

I have detailed notes covering my discussions with Senator Fong, Andy, and others in mid-1973 concerning who would run for governor in 1974. I tried my best to interest Fong in the contest and vowed that I'd run for lieutenant governor with him. Nevertheless, Fong called a press conference on June 1, 1973, in which he announced his decision not to run. For another month or two Andy and I fenced actively with each other about who might run for governor. Andy's supporters pushed for a team with Andy for governor and me for lieutenant governor. At one point Andy said, "It's your option." But I was not confident that I would be able to raise the necessary funds. I did not take the ball and run with it.

This Alphonse-Gaston act continued until we were both taken aback when Randolph Crossley announced his candidacy, along with former territorial senator Ben Dillingham for lieutenant governor. Ariyoshi dealt with them handily at the ballot box.

Our paths were to cross again—for the last time—after I moved to Maui. (See Chapter 7, Various Causes, the Fagan Campaign.)

Cecil Heftel

A sometime politico with whom I did not have cordial relations was my opponent in 1976, "Cec" Heftel. To this day I reproach myself for losing the 1st District Congressional seat to a man who bought his way into office. Were it not for Heftel's early run against Fong, in which Inouye touted him at great length, I believe I would have won in 1976 despite my flawed effort. (See Chapter 2 and Appendix 1.) Heftel's last-stage collapse in the later Democrat contest with Waihe'e for governor was, for me, a catharsis.

Pat Saiki

Pat Saiki remains to this day one of my favorite people (both politically and non-politically). I first met her when as House GOP leaders we needed someone to fill in for an ill minority staff employee. Rep Ken Nakamura, my law associate and fellow House member, recommended Saiki. She did a great job. (Ken had dated her when they were both attending U.H. Mānoa).

Later, in the early sixties when D.G. Anderson and I were on Maui at a state GOP convention and were looking for a candidate for secretary of the state Republican party, we talked her into jumping on the next plane and joining us. We introduced her to the assemblage, and she was elected overwhelmingly.

Pat later offered to help me in my race for the State Senate in 1965. She walked house to house with me in Kaimukī/Pālolo during August of that year. She was a key part of the strategy team as well, joining many a meeting with PR types Patt Patterson and his girl Friday. His slogan was "Do it!"

When we won, I hired Pat as my principal aide for the 1967 Senate session. Later she joined our Senate minority staff along with Kinau (Boyd) Kamali'i, who also later became an elected official. Pat went out on her own in a run for con-con, and I walked house to house with her. Upon election to con-con she developed a working relationship with Senator Porteus and, because she was a Porteus backer, also became close to Andy. She then ran for lieutenant governor with Anderson, and she eventually won the U.S. House seat from the First District, the one that I had failed to win in '76. She did a workmanlike job in U.S. Congress. When Senator Matsunaga died, she made the effort to be elected to the U.S. Senate but lost to Akaka.

Hawai'i lost a lot with that result, as she would have balanced off Senator Inouye in the Bush-41, Clinton, and Bush-43 years.

Sakae Takahashi

Sakae became one of my friends "across the aisle" (as they say in Washington). He was a veteran of World War II and had attained the rank of captain in the Army (equivalent to full lieutenant in the Navy). He was a liberal, and he followed Tom Gill on many issues. I was pretty supportive of Gill's positions on land reform and mass transit, so Sakae and I could talk issues easily. He was easy to talk with about anything. I worked with him on the collective bargaining act for public employees. One night he called a hearing, and none of the members of his committee showed up, including me. My excuse, a bad cold. But we caught hell in the press and Sakae was legitimately angry. "Cec" Heftel was at the meeting to testify and was very critical of our absence.

Later, when I ran for Congress the second time, Sakae wrote letters and signed endorsements on my behalf. He was a solid contributor to a better Hawai'i and a loyal friend.

Ben Cayetano

I got to know Ben initially when he became an associate attorney with Padgett, Greeley, and Marumoto, from whom I rented space in the Hawaiʻi Building. I liked Ben personally. I remember cooperation from him on the house side in 1974-75 on bills to improve the plight of residential leaseholders.

In early years he had trouble "making nice" the way politicians are expected to do. This was accompanied by his unique "Prince Valiant" haircut and a propensity to be on the most liberal side along with Abercrombie. Later, when he was lieutenant governor and I had moved to Maui, we exchanged views on ways to improve our public schools, including use of charter schools and vouchers.

As governor he earned my respect by confronting excesses of the government employee unions and by his handling of the State's investigation of the scandalous Bishop Estate trustees and Supreme Court justices. He gave his attorney general, Margery Bronster, the ball and backed her up despite his past alliances with Dickie Wong and Henry Peters. He also signed our Maui Vets bill to right the injustice of the state retirement system (See Chapter 7). I have thoroughly enjoyed his book (*Ben*) which documents Capitol events subsequent to my retirement in 1984.

Frank Fasi

This will be brief because most everything there is to know about Frank you already know! I always liked the guy even though there were times when his flamboyance was a bit overwhelming.

He did a good job as mayor, and he ran a great bus operation. Little known is the fact that Fasi once offered me the job of Honolulu public prosecutor when it was still an appointive position. I declined, saying that criminal law wasn't my thing—but if the corporation counsel slot was open, I'd be interested. At the time that post was occupied by Fasi loyalist Richard Sharpless.

Later on, however, when the office of the prosecutor became an elected office, I did take a close look at running for it. This action had been recommended by Rich Frias, a GOP hired gun, and by other associates. I even made a trip to American Samoa to try a criminal case in order to meet electoral requirements. In the final analysis I decided to keep my eye on my lifetime target, U.S. Congress.

After I moved to Maui, Fasi won election as mayor with the help of Andy. At the latter's invitation I interviewed for the job of corporation counsel, Honolulu County. But Fasi chose Richard Wurdeman.

Sparky Matsunaga

Sparky Matsunaga was a personable man and a good legislator. I met him first when he appeared before committees of the house in the first State Legislature as a private attorney. He often represented State Savings and Loan, which did a lot of media advertising.

My main differences with him stemmed from my view that he should be doing more for Hawai'i—as he incessantly claimed to be doing —as a big shot on the U.S. House Rules Committee. My campaign gang and I ran a better campaign against Sparky than against Heftel, as we moved from 22 percent of the vote in June to 43 percent at election time. Spark was a little too soft on military issues for me—and yet he was a World War II vet.

Hannibal Tavares

Another one of my favorite people in political and legal life was Hannibal Tavares. I knew Hannibal first at the State Capitol as an intrepid lobbyist for the HSPA, an organization sponsored by the sugar companies. He was a bulldog who worked tirelessly for his principals.

He was often seen both socially and politically in the company of longtime Republican Arthur Woolaway, who was also from Maui and an executive of A&B Corporation. These two regularly occupied an outside wall table at the Ala Moana Tropics, where Jack Hall and others in the labor relations business had lunch frequently. My law-firm senior partner

Ernest "Bud" Moore hosted a firm lunch at the Tropics once a week, and I soon learned not to have more than one martini, if that, should I want to be productive in the afternoon.

I later got to know Hannibal even better (as my overall boss) when Rodger Betts recruited me for his Maui County corporation counsel's office in 1984. Hannibal's right-hand man was County managing director Howard Nakamura. When Hannibal wanted anything from me, he'd tell Howard, who would tell me. Howard would get it as soon as I could deliver. An example was the ordinance establishing the Research & Technology Park in Kihei, where a highly successful operation is continuing to this day. Also, we moved expeditiously when Hawaiian Airlines (in the Jack Magoon era) wanted to build an airport on the west side of Maui. I wrote a (long-winded) 35-page opinion on our authority to do this. Hawaiian Airlines should have given me at least 100,00 miles of credit for that service!

My wife Patty's cousin, Manuel "Junior" Moniz, was Hawaiian's manager on Maui and was a prominent Democrat party advocate. Moniz and Eddie Tangen (former ILWU leader) spent a lot of time arguing their transportation causes in my office. (Tangen represented a helicopter operator. He and his wife became close personal friends).

The biggest test of my relationship with Hannibal was the Kapuni Moloka'i cruise special-use permit situation. Hannibal and Howard wanted me to back off honorably from the showdown between the County Council (Velma Santos) and the planning commission, which was building to a crescendo in the 2nd Circuit Court. On the merits I was sure that the council was right and that the commission was wrong. But I followed his directions and cooled involvement of my corporation counsel's office. Within a month, however, I resigned and returned to private practice. I did not like being pulled in opposite directions by my two bosses (mayor and council).

Hannibal was a no-nonsense, dedicated public servant who was loved by the people of Maui (and me).

Linda Lingle

My initial encounters with Linda occurred when she was one of two Republicans out of nine members on the Maui council and I was a Maui deputy corporation counsel (1984-87). I was impressed with her because she did her homework and was not afraid to take on the establishment. Sometimes this led her to work over our administration testifier, thereby causing "grumbles" on the 9th floor (the mayor and managing director's offices).

She was a good Maui mayor, and she later did a super job building the Republican Party of Hawai'i, having moved to O'ahu.

The Lingle gubernatorial years have been productive despite frequent standoffs with the overwhelmingly Democrat-controlled Legislature.

While I am somewhat disappointed by the modulation in recent years of her earlier call for a much-needed overhaul (via decentralization) of the state school system, generally speaking Linda has done a fine job as our governor.

Linda's political future depends on the electoral status of our U.S. Senators—in particular, Senator Akaka, whose next re-election bid will take place in 2012. Both senators are in their eighties. Unless they have a formula for immortality, they are subject to life's vagaries as well as the whims of the electorate.

(Ethics considerations require that I disclose that I am a Lingle appointee to the Statewide Health Coordinating Council and therefore may qualify as a member of Linda's administration.)

Charles Djou

I close this review by looking forward, to the future.

I have been very impressed with this young man's forthright leadership on the Honolulu City Council. Charles is diligent, analytical, thorough, insightful, and very articulate. He has a natural charm, and he exudes sincerity of purpose. (I listen to his radio appearances on the Rick Hamada show, 830 on the dial, regularly.)

Djou is running for U.S. Congress from the first district on Oʻahu. He has filed for a special election and the general. In the November general election he will go to the wire against State Senator Colleen Hanabusa and the Democratic establishment.

The decisive factor in choosing whom to support should be which of these candidates can do the most for the people of Hawaiʻi. One more Democrat would be redundant for our small delegation in Washington.

Hawaiʻi can secure much-needed access to GOP members of the U.S. House only by electing Djou. Experts are saying that the Republicans will make major gains in 2010 and could conceivably return to majority status in the House. So it is a "no-brainer." Charles Djou is the man we need in D.C.

LIFETIME SPORTS

My Philosophy re: Physical Fitness

My dad told me early on that if you give up doing physical exercise, you will never be able to regain good physical condition. I took that advice to heart. Up until the last several years I worked out regularly. While I lived in Honolulu, I belonged at various times to the Central YMCA, the Nuʻuanu YMCA, and the Center Health Club (which eventually became Clark Hatch Fitness Center). I usually exercised in the morning before work so that late-afternoon meetings would not deprive me of a workout. During the years I worked for the County of Maui, I used to swim either in the morning at the War Memorial Pool or at lunchtime in the small pool by the Armory. After leaving the County's employ, I became a member of Valley Isle Fitness (and its various successors), where I would do a two-hour workout. Unfortunately my back problems now have restricted me to golf (with cart) and light swimming at a county pool near my home. My days of masters swimming are now over but remain fond memories.

Swimming

It was sometime in the late 1960s that I read about a masters swim meet being held at Punahou School on a Sunday afternoon. I was in my forties at the time. I decided to enter a 500-yard freestyle event. I took a look at my competitors—Jim Welch (age fifty-one) and Lloyd Osborne (mid-sixties and a former Yale swimming captain)—and figured I could handle them. WRONG! Both beat me. I dragged into the finish. This led me to commit to serious training.

My best event was the backstroke. After a few warm-up meets at home, I joined the state masters Humuhumunukunukuapua'a team in several national competitions. These were held in Santa Clara, California, and in Irvine, California. In 1984, competing in the fifty-five to sixty age group, I finished fourth in the 200-yard backstroke with a time of 2:53.23, and I came in third in the 100-yard backstroke with a time of 1:16.86.

The Waikiki Roughwater Swim was revived a few years before my 1976 congressional campaign. John Craven, a well-known ocean sciences professor at the University of Hawai'i, entered the campaign against "Cec" Heftel on the Democratic side of the ledger. He challenged me and Heftel to the Roughwater in 1976. I accepted. Heftel declined. I finished in the time of 1:06, taking third place in my age group (forty-five to fifty) and beating John decisively. I swam the Roughwater thereafter in 1977, 1979, 1984, 1986, 1989, and for the last time in 1999 at age seventy-one. My most memorable Roughwater was the 1984 race, in

MY SONS 'FRITZ', BRAD, AND KARL ACCOMPANY ME ON A RUN AFTER BODYSURFING AT MAKAPU'U.

which I finished a close second to our age-group's perennial winner, "Mo" Mathews, with a time of 1:04.

I encouraged my sons to take up athletic endeavors as well. My eldest (Fritz) played t-ball and baseball in the Kalanianaole League and ran cross-country at Punahou and Dartmouth. He wanted to play football but injured his back early on. Despite a busy attorney's schedule he makes time for exercise. Karl and Brad weren't too enthused about ball-playing but they excelled at skateboards and surfing. Today Karl is a high-qualified kite-board rider and does the full variety of water sports...it helps that he is an employee of Hawaiian Islands Surf & Sport on Dairy Road near the Maui Airport.

Over the years I also frequently swam in the North Shore Challenge, a beautiful course along the north shore of O'ahu with a finish at Waimea Bay. In the 1986 challenge I placed first in the fifty-five to sixty age-group with a time of 1:06. I entered Maui roughwaters during the nineties, winning my age-group in 1994 off Ka'anapali (with a time of 35.5) and in 1998 as part of the Wailea coast race (a time of 1:12).

One year I joined O'ahu swimmer friends Diane Stowell, Pete Schlegal, Jim Anderson and several others to compete in a Maui-Lana'i cross-channel relay race. Each swimmer swam two half-hour shifts. My second shift was the finish effort. I almost got swamped by a Chinese-junk cruise boat, which decided to exit the harbor just as I was coming in!

Skiing

My skiing history goes back to my college years, with excursions to Vermont and New Hampshire, also to my early married life when as a family we took trips to places such as Mount Hood, Mount Rainier, Big Mountain in Montana, the Colorado Rockies, and Lake Tahoe.

More recently my skiing all took place in Whistler, Canada. I was originally invited there by my Punahou classmate Peter Nottage and his friends. These trips began as early as 1989. For a span of twelve years thereafter (except 1991) I joined the gang every year. We called ourselves the "Royal Hawaiian Ski Team" (but some people just called us those "old

geezers" from Hawaiʻi). Photo above includes ski team members George Nottingham, Keith Steiner, Peter Nottage, me, Peter Wilson and Jim and Paule McConkey. Other members of the RHST not pictured are John Walker, Jr., Hal Henderson, Warren Clark, and Henry Rice. McConkey is a legendary Canadian downhill racer/helicopter skier who led us on challenging trails with the cry of "follow me!"

Straight Talk about the Need for a Hawai'i Republican Party "Big Tent"

Excerpts from speech given by Senator Fred W. Rohlfing to the Young Republican State Convention on March 1, 1969, at the Princess Ka'iulani Hotel, Waikīkī. See discussion on pages 38 to 40 of this book for the context in which this speech was made.

"...I was originally going to talk to you about URBAN PROBLEMS and the hang-up of the Democratic Party in meeting those problems. But time and events have largely caught up with that theme. Instead, I am going to talk about whether the Republican Party of Hawai'i is really ready to conscientiously discuss and respond to these challenges. Or does the Republican Party again choose to claw itself into oblivion in an ideological blood bath?

"...Does it return to 1964 and thereby abandon the challenges to the panaceas offered by the Democrats?

"Let us examine in more personal terms the events of the past week, for these events comprise another turning point in Hawai'i politics.... [But first] I'd like to tell you the kind of Republican tradition that I come from. My grandfather was at one time postmaster of Placerville, California, (known to many as 'Hangman's Town') during the Hiram Johnson era. Johnson controlled postmaster appointments. Hiram Johnson was a great Republican California U.S. senator who fought monopolistic railroads and was a believer in true democracy. Essentially he was a 'populist' or 'progressive.' He strongly opposed the U.S. entry into World War I.

My parents came here as immigrants from this area of California. [They] instilled in me a philosophy of honest questioning of the 'sacred cows' of any era. Also, they transmitted a basic sensitivity for those who are less fortunate—not by choice but by circumstance.

"I was born in Hawai'i about the same time as [newly Democrat Senator] Jim Clark. He and I were schoolmates and played on the same football team in 1945. We have played and have sung Hawaiian songs together at his parents' home in Papakolea. We have had a few Primos together, too. I have served six years with him in the House and the Senate. On more than one occasion I have seen him quietly demonstrate moral courage that lots of other people get certificates for.

"I am deeply saddened both emotionally and intellectually by Jim's decision [to change political parties]. Those who would be quick to throw verbal brickbats and those who would gloat have missed the underlying message of this event. In my judgment Jimmy Clark will ultimately suffer the most from this decision.

"The local talk-talk element is now deliriously happy with the implications of victory of the so-called Republican 'conservatives' over the so-called GOP moderates and liberals. But I ask you how many Republican office-holders in the legislature or the party were raised in Papakolea (i.e., Hawaiian Homestead lands), were professional football players, and prominent employee leaders? Whether you know Jim or not, was not his departure a grievous defeat for two-way internal communications of ideas within our party?

"The real message for Republicans in Hawai'i is whether the Republican Party is now to undergo a *purge* so it can be made up of all the same kind of people? Senator David McClung says we still suffer from the plantation image, but that is an old wives' tale. Our problem today is [instead], an intolerant, loud, and abusive dissident—but minority—element that is either unwilling or unable to really understand the people of these islands or their needs.

"Don't misunderstand me. We need new blood from wherever in our party. There is a need for legitimate, *responsible* conservatism. On many occasions I have voted a conservative viewpoint. I have faced Speaker Cravalho and thirty-nine other line Democrats on the house floor on many a sacrificial conservative issue 'for the party'—always on their initiative, at times of their choice. I will never accept that negative role again....

"Remember this—a Republican legislator, once elected, represents all of the people of his district, not just the Republicans. He may represent people whose backgrounds and environmental conditions are often as disparate as Pālolo Public Housing on the one hand and Wailupe Circle on the other.... The people on Wailupe are better able to represent themselves or employ lobbyists than are those that have the greatest need and who must count on the understanding of their legislators. It is in this context that those who talk the loudest about their hundred-percent Republicanism make me sick.

"A political party loses the reason for its existence if it doesn't seek to win elections in as many a district as it can find candidates.

"The Republican Party of Hawai'i has reached a time of decision. We have to prove that the Republican Party has the leadership capability, the intellectual fiber, an understanding of the needs of our people, and the moral courage to tread new paths—to chart new courses in meeting people problems of our time. We can't just stay in our friendly areas of Kāhala and Lanikai. And...if we fail to make our party representative of our diverse population (and of people like Jimmy Clark), it will be twenty years* before a two-party system comes back to Hawai'i."

* Note: It is now forty years since I delivered this talk.

INDEX

MICHELE MALIA BOND

Fred Rohlfing was born in Honolulu, Territory of Hawai'i in 1928. A graduate of Punahou School, Yale, and George Washington Law School, Rohlfing stayed in the Naval Intelligence Reserve for 33 years after serving on active duty at the Pentagon during the Korean War. Elected as a Republican to the Hawai'i First State Legislature upon Statehood, Fred served 21 years in Hawai'i's House and Senate. He ran for Congress from O'ahu's 1st district twice, losing close races to Democrats Matsunaga and Heftel. Thereafter he served as Attorney General—and Honolulu Liaison officer—for American Samoa, and two terms as U.S. Alternate Representative to the South Pacific Commission (New Caledonia). After moving to Maui in 1984 he became Maui County Corporation Counsel. Retiring from the County and the naval reserve in 1987/88 Fred was awarded the U.S. Meritorious Service medal. In "retirement" he has served as a Federal Magistrate Judge, as a member of the Maui Apportionment Advisory Council, the Maui Salary Commission, and currently the Statewide Health Coordinating Council.

Father of three sons by his first marriage, and grandfather to six offspring, Rohlfing now lives in Kula with his wife of 27 years, Patty, and their Australian Shepherd mix, Koa.